Gospel of the Living Dead

GOSPEL OF THE LIVING DEAD

*George Romero's Visions
of Hell on Earth*

Kim Paffenroth

Baylor University Press
Waco, Texas 76798

Jacket Design by William Lebeda, William Lebeda Designs
Jacket Photography © iStockphoto.com
Zombie Photography © William Lebeda
Zombie Effects by Cerberus Creations
Author Jacket Photograph by William Lebeda & Cerberus Creations

Library of Congress Cataloging-in-Publication Data

Paffenroth, Kim, 1966-
  Gospel of the living dead : George Romero's visions of hell on earth / Kim Paffenroth.
      p. cm.
  Includes bibliographical references and index.
  ISBN-13: 978-1-932792-65-2 (hardcover : alk. paper)
  1. Romero, George A.--Criticism and interpretation. 2. Zombie films--History and criticism. I. Title.

PN1998.3.R644P34 2006
791.4302'33092--dc22
                                        2006021263

Printed in the United States of America on acid-free paper with a minimum of 30% pcw recycled content.

CONTENTS

ACKNOWLEDGMENTS

Few of my friends share my enthusiasm for the zombie movie genre, but those who do—or, more often, who at least tolerate reading what I've written about it—have provided valuable feedback as this book has progressed, especially W. Scott Field, Victor Gibbs, Robert Kennedy, and John-Paul Spiro.

At my institution of Iona College, thanks are always due to my colleagues in the Religious Studies Department—Brian Brown, Kathleen Deignan, Robert Durning, and Elena Procario-Foley—and to my dean, Alex Eodice. The staff at Ryan Library also deserves special thanks, particularly Richard Palladino, Kathleen Pascuzzi, Matt McKee, and Ed Helmrich.

I would like to thank my editor at Baylor University Press, Carey Newman. His enthusiasm for the project made it a reality and a success.

Very special thanks go to the team who produced the cover: design and photography by William Lebeda; photography by David Midgen; zombie makeups by Greg McDougall and Cari Finken of Cerberus Creations; and the zombies themselves—Hillary Bauman, Anne Coleman, Crystal Deones, Grant Nellessen, Josh Novak, and Jeffrey Schwarz. The living dead have never looked so good or behaved so well.

And, of course, one's family always bears the biggest share of the burden of one's idiosyncrasies, whether those idiosyncrasies are in entertainment or intellectual pursuits. My son Charlie rather enthusiastically discusses zombies with me, talking fine points of tactics, stockpiling food, the advantages and disadvantages of various weapons, etc. When we do so, my daughter Sophia, on the other hand, simply keeps playing with Barbie and saying, "Zombies don't exist, daddy." (She has, however, learned to phrase her commentary that way, since when she used to say, "Zombies aren't alive," I could respond, "Of course they're not: they're undead.") I know that, even if their preferred subject is not zombies, they will both find their own way to relate imagination and rationality to understand the world and its meaning, which is the most high-minded description I can offer of what I'm trying to do here and in my other work.

Kim Paffenroth
Cornwall on Hudson, New York

PREFACE

In each chapter, both in the synopsis and analysis of the movie being discussed, there will be what people usually call "spoilers"—i.e., I will give away
the ending or key points of information that will make the movie less sus-
penseful if the reader has not already seen it. If a reader wishes to see the
movie with all the suspense it has for a first-time viewer, then he should not
read those parts of the book before viewing it.

All the movies being discussed were either rated R in the United States,
or were not submitted for rating at all, so as to avoid the X or NC-17 rating.
They contain scenes of graphic, usually unspeakable violence, often including the most sickening acts of cannibalism and dismemberment, depicted
in excruciating detail with rivers and geysers of blood. Under no circumstances would I recommend that anyone under the age of fourteen see the
uncensored versions of these movies, though every time I have seen them
at the theaters, people have been there with small children, which I find
inconceivable—nearly criminal, I would say. These films give me nightmares, to be honest. It is part of their appeal, the catharsis and edifying
ordeal that horrific, dramatic experiences put us through, but one should
certainly be circumspect about viewing them, and even more so in allowing
children to see them. All the films also contain a frequent, often pervasive
use of expletives; I will omit the middle letters of the most vulgar of these
when including them in the text.

Introduction

THE THEMES OF THE CURRENT ZOMBIE MOVIE GENRE

THE CURRENT STATE OF ZOMBIE MOVIES

When one speaks of zombie movies today, one is really speaking of movies that are either made by or directly influenced by one man, director George A. Romero (b. 1940),[1] an avuncular, now grandfatherly figure with thick glasses and a big smile, whom it is nearly impossible to imagine crafting images of such horror and grotesquery. His movies and their related progeny are enormously popular in the United States and even more so worldwide, despite their very low budgets and lack of any bankable stars: only Romero's most recent, *Land of the Dead* (2005), and the recent remake of *Dawn of the Dead* (2004), included even B-list actors.[2] Romero's landmark film, *Night of the Living Dead* (1968), has defined the zombie genre since its release, and has even spilled over into the depiction of zombies in any medium, including books, comic books, video and board games, and action figures. Sometimes the influence can come full circle: Romero-influenced zombies populate the immensely popular and violent video game *Resident Evil*, which was then made into films (2002 and 2004), and also influenced the remake of *Dawn of the Dead*, which some critics then accused of looking too much like a video game.[3] In this analysis, we will be looking at the four movies of Romero's zombie "trilogy," together with the remake of his classic *Dawn of the Dead*. I will skip the remake of *Night of the Living Dead*

(1990), which Romero oversaw, as too identical to the original to need further comment. I will make passing reference to other popular movies in the genre, especially *28 Days Later* (2002) and *Shaun of the Dead* (2004), all of which clearly show that their depiction of zombies is dependent on how Romero defined these horrific beings, even within their variations.[4]

Although Romero is said to eschew the idea that his movies have meaning or significance,[5] they are widely acknowledged, by reputable critics and not just fans, to be thoughtful and serious examinations of ideas, not just exercises in shock and nausea. Even the gruesomeness and violence may be a vehicle for catharsis and not sadistic voyeurism,[6] for Romero uses horror rather more as it is used in the tradition of American Gothic literature, which includes such luminaries as Edgar Allen Poe, Herman Melville, and Flannery O'Connor, where shocking violence and depravity are used to disorient and reorient the audience, disturbing them in order to make some unsettling point, usually a sociological, anthropological, or theological one.[7] It is also a telling anecdote as to the religious meaning implicit in these films that *Dawn of the Dead* (2004) was the first movie to edge Mel Gibson's *The Passion of the Christ* (2004)—another low budget movie with plenty of gore and no big stars—out of the number one place in box office sales. Without jumping into the fray about Gibson's film, it is the contention here that zombie movies may also usefully and constructively inform our ideas about human beings and God.

The basic characteristics of zombies were laid out in Romero's first film, with some room for elaboration or development, especially in the most recent revival of the genre in the last two years:

- For some reason, recently dead human beings suddenly start getting up and walking around again. They no longer have human minds, however. They are zombies, though they are almost never referred to as that by the characters in the movies themselves, who usually use more terse and ominous terms such as "them" or "those things." The exact cause for this outbreak is usually left unstated, but is sometimes briefly and cryptically described as "mysterious radiation" from a space probe returning from Venus (*Night of the Living Dead*), or divine judgment (*Dawn of the Dead* [both 1978 and 2004]), or, more scientifically, some kind of disease or virus (*Dawn of the Dead* [both 1978 and 2004]), or most likely a biological weapon that got out of hand (made explicit in *Resident Evil* and *28 Days Later*). In every case, the plausibility of an explanation is irrelevant, as the movies are always about some small group dealing with the effects, not the causes, although the more recent movies do make more of an attempt at plausibility.[8] This last rationalization of a biological weapon may be a symptom of a post-9/11 world nervous at the possibilities of bioterrorism,[9] as a previous generation lived constantly in the shadow of nuclear war, and zombies were then depicted as the outcome of radiation.[10] Both nuclear zombies and bioterror zombies are then a symbol of our own mad urges to destroy ourselves, and a terrifying portent that we might succeed. But in the movies, the cause is, of course, more or less irrelevant: it is only a necessary plot device to get us to the point of, "What would happen if corpses got up and started walking around?" And the story that each movie offers is to look at one very small band of survivors in their struggle to survive, not to find explanations.

- Zombies are autonomous beings, not under the control of someone else. This makes them quite different than most earlier movie zombies, who were usually under the control of a mad scientist, alien, sorcerer, or witch doctor (usually "voodoo"),[11] though, like Frankenstein's monster, they could sometimes get inconveniently out of the hands of their creators. Such zombies are more victims than monsters, and can usually be released from the malevolent control by killing the agent that is controlling them, thereby returning them to human status, or to the peaceful rest of death. The new type of zombie, on the other hand, is a horrifying killing machine in its own right that can never revert to "human." As soon as they reanimate from the dead, zombies immediately begin savagely attacking and killing the living around them.

- After the initial cause, whatever it is, zombies rapidly increase their numbers by killing living people, who then also become zombies. In most of the movies, anyone who dies in any way will also become a zombie (as above). The exceptions are in those movies where the cause of becoming a zombie is an "infection" (*28 Days Later, Dawn of the Dead*

[2004]), a heretofore unknown one, and one that spreads with unheard-of speed and virulence, but one that bears at least some semblance to normal, terrestrial diseases, and therefore must be spread through contact. (Though the mechanics are often implausibly stretched to fit dramatic needs: several times *Dawn of the Dead* [2004] shows dying, infected people being kissed goodbye on the lips just minutes before their death and reanimation—without harm to the other person—when their bite will be fatal just a few moments later.) But in all the movies, the zombies' most preferred method of attack is to bite their victims, thereby assuring that everyone they attack will become a zombie, so the distinction in these more "rational" movies carries little difference. Even if the bite is not immediately fatal through blood loss, the ensuing infection will inevitably be so; most every movie shows this in horrifying scenes of contamination and lingering death, followed by a shroud-covered body sitting up in its deathbed to attack its former friends and family.

- Zombies partially eat the living. They thereby resemble the traditional depiction of ghouls, mythical monsters that hang around crypts and graveyards to eat corpses. It would be better for the remaining human survivors if zombies ate all of their victims (as a scientist observes in *Dawn of the Dead* [1978]), but they actually only eat a small amount, thereby leaving the rest of the person intact to become a zombie, get up, and attack and kill more people, who then likewise become zombies. Zombies derive no nourishment from eating people, since they function exactly the same even if they don't eat, and they never tire or sleep or slow down, regardless of their diet or lack of it; so the whole theme of cannibalism seems added for its symbolism, showing what humans would degenerate into in their more primitive, zombie state. As the series of movies progresses, this theme becomes more and more prominent: we, humans, not just zombies, prey on each other, depend on each other for our pathetic and parasitic existence, and thrive on each others' misery. It is Romero's most potent image, and what lifts him out of the category of a mere craftsmen in gore and makes him an artist,[12] though ironically, cannibalism is exactly what has given him so many opportunities over the years to engage in such epic gore-splattering across the screen.

- Zombies are tenacious and will never relent in their attack (except in the final scene of *Land of the Dead*), but they are fairly easy to kill: most all zombie movies follow Romero's depiction that a zombie's brain is what has really been "reanimated" or "revived," and therefore a blow or bullet (or any projectile or penetration) to the head will permanently "kill" a zombie.

- Perhaps because individually zombies are not too threatening, the suspense in zombie movies comes more from how the human characters interact. Each movie has the suspense, paranoia, and claustrophobia of a movie about a siege, or a lifeboat full of survivors with limited supplies: the besieging army or the sea is a "given" and is not really the enemy, the real enemy is within the group, with the fear and ignorance that tears them apart and sets them against one another. More than other genres of horror, zombie movies are deeply psychological dramas.

Besides these points of agreement between all the movies, there are several points of difference that show some development in the genre:

- Zombies are almost always slow, shuffling, uncoordinated creatures, except in *28 Days Later* and *Dawn of the Dead* (2004), where they are suddenly possessed of the speed and agility of jungle cats.[13] (In the new *Dawn of the Dead* they also sound like large wild animals.) This seems to fit an overall pattern in recent monster movies of speeding up slow monsters to make them more threatening: think of how fast the dinosaurs are in *Jurassic Park* (1993), or the monster in the new *Godzilla* (1998), compared with their predecessors.

- The plots of the first two movies, *Night of the Living Dead* and *Dawn of the Dead* (1978), rely on zombies being afraid of fire; in *Night of the Living Dead* this is even generalized to zombies being afraid of any light source. But the zombies are utterly fearless of fire in the more recent films, especially in *28 Days Later* and *Dawn of the Dead* (2004), where they are shown continuing to attack humans even when completely engulfed in flames. This is probably a point where Romero and his followers have developed zombies to be less like animals, which are always afraid of fire, and more like humans.[14] This change is similar to the following points of development.

- How zombies act towards animals other than living human beings is left ambiguous. Most of the movies never address the question, but the plot of the new *Dawn of the Dead* relies on zombies not attacking animals, while *Land of the Dead* states explicitly that they will eat other animals, although they greatly prefer living human flesh, and the original *Dawn of the Dead* (1978) specifies that they will only consume human flesh, not animals or other zombies. As with the preceding point, this difference seems mostly plot-driven, though as with the zombies' cannibalism, there may be a symbolic point about human nature here, but one that could be taken either way, and hence the ambiguity: either humans are ironically and self-destructively only violent to one another and not towards other animals, in contradistinction to practically every other "natural" species, whose murderous violence is usually curbed around members of their own kind, while human violence flares up most virulently around other humans; or humans are so violent that their violence indiscriminately spills over onto all species, even if their mad preference is to devour other humans.

- Zombies are usually completely imbecilic, incapable of making plans, coordinating their attacks, or learning from their mistakes. They are frequently shown picking things up to use as clubs, but their dexterity and planning seems to stop at that level. Romero himself seems particularly interested in undoing the idea of unintelligent zombies, making their increasing intelligence the theme of his last two zombie movies, *Day of the Dead* and *Land of the Dead*.

On the one hand, such developments are easy enough to explain. They develop to make the movies, or, at least, the monsters in them, scarier: a fast, agile, fearless, intelligent zombie who tears apart anything that comes near it is much more potent than the plodding, stumbling, oblivious imbeciles of the first movie. (Though it does sometimes seem that increasing zombie speed misses the point of their monstrousness, and Romero has refused to make his zombies fast in *Land of the Dead*.) But on the final point of increasing zombie intelligence, Romero seems to be working on the symbolism of zombies, as he did by making them cannibals, or as the other directors did by making the zombie menace a creation of our own mad, foolish intellect. In the end, Romero is asking what is a smart zombie, other than . . . a human being, a bestial slave to its appetites that struggles to be more? Or what are we, other than . . . slightly smart zombies, a tribe of deranged, self-destructive cannibals preying on one another? It is this overlap and crossover between zombies and humans that makes zombies different than other movie monsters, and makes zombie movies more potent and deeper explorations of human nature and theological questions, as we shall now see.

THE SYMBOLISM OR MEANING OF ZOMBIES

Being a combination of two creatures or being between two physical states is a common characteristic of monsters, frequently seen in classical mythology, where many monsters are a combination of two creatures: the Minotaur, chimera, harpies, satyrs, and centaurs. They are usually created by someone foolishly and impiously crossing the boundary between species and mating with a member of another species, or by the equally foolish gods transgressing the boundary between human and divine to mate with humans. And in modern movie monsters, influenced more by Christian mythology, monsters are also frequently such borderline, hellish creatures that straddle the threshold between human and nonhuman (werewolves and all victims of lycanthropy; or, in the modern science fiction genre, any victim of horrible experiments that combine species, such as *The Fly* [1958 and 1986]; or diabolical machines that are nearly human, but not in a nice way, as with HAL in *2001, A Space Odyssey* [1968]), or between living and dead, whether through supernatural means (ghosts, hauntings, possessions, and vampires), or by hubristic human intellect (the Frankenstein monster or any of its equivalent attempts to cheat death through technology). Such monsters do not quite belong in either of the two species, and they usually possess the worst but most potent qualities of both species: brute strength, diabolical intellect, deceit, lechery, lust for power, and savage disregard for life.

What makes such hybrid or divided beings even more interesting, however, is that they are not always just monstrous, but their combined nature is also frequently a quality of what humans consider holy and sacred. Sacred places, temples, groves or mountains, and sacred cities, such as Jerusalem and Mecca, are often considered the gateway between heaven and earth, a combination of divine and mundane. They are not quite like ordinary places, and are to be treated with special care and reverence. Similarly, there are many beings who straddle the boundary between human and divine, including saints, angels, and even saviors, like Jesus or Buddha, who are not monstrous, but who are definitely somewhat dangerous and beyond our control, and therefore not to be treated the way we treat "regular" people, for that would be both imprudent and blasphemous. Going in the other direction in the hierarchy of beings, animals often elicit our compassion and sometimes even awe because, unlike rocks or plants, which can be just as beautiful and sublime as any animal, animals often seem almost human. So, too, a human corpse is considered simultaneously both gruesome and sacred by any normal human being, because it is both still human, and yet no longer human: it cannot be treated just like a piece of trash, but also it should not be kept around (though relics go even further by violating this rule). It must be disposed of in a way that will respect and maintain its humanness and its sacrality, even while disposing of its impurity and contagion.[15] Straddling the boundary between human and divine, or human and subhuman, is not just monstrous, it can also be mysterious, holy, and life-affirming to humans.

With such observations about monsters, the mysterious, and the sacred in mind, the potency of zombies as a symbol is even more apparent.[16] Although they resemble vampires and werewolves in several ways, being humanoid monsters who turn other humans into creatures like themselves by biting them, zombies are more ambiguous in their state between human and nonhuman. Zombies possess none of the supernatural qualities of other such monsters: they cannot fly; they cannot turn into a vapor, bat, or wolf; they are not possessed of superhuman strength; they don't have fangs. As one critic has put it, this means that we do not have "admiration" for them the way we often do for more powerful, superhuman monsters.[17] While this makes zombies less formidable as opponents, it makes them rather more fully and disconcertingly human. This often gives zombies a noticeable advantage, for they frequently get the jump on a person who has not yet realized that she is dealing with a zombie and not a human being, such as in the horrific scenes with little girl zombies in *Night of the Living Dead* and in the opening sequence of *Dawn of the Dead* (2004).[18] No masters of stealth, zombies are nonetheless able to sneak up on humans just by their fully human appearance, adding to their scariness.[19] While we cannot admire the slow and clumsy and all-too-human zombies, they are scarier because we identify and sympathize with them in a way that we never could with more powerful and demonic monsters.

But what makes zombies more terrifying than other monsters is that this confusing resemblance of zombies to normal people never goes away. Unlike vampires, zombies do not sleep in coffins, and unlike werewolves, zombies do not go back and forth between their human and monstrous states: what is especially terrifying with zombies is that their monstrous state *is* their human state, it never transforms or goes away.[20] This adds much to the movies' grotesquery, as it is much more gruesome to watch human zombies devouring other humans than it would be to watch alligators, sharks, piranhas, or scarab beetles doing so, though enough movies traffic in these other kinds of devourings to show that *any* image of being eaten alive is pretty frightening.[21]

The real psychological terror of zombies, however, lies in the reverse prospect: it is not just horrible to watch zombies devouring humans, but it is more subtly and insidiously horrible to imagine the human characters in the movies slaughtering hundreds of zombies who look, and, to some extent, still act, exactly like human beings. It is a moral dilemma at which the human characters frequently express their dismay in several of the movies. Driving a stake through Dracula's heart or shooting a slavering werewolf with a silver bullet is one thing: putting a bullet in the forehead of a zombie who looks like an elderly lady or a little girl is quite another.[22] (And, it should be noted, though these movies are rightfully known for their gore, they also obey certain limits of decency, at least in Romero's versions:[23] zombies and their human victims, especially those zombies and humans who are killed onscreen, are almost always fit, young adults, and often, in the case of the humans, have been behaving either foolishly, or despicably toward the other characters.) Zombie movies imagine a scenario far worse than nuclear war or a cabal of vampires taking over the world: they present us with a world in which humans and monsters become very hard to distinguish, and therefore the moral rules that guide our dealings with other humans—it is better to suffer injustice than to commit it, thou shalt not kill, love thy neighbor, turn the other cheek—are discarded as irrelevant and unfeasible. Even "eye for an eye" would be considered impractical in a world full of zombies: the only way to stay alive and continue some kind of human "civilization" would be to shoot any suspicious person in the head before he tries to tear out your throat and eat you alive. This rule made explicit in the more recent movies, *28 Days Later* and *Land of the Dead*, in which bitten or infected humans are routinely and heartlessly killed, rather than waiting for them to turn into zombies. Several times it is said that infected humans and zombies must be "exterminated" (*Dawn of the Dead* [1978]) or "put down" (*28 Days Later* and *Dawn of the Dead* [2004]), wording more usual for how one deals with a nonhuman pestilence, like cockroaches or rabid dogs, not human beings. Again, the more recent directors probably want to draw parallels with the modern situation of terrorism, to which "civilized" countries cede some of their "civilization" when they fall into the rhetoric and behavior of, "We've got to get them before they get us, no matter what it takes." The use of nuclear weapons is debated in the original *Dawn of the Dead* (1978), and on the DVD bonus features of the new version, they are said actually to have been used, with all the resultant loss of human life. The horrific nature of zombies, and, many would say, terrorists, is that they may force us to act as barbarically and impetuously as they do.

The zombies' bordering between human and nonhuman is even deeper and more ambiguous, however. Zombies do not just look like humans, thereby making it more uncomfortable to shoot them in the forehead: the point in the movies is that zombies are human, and humans are zombie-like, as one character exclaims explicitly in *Dawn of the Dead* (1978), "They're *us*!" Romero also displays it graphically in *Dawn of the Dead* (1978) by having the camera shoot from the point of view of the zombie, as though the audience are zombies looking at the human characters in the film.[24] This *mental* and *psychological* similarity of zombies and humans is so deep that the implications of such a horrible resemblance have become a field of research and hot debate in the modern philosophy of mind.[25] The abstract, theoretical possibility of a zombie, not the cinematic depiction of it, it should be noted—but with implications for the movies, to be sure—has been seen to raise vexing and interesting questions about the human mind and existence. Some philosophers have claimed, in effect, that zombies prove that we humans are not just material beings, an important claim and one that outrages other philosophers, who are heavily invested in the belief that we are only physical and that there is no such thing as an immaterial "soul" (or spirit, atman, Brahman, or self). The argument, basically, follows the implications of a thought experiment. First, imagine a being who acts like a human in every physical way, even all the way down to the internal physical processes that accompany sense and cognition. If it is then possible, without some logical inconsistency or baseless assumption, to imagine that such a being might still lack consciousness, that it would be a "zombie," then it has been "proved" that humans have something immaterial about them, that they are not just machines. In a wonderful bit of irony and rhetoric, the monstrous zombies created by our imaginations, whether in a logician's thought experiment or a director's frame, may yet save us from our own misguided and arrogant urge to degrade and dehumanize ourselves into soulless machines.

Philosophical conundrums and "proofs" aside, zombie movies seem mostly interested in the moral implications of the resemblance of zombies to humans, the disturbing implication that even if we are conscious and the zombies are not, our consciousness does little to make us "better," even if it makes us epistemically different or more complex. The various movies play this theme out in different ways, and it is clearly one that has developed a great deal since the first movie, becoming the predominant theme in the genre. Unlike aliens, robots, or supernatural beings, such as demons, the distasteful and horrible aspects of zombies cannot really be discounted as unhuman, but are rather just exaggerated aspects of humanity. Zombies are essentially primitive humans, humans without, or without much, reason and intellect. But they are far from noble savages. They are old-fashioned savages, descending immediately to cannibalism and irrational, uncontrollable violence. They are completely self-centered, showing no concern for their fellow zombies or mercy to their human prey, at least not until the final installment, *Land of the Dead*. But the humans in the films are, for the most part, little better than their zombie counterparts and tormentors. Many of the human characters are more petty, predatory, and selfish than any zombie could be, for their intellect does not undo or diminish such bad characteristics, it only enables the humans to act on such urges with greater cunning, subtlety, and effectiveness. It is, to be sure, one of the most cynical portrayals of human nature in any film genre, and, indeed, I would say it makes these movies more inappropriate for younger viewers than does the bloodshed, but it is not an estimation without redeeming value: expecting, depicting, and criticizing the worst aspects of humans may be a necessary part of the diagnosis of their sin and disease.

Besides being on the threshold between human and nonhuman, zombies also clearly straddle the line between living and dead in a perverted version of the Christian idea of bodily resurrection. Like other monsters, such ambiguity, or the hybrid or oxymoronic nature of being "living dead," means that zombies violate the natural order, both of the physical world and of human society. In zombie movies, human society is in a shambles not only because there is a deadly threat, but because there is a threat of turning into something that is neither alive nor dead. Such a prospect of becoming neither alive nor dead diminishes the human characters' ability to deal with mortality, which is already a deep enough psychological strain for most of us.[26] Several times human characters are shown being unduly reckless, or, at the other extreme, committing suicide, regarded as a grievous sin or psychological disorder by many, rather than become one of "them." And the fact that a loved one who dies will immediately rise up and try to kill you means that the normal rites and ceremonies of funerals, saying goodbye, grieving, and "moving on" must be discarded, or, much more horribly, replaced with a new expedient of shooting the loved one between the eyes,[27] followed by unceremoniously setting the body on fire.[28] Several times, not surprisingly, the movies show this as putting a terrible, painful psychological strain on the human characters. As noted above, humans need to feel the sacredness of a human corpse, but if that corpse is suddenly a great physical danger, such feelings must be ignored. That does not mean that the feelings will conveniently go away; they will just go deeper down into a person and probably fester. Zombies dehumanize humans by eliminating their chance to experience normal feelings of grief, mortality, or sacredness, and forcing them to substitute callous, unthinking, reflexive violence. It would be similar to what soldiers feel with battle fatigue and post-traumatic stress, but like none experienced even in the worst of human conflicts so far.[29]

Zombies also violate the natural world of physical and biological laws. Since they are not fully alive, zombies, unlike other species, cannot reproduce on their own. They are more like a cult of cannibalistic Shakers (an eighteenth- to nineteenth-century Christian sect who believed in celibacy for all members, not just clergy), who must rely on "converting" others to their lifestyle in order to perpetuate themselves. And unlike the peaceful Shakers, the zombies' tactics of "conversion" are very aggressive and convincing indeed. And since zombies are not fully dead, they upset the essential balance of nature: no animals eat zombies, apparently, and zombies do not seem to decay, at least, not to the point of disintegration and reintegration back into the soil, so the food chain, or the circle of life, seems to end or be short-circuited by their existence. Zombies fulfill the worst potentialities of humans to create a hellish kingdom on earth of endless, sterile repetition and boredom.

More than any other monster, zombies are fully and literally apocalyptic, as the movies acknowledge (especially *Dawn of the Dead* [2004]): they signal the end of the world as we have known it for thousands of years. Also, in the original meaning of "apocalyptic," they "reveal" terrible truths about human nature, existence, and sin.[30] The dead roam the earth, never at rest, and they never leave the living alone to enjoy "life," but constantly and savagely try to drag them into a shadowy realm that is neither alive nor dead. Zombies thereby bring the complete breakdown of the natural world of food chains, social order, respect for life, and respect for death, because all those categories are meaningless and impossible to maintain in a world where the most fundamental limen, the threshold between alive and dead, has become a threshold that no one really crosses all the way over, but on which everyone lives suspended all the time.[31] It is this endless, eternal suspension between two equally horrible states that is the real horror of zombies, not the few seconds of violence that it takes to cross over from human to zombie status, a boundary that signals little real change in their hellish world.

ZOMBIES, HUMOR, AND RELIGION

Part of the appeal of zombie movies also lies in their undeniable humor. Unlike other monsters, zombies do not need any separate comic relief, such as a comic sidekick like Igor or Renfield: they are their own comic relief. But as with the other aspects of zombies, this too is not merely a part of why they are entertaining, but also contributes to the movies' deeper meaning. And although *Shaun of the Dead* is the outright comic version of this, together with other parody/tributes like *Return of the Living Dead* (1985), all the movies participate in it, especially the original *Dawn of the Dead*, which even has human characters throwing cream pies at zombies and squirting them with seltzer bottles. Part of their appeal and meaning is that no good zombie movie takes itself, or us, entirely seriously.[32] A pretentious zombie movie is really an oxymoron.

The most basic kind of humor that zombies bring to the screen is simple slapstick, physical gags based on the zombies' lack of coordination and intelligence. All of the movies are full of zombies bumping into things, knocking each other over, trying to go the wrong way on escalators, taking various pratfalls, and accidentally electrocuting or decapitating themselves by staggering into things that they should not. It is macabre, black humor, to be sure, and not to everyone's taste, but it is a boon to the pacing and tone of the movies that zombies can alternate pretty seamlessly between making us scared and making us laugh, most expertly played in the original *Dawn of the Dead*, where the climactic scene of carnage is immediately preceded by the pie-throwing scene. But since zombies are not just amusing imbeciles—they are more essentially the walking damned—their comedy is also meant to make us laugh at the sin and damnation they embody. This is a common strategy of older religiously based spectacles, such as medieval passion plays, which likewise combined savage violence, ethical warning, religious education, and bawdy, low humor: watching Judas and the impenitent thief being disemboweled and torn to pieces was considered especially entertaining and edifying in these plays.[33] And just in case one would discount such humor as merely a symptom of low cultural achievements, whether religious or not, the *Inferno*—the classic description of hell written by the medieval Italian poet Dante Alighieri (1265–1321)—is also a careful blending of seriousness and comedy (though the book's overall title, *The Divine Comedy*, does not refer to this aspect, but simply means that the book has a happy and not tragic ending). One minute Dante is frozen in terror by the demons, who he fears will tear him limb from limb, and the next minute we see the demons taking a pratfall into a lake of boiling pitch and degenerating into a Three Stooges' routine of hitting and clawing each other until their wings are too fouled with pitch to allow them to fly out. The humorousness of zombies is not just comic relief, a matter of dramatic pacing: it also stands in a long tradition of laughing at evil, defusing its power and its hold on us through laughter.

Such humor at the expense of zombies and other monsters does run the risk, however, not only of defusing or defeating evil, but also of discounting or trivializing it as merely something funny. To use laughter to deepen our appreciation of evil's power, some of the jokes would have to be self-deprecating at the expense of the human characters and audience, and not just directed at the alien, evil "other" to whom we like to imagine we bear no resemblance. Zombie movies are full of this kind of humor, too. If zombies are shown as humorously and fatally distracted by shiny objects (*Dawn of the Dead* [1978])[34] or fireworks (*Land of the Dead*), the human characters frequently are just as funny in their dullness and shallowness. In *Shaun of the Dead* this is the most obvious, for the human characters hilariously do not even notice that zombies are taking over the earth for much of the movie, because they are all so drunk and/or self-absorbed. But the more straightforwardly serious movies frequently play with the same idea, epitomized perhaps in *Dawn of the Dead* (2004), when one character, while stuck in an elevator, leaving one scene of unspeakable horror and violence on his way to another, smiles when he hears the mind-numbing Muzak, which, as a mall employee, he must have heard thousands of times, and says, "I like this song!" Zombie movies are more meaningful because we do not just laugh at the hideous, evil vacuousness of zombies, but we laugh a little uncomfortably at our own empty, selfish pettiness. If zombie movies do not, or should not, take themselves too seriously, then they also help us not to take ourselves too seriously.

Another type of humor is the comedy of reversal, especially the reversal of social roles and status. As with the other types of humor, this can be seen in common, low cultural settings, such as the ubiquitous sitcom fallback plot used when the writers cannot think of anything better: it is funny whenever you dress up men in women's clothes, a subcategory of a cliché so common it has its own name, the "fish out of water" plot. But it is also frequent in humorous religious festivals, such as Mardi Gras and Purim, which include a lot of drinking, violating of social rules, and people masquerading as things they are not. Again, *Shaun of the Dead* is the most obvious example of this, with a protagonist who is a total cutup and failure in his regular, pre-zombie world, but who must rise, imperfectly and hilariously, to try to save the human race. But all the serious movies contain similar protagonists: even though the scenario of a zombie takeover would make it seem much more likely that most survivors would be the rich and powerful in well-designed bunkers or enclaves, every movie presents us with a group of blue-collar, lower- to middle-class people who are suddenly the last hope of humanity. One of the funniest scenes in all the movies is in *Dawn of the Dead* (2004), when the characters play a very sick and hilarious game. They, or, more accurately, the male characters, stand on the roof of the mall and hold up a dry-erase board with a celebrity's name on it, and their friend across the street then uses a high powered rifle to blow off the head of the zombie who resembles that celebrity: it is an obvious and hilarious parody of class envy, with commoners getting their revenge against the rich and famous.

It is the zombies themselves, however, who are the biggest example of this pattern of humorous reversal. Zombies are the lowest, most "peasant" type of monsters,[35] especially in comparison to vampires, who are always very sophisticated and effete,[36] but zombies enjoy greater success at annihilating humanity than any previous monster ever did. Zombies do not take over a person (as in *The Exorcist* [1973]), or a home (as in *The Amityville Horror* [1979 and 2005]), or a town (like *Salem's Lot* [1979 and 2004] or *Jaws* [1975]), or even a whole region (like Transylvania in all the Dracula stories). In all zombie movies after *Night of the Living Dead*, zombies take over the entire planet in a matter of days. It is the most extreme and funniest reversal that the world once dominated by humans—who so arrogantly and stupidly suppose that they are the smartest, most advanced, and most important life forms in the universe—is destroyed pretty easily by an apocalyptic army, not of powerful, supernatural beings, like Satan or the Antichrist, but of slow, clumsy imbeciles who can barely stand up. The whole idea of zombies taking over the world is both a funny and potent parable against human hubris, arrogance, and self-sufficiency.

ZOMBIES AND SOCIAL CRITICISM

Zombie movies of the past forty years have rightfully gained much of their respectability and invited so much serious analysis by engaging in social criticism, another point that distinguishes them from more forgettable entries in the horror movie genre.[37] Although the zombie epidemic is said to be worldwide in some of the later movies, the world that the undead are shown devouring onscreen is always modern, western culture, especially American culture,[38] though two of the recent, related movies, *28 Days Later* and *Shaun of the Dead*, show that the British have similar anxieties and misgivings about their society. Romero visually signals the target of his horror and humor at the beginning of *Night of the Living Dead*, with the American flag prominently displayed over the graveyard in the opening sequence,[39] and American flags are often and jarringly thrust into the foreground at other points in these films,[40] to remind us that it is America that is eating itself alive. The ability of the zombies to wreak so much havoc so quickly, and the humans' ineffective response to the threat, show in each case that the society being destroyed is rotten from within to begin with,[41] as one character exclaims at the beginning of *Dawn of the Dead* (1978), "We're blowing it ourselves." Romero and the other filmmakers use the fantastical "disease" of zombies to criticize the very real diseases of racism, sexism, materialism, and individualism that would make any society easy prey for barbarian hordes.[42] And the portrayal is so powerful and compelling in these films, that it is impossible to discount it as some thoughtless anti-American screed: it is a real, if extreme, diagnosis of what ails us.

Racism is perhaps the social ill most consistently decried in the series, appearing prominently in nearly every installment. Part of what gives the first movie, *Night of the Living Dead*, its haunting power is that it features a black protagonist—at a time when such were rare in American films—who survives the horrific rampages of the zombie hordes,[43] only to be thoughtlessly shot in the head by a roving posse of white zombie hunters at the end of the movie, who clearly evoke a white, American lynch mob more than they do any force of law and order.[44] Romero likewise featured black protagonists prominently in his sequels *Dawn of the Dead* (1978) and *Day of the Dead*, as did director Zack Snyder in the remake of *Dawn of the Dead*. Romero also put in a racist rampage at the beginning of *Dawn of the Dead* (1978), in which an out-of-control cop uses the excuse of the zombie menace to shoot blacks and Hispanics indiscriminately. In his final installment, *Land of the Dead*, Romero makes his point even more emphatically, with a Hispanic protagonist, Cholo, battling against the zombies, as well as against the evil capitalist who murderously and sadistically runs the city of surviving humans. In the end, Cholo is helped in his class struggle by an undead army led by a black zombie whose gas station attendant name tag identifies him as "Big Daddy"; together they bring about an end to the evil, racist human empire. The zombies' victory is facilitated in all the movies by the humans' constant inability to cooperate with one another,[45] an inability frequently exacerbated by racism, while the zombies themselves, though usually oblivious to one another, are always a multi-ethnic mob whose violence is always directed outwards.[46] The barbaric cannibalism of zombies is an effective and appropriate parallel to the barbaric, parasitic practice of slavery. The zombies' violent, successful destruction of our society is also an effective indictment of the senselessness and brutality of racism, a hideous punishment for its continued presence in our supposedly "civilized" society, inflicted on it by the primitive but in a way more peaceable and communitarian zombies.

The critique of sexism in zombie movies is not nearly as prominent, and seems more a mocking jibe directed at the audience's expectations, than it is an indictment of the characters and the audience. Every movie after the first features strong women characters who are nearly as effective at killing zombies as the male characters, and who are much more compassionate, caring, and cooperative with other humans than their male companions.[47] If anything, the depiction of women as caring nurturers tends in the direction of stereotypes, and when Romero tries to undermine it, he sometimes steps into another stereotype, such as the "prostitute with a heart of gold" (in *Land of the Dead*).[48] But in his depiction of men, his instinct for social satire treats his material with real wit and subtlety. The men in the movies are as hysterical, disorganized, vain, and superficial as any female stereotype has ever accused women of being. The epitome of this is in the original *Dawn of the Dead* (1978), in which it is the three swaggering, macho, male characters who extravagantly swoon over the idea of living out their days in a shopping mall, foolishly risking their lives to do so, while the lone female character is the one who wants to strike out into the wilderness to found a new colony, first chastising them that, "This is exactly what we're trying to get away from," and finally breaking down with the wretched lament, "What have we done to ourselves?" The zombies, on the other hand, being utterly sexless beings,[49] are as immune to sexism as they are to racism. In zombie movies sexism does not seem to taint and damn human society as poisonously as racism does: it just makes men expect women to act like idiots, while blinding them to their own foolishness.

The self-destructive materialism displayed by the male characters in *Dawn of the Dead* (1978) is repeated in a more subdued way in the remake, and then is taken to greater heights in *Land of the Dead*. In each of these movies, the characters create an equivalent of a Noah's ark adrift in a sea of the undead, but theirs is not a God-given mission to save human and animal life as we know it against the forces of evil and chaos; their goal is just to stay alive so that they can consume more stuff, at the expense of both the undead and the less fortunate living. They do not set up farms or develop new technologies to become self-sufficient; they just scavenge off of the leftovers of the now dead human society. They act as though endless stuff—not ideas, not relationships, not even new experiences or pleasures, but just plain *stuff*—will somehow compensate for living in a cage, surrounded by cannibal corpses that could at any moment break in and eat them alive. Both *Dawn of the Dead* (1978) and *Land of the Dead* show this reaching its most ridiculous and evil extremes when the characters gleefully kill other humans to protect their supply of stuff (never mind the hundreds or even thousands of zombies that are killed along the way to satisfy the humans' greed). These two movies even show them hoarding paper money in a world where money must have awfully little significance. It is a measure of the much greater optimism of the new *Dawn of the Dead* that the humans are able to overcome this blinding materialism on their own, while in the two movies by Romero himself, only the zombies wrecking their playground and feeding trough finally shocks the humans out of it by necessity. Almost more than racism, our addiction to stuff, no matter how we get it or whom we hurt to get it, sickens these filmmakers as they bring down the wrath of the zombie army onto the greedy, grasping, selfish, predatory humans.

Differently than with racism or sexism, however, zombies are, in a way, also guilty and symbolic of materialism, because, as noted, they remain human at some deep, primitive level. They are not, of course, literally materialistic. They may be gluttons, but zombies do not really try to get stuff, they are utterly content to sit around and "enjoy" what little they have. But in both versions of *Dawn of the Dead*, it is emphasized over and over that the zombies want desperately to get into the mall, not just or even primarily to eat its inhabitants, but because they intensely remember and long for the shopping experience, more than anything else from their pre-zombie existence. In both *Dawns* and in *Land of the Dead*, the zombies are the class envious and outraged have-nots, toppling the spoiled and decadent haves.[50] The zombies' materialism and consumerism in life have outlived their personality, reason, and emotions, and are now the "motorized instinct," as a scientist in the original *Dawn of the Dead* puts it, that still drives them, even in death, to long to consume and possess. According to these movies, materialism and consumerism have saturated our being much more thoroughly than racism and sexism, so much so that we could remain sinful, grasping, parasitic wretches for the rest of eternity, content always to wander the mall with startled, stupefied looks on our faces.

Finally, zombie movies appreciate and mock that uniquely modern and particularly American predilection, fierce individualism, as something that can sometimes temporarily save us in a crisis, but which can also doom us in the long run. Considering the scenario of a zombie takeover, or any civil unrest or natural disaster, U.S. citizens, self-reliant individualists who are deeply suspicious of the government and intellectuals and who are armed with a number of firearms that Europeans find incomprehensible among "civilized" people, would probably fare better than people in other countries. We would all barricade ourselves in our individual houses and start shooting. Or, better yet, we would all use that other quintessentially American machine, the automobile, to drive around and shoot zombies. We would probably gain the upper hand over the zombies in some places in the short term, as is shown in *Night of the Living Dead* and *Dawn of the Dead* (1978). But as the crisis continued, unless our individualism could give way to feelings of trust, sharing, and community, we would be doomed as our individual supplies of ammunition and food gave out and we fell to fighting amongst ourselves: reports after Hurricane Katrina of people looting and shooting at rescue personnel, thereby stopping them from doing their jobs, sadly confirm this. Our American myth of a lone wolf, a tough guy who solves all of his problems with his fist, or, more often, his gun(s), is not very realistic or helpful in our real world;[51] if it excludes community, compassion, and helping others, it is downright sinful, one might say. In zombie movies, such an attitude is epitomized by Ving Rhames' character in *Dawn of the Dead* (2004), who almost leaves the group, spurning their request for and offer of assistance by saying simply, "F**k y'all." It is only when he overcomes this base and foolish urge in himself that he and the group have any chance of survival, a heroic move of putting community ahead of oneself repeated by Riley in *Land of the Dead.*

Anyone who watches zombie movies must be prepared for a strong indictment of life in modern America. It is not just because of the dismemberments, decapitations, and disembowelments that these films are not "feel good" movies, but because of their stinging critique of our society. It is this pointed critique that lifts them above the ranks of other horror movies. But it is a critique that is not wholly unbelievable or misguided. Anyone who says that racism, sexism, materialism, consumerism, and a misguided kind of individualism do not afflict our current American society to a large extent is not being totally honest and accurate. It is, moreover, a critique that could be characterized as broadly Christian, but which many modern American Christians may now find uncomfortable or unfamiliar. Many of us have been rather lax of late in offering critiques of American society, and have more often been enlisted to cheer for our wars and our "values," while perhaps scapegoating a few people, such as homosexuals or doctors who perform abortions or teachers who teach about evolution, as both un-American and un-Christian. But if it is a more fundamental and important description of Christian beliefs to say that Christians believe all people are equal, regardless of their race and gender—and that the only way for people to be really happy is by loving God in community with other human beings, and not by selfishly loving and accumulating material possessions on their own—then the moralizing of zombie movies should not strike us as threatening at all, but as a most welcome corrective, even if presented in unfamiliar and frequently grotesque images.

ZOMBIES AND THEOLOGY

Zombie movies are especially suited to presenting theological ideas of human nature and human destiny because of the nature of zombies and the threat they pose. Zombie movies deal not just with a deadly attack of monsters, but with a situation in which all humans are quickly reduced to a hellish existence, either as zombies, who are the walking damned, robbed of intellect and emotion, or as surviving humans, barricaded and trapped in some place from which there is no escape. Either way, people are doomed to a shadowy, trapped, borderline existence that resembles hell. It is probably no surprise, then, that much of the imagery of zombie movies is borrowed, consciously or unconsciously, from Dante's *Inferno*.[52]

First, there are the zombies themselves, who eerily resemble the description of the damned that Dante gives as he begins his descent into hell: they are "the suffering race of souls who lost the good of intellect."[53] This is exactly how zombies act in all the movies, humans devoid of intellect and reduced just to appetite. They are also, in many ways, embodiments of several of the seven deadly sins.[54] These are for the most part sins of uncontrolled appetite, which Dante presents in the first five circles of hell. Zombies are the nadir of gluttony, eating whenever they can and as much as they can, even though it does not nourish them; they frequently get so distracted in their ghoulish feasts that other humans can easily slaughter them. They are overcome with uncontrollable rage, frequently shown snarling and attacking one another in all the movies when there are no humans around to kill and eat, and there is a shinbone or entrails over which to fight. When they are not fighting or killing, zombies are just as likely to lapse into complete sloth, sitting around doing nothing if there are no humans in sight. More than any other movie monster or mythological creature, zombies vividly show the state of damnation, of human life without the divine gift of reason, and without any hope of change or improvement.

This would perhaps make zombie movies slightly more interesting than the average horror movie, but it is again the human characters who round out and complicate the ideas presented even more. For it is the human characters who in fact embody the majority of the seven deadly sins. Their reason has done little to control their urges, but only allowed them the cunning and skill to survive longer to satisfy their appetites, and even to develop more exotic and evil desires, like cruelty and treachery. Most of the movies are extremely restrained in their depiction of sexuality, but the most despicable human character in the new *Dawn of the Dead*, Steve, is shown flagrantly indulging in the sin of lust, as well as others. As already noted, greed or avarice is frequent among the human characters. If anything, it is their besetting sin, driving them to the utmost of cruelty and violence. It also brings with it envy, as humans foolishly and sinfully risk their lives to take what other humans have. And all of these are symptoms of pride, which is a peculiarly intellectual sin. It does not come from physical appetites, but rather gives rise to them: when one is prideful, one has it in mind that one is superior to others and above their petty rules and limitations, and therefore one's desires do not appear to be indulgences, but things to which one is entitled as a superior person. In contrast to the bestial zombies with their bestial sins, the human characters are frequently conniving and cruel, like the sinners deeper down in Dante's hell, guilty not of lacking reason, but of perverting it to satisfy their sinful desires. The description Dante gives of the sinners lower in hell could just as accurately apply to most of the human characters in zombie movies: ". . . since fraud belongs exclusively to man, God hates it more and, therefore, far below, the fraudulent are placed and suffer most."[55]

In all this, zombie movies have picked up on what is perhaps Dante's greatest and most surprising notion, that hell is not so much a place of external torments, tortures or punishments inflicted on the damned from some force outside of themselves, whether it is demons or God. Rather, both Dante's hell and the hell of a zombie-infested earth are places where the hell is primarily internal, of our own making. Again, in this depiction, zombies come off as the lesser sinners than humans, for zombies merely behave like animals, unthinking slaves to unrestrained, bestial appetites. Though they exaggerate and parody human urges, we can easily excuse them, for they do not seem to know any better. But there is nothing in these movies that makes the humans behave so badly, except their own sinful natures: they, we feel, should know better, and do not. We therefore blame them more, just as we are more aghast and outraged at the sinners deeper in Dante's hell.

An important corollary to this is that in both Dante's hell and a zombie-infested earth, the really horrifying part is not the tortures or punishments, but the endless boredom and repetition; or, rather, the endless repetition *is* the punishment of sin. In Dante's hell, the damned are not punished by withholding their heart's desire from them: the lustful can still be with those after whom they lusted, the wrathful can rend each other limb from limb over and over, and the thieves can steal from each other for all eternity, though none of this brings them any satisfaction, let alone joy. Likewise, zombies go through the motions of their earthly existence, wandering about the mall, going to work, for whatever good it does them.[56] And the surviving humans set up a similarly boring and repetitive world, either in the mall which the undead also crave in *Dawn of the Dead* (1978 and 2004), or in the city/mall/high-riser haven of *Land of the Dead*, rapturously extolling "Life goes on!" in a television ad at the beginning of the movie, beguiling people with advertisements of a life of boring leisure while others starve in the streets and the undead are always just outside the gates, ready to attack. It is a terrifying vision because it proposes that our choices now might have eternal significance, and that death may well resemble and be based on how we live our lives now, as stated more optimistically in another recent movie, *Gladiator* (2000), "What we do in this life, that goes, for eternity!" As Dante has retained his popularity and relevance while many other visions of the afterlife have long been forgotten, zombie movies get their edge and relevancy by asking us uncomfortably whether such an afterlife sounds more like heaven, or more like hell.

Chapter 1

NIGHT OF THE LIVING DEAD (1968)
ROMERO'S FIRST LOOK AT HELL, SIN, AND
HUMAN NATURE

Romero's first zombie movie is one of the great success stories of film history. Shot in rural Pennsylvania on a budget of $114,000,[1] it immediately attracted controversy for its scenes of graphic and unremitting horror, including zombies ravenously eating intestines and other body parts in close-up shots. Even more shocking was the scene of a zombie child eating her father and murdering her mother, stabbing her mother repeatedly with a trowel in a scene deliberately reminiscent of, but infinitely more horrible than, the famous stabbing in Alfred Hitchcock's *Psycho* (1960).[2] *Reader's Digest*, that American bastion and arbiter of bland propriety and taste, rather predictably denounced the film, though it did so with a review by the thoughtful Roger Ebert,[3] who would go on to much greater fame and influence, and whose subsequent evaluation of the film and its sequel, *Dawn of the Dead*, would be much more praising. The review in *Variety* is often quoted at length to show the level of shock and outrage:

> Until the Supreme Court establishes clear-cut guidelines for the pornography of violence, *Night of the Living Dead* will serve nicely as an outer-limit definition by example. In a mere 90 minutes this horror film (pun intended) casts serious aspersions on the integrity and social responsibility of its Pittsburgh-based makers, the film industry as a whole and

[exhibitors] who book [the picture], as well as raising doubts about the future of the regional cinema movement and about the moral health of filmgoers who cheerfully opt for this unrelieved orgy of sadism.[4]

However, they say that there is no such thing as bad publicity, especially not if it is free, and controversy only furthered the film's commercial success. It was a hit first at drive-ins, then an even bigger success in Europe, and finally settled into decades of popularity, profit, and veneration on the midnight movie circuit.[5] Its success has been enshrined now, having been placed on the American Film Institute's list of "Top 100 Thrills" ever seen on film.[6]

The film's success, however, has not only been commercial, but also critical. Reviewers began to recognize that the film did not just shock and disgust, but that it disturbed and perplexed viewers, and demanded more of them at some deeper, more thoughtful, and more introspective level. By the time the sequel, *Dawn of the Dead*, was made a decade later, *Night of the Living Dead* could be hailed as "among the most powerful, fascinating and complex of modern horror films."[7] Critics would also subject the film to detailed and scholarly analysis. As it was analyzed as part of the larger phenomenon of horror films in general, or even of movies in general, *Night of the Living Dead* would be placed at the beginning of a new epoch in horror films, the first of what critics would now recognize as the "modern/contemporary U.S. horror film."[8] The film even seems satirically aware of its epochal and pivotal status, beginning with a character doing an impression of the classic horror movie icon, Boris Karloff, as though to say that the old genre is due for a big shake-up and redefinition here, for new horrors would be offered that would make the old look like a sad, stale joke—aesthetically, emotionally, intellectually, or spiritually.[9] No false modesty from the fledgling director Romero; I think any viewer will have to admit that his premonition of how meaningful and influential his work would be proved entirely justified.

SYNOPSIS

On an overcast day, we see a car approaching in the distance, as we hear the sound of ominous music. The car enters a cemetery, where a young man and woman get out. As they get out of the car, the car radio mysteriously comes on by itself, the typical kind of harbinger that suggests something is not quite right on this day. The man and woman are brother and sister, Johnny and Barbra,[10] and they have driven 200 miles to lay flowers on their father's grave. Johnny complains constantly of this task and of how late they will now get back, while Barbra notes that it is his fault they got there so late. She comments on how light it is at eight o'clock, because of daylight saving time. As she kneels by the grave to pray, he continues to complain, and it begins to thunder and rain. As they are returning to the car, they see what appears to be a man ambling toward them, and Johnny teases his sister with a Boris Karloff imitation, "They're coming to get you, Barbra!" The "man" is, in fact, the first zombie we see in the movie, and it attacks Barbra. She escapes as Johnny fights with the zombie. Johnny falls and hits his head on a tombstone, which apparently kills him.[11] The zombie then pursues Barbra in a long chase sequence, till she finds refuge in a nearby farmhouse.

Inside the house, Barbra arms herself with a knife from the kitchen, and is startled by a trophy room full of the stuffed heads of animals hanging on the wall. When she climbs the stairs to explore the upper floor, she finds a rotting corpse. As she flees this new horror, she opens the front door to see more zombies gathering outside, and the headlights of a truck coming right up to the door. A black man, Ben, armed with a tire iron, jumps out of the truck and quickly pushes Barbra back into the house. Because the zombies in this version are afraid of any light source, they attack the truck with rocks and smash the headlights. Ben, assuring Barbra that he can take care of "those things," goes outside and kills two of them with the tire iron. But the undead, extremely slow and clumsy in this version, still are capable of putting up quite a fight, each one requiring repeated, savage blows with the tire iron before expiring.[12] Ben, exhausted from the fight and with more of the living dead closing in on him, now has to retreat into the house to save Barbra, who is being menaced by another zombie. Ben dispatches this one as well and drags it outside. Sensing Barbra's rising panic, he shouts at her, "Don't look at it!"[13]

Ben now prepares defenses, moving about the house with feverish, frenetic motion, never stopping, while Barbra is completely inert.[14] He drags a stuffed chair outside and sets it ablaze, temporarily frightening the undead who cower and retreat from the flames. He starts breaking up furniture and removing interior doors, using the pieces to barricade the windows and exterior doors. As Ben moves about, he tells of how he came to the house. He had been at a diner, and had seen a tractor trailer being attacked by zombies until the driver crashed the truck. Ben had gone outside and gotten into a pickup truck to try to learn what was happening by listening to the radio, and had been thereby cutoff from those inside the diner, who were surrounded and killed by "those things." He had then escaped in the truck until he found the farmhouse. Barbra then also tells her story of the attack in the cemetery, though she gets increasingly frantic in the retelling. Ben, masterful at building and working with objects, seems to have no clue how to deal with her, and can only ineffectually repeat, "You should just calm down!" She finally starts screaming hysterically that they have to go outside to save her brother, hitting Ben in her mad fit, until he retaliates and punches her. In an extreme but altogether believable piece of "psychological verisimilitude,"[15] Barbra collapses and remains more or less catatonic for the remainder of the film.

Ben continues his furious activity, finding useful objects like a radio and even a rifle and bullets. The radio informs them of an "epidemic of mass murder" that has engulfed the eastern third of the United States. It urges all people to remain where they are and not attempt to travel. The broadcast's description of the zombies, however, does not quite match up with what we have seen of them: the radio announcer tries inaccurately to fit the zombies either into a human category—calling them an "army of assassins"—or to overlook their obvious humanity completely by calling them "misshapen monsters." The zombies we see in this film are clearly neither of these things: they are human, yet monstrous; monstrous, yet still somehow human.[16] That is what so terrifies Barbra that it drives her into madness—the visage of a human monster, like the zombies or the corpse upstairs. In a world with the living dead outside the house and rotting corpses within, nothing "fits" or makes sense to her anymore.

With the radio's approval of his preparations, Ben completes the barricades downstairs, and then moves upstairs and drags the corpse into a room, trying to hide it from Barbra and spare further hysterics. But as he is doing so, Barbra watches in terror as a door opens and hands reach around it into the room. The suspense is unbearable, but it is not the threat that we expect: the door leads to the basement, and two white men who had been hiding there emerge, a middle-aged man, Harry Cooper, and a teenager, Tom. Down in the basement are also Harry's wife, Helen; his daughter, Karen, who has been bitten by zombies; and Tom's girlfriend, Judy. The joining of forces between the group in the basement and Ben and Barbra begins badly, for Ben is deeply suspicious and accusatory of these people who hid in the basement and ignored them, despite Barbra's earlier screaming. Ben and Harry immediately begin to argue and vie for control of the group, with only Tom advocating for cooperation.[17] Harry wants to retreat back to the basement, while Ben, so proud of his accomplishment of barricading the first floor, wants to stay there. Romero makes it clear that the humans can expect little help from one another in their attempts to defend themselves from the living dead, who show no signs of any similar dissent or disorganization in their group or in their steadfast resolve to destroy the living.[18] Indeed, with their anger and fighting amongst themselves, the living may even have as much to fear from one another as they do from the ghouls outside.

When not bickering, the group gets more news, first from the radio, then from a television they also find.[19] They learn first that the attackers are also eating their victims, adding a new dimension to the horror they face—that they will not only be killed, but eaten alive. The authorities have now figured out that the creatures are animate corpses, and they connect this phenomenon with a space probe that had returned to Earth with a "mysterious, high-level of radiation." In the face of this threat, the broadcast now reverses the previous advice of staying in homes, and urges people to go to rescue stations, listing the names and locations of such stations on the screen. Authorities also demand the immediate burning of all dead bodies to prevent their reanimation.

Ben now tries to formulate a plan to follow this new advice to flee to a rescue station, over the protests of the craven Harry, of course. The plan they concoct seems difficult, but workable, though only if everyone cooperates. Harry must throw Molotov cocktails from a second floor window, driving back the crowds of the undead that are now staggering all around outside the house. Ben and Tom will then rush to the truck and drive it to the nearby barn, where Ben saw a gas pump, while Harry runs downstairs to bar the door from which the other two have run. After refueling the truck, they will drive back to the farmhouse to pick up the others, and escape to the nearest rescue station.

The plan goes awry almost as soon as they start, in the quasi-comic, all-horrific manner at which Romero has excelled throughout his career. Judy, fearing for Tom, follows him out the door, thereby complicating the mission. Despite this, Ben, Tom, and Judy do succeed in getting into the truck and driving it to the gas pump, while Harry secures the door behind them. At the pump, however, Tom spills gasoline onto the side of the truck, and it catches on fire from the torch that they brought. The truck is engulfed in flames, right next to the gas pump, with Judy still inside the truck. Tom gets back inside to drive the truck away from the pump, then stops it, attempting to escape before it explodes. But Judy's jacket is caught on something, and as Tom helps to free her, the truck explodes and kills them both. This leaves Ben alone, hundreds of feet from the house, with the living dead closing in on him. He fights his way past the slow moving zombies, but Harry, quite predictably, refuses to let him back in. Ben breaks down the door and savagely beats Harry for trying to keep him outside with the undead. Meanwhile, we behold the spectacle of the zombies feasting on the burnt bodies of Tom and Judy in lurid and shocking detail, all of it bathed in moonlight, eerie and unearthly, "a macabre sort of picnic."[20]

Inside the house, the survivors watch the television, which shows the success of a posse of zombie killers led by a sheriff named McClelland. Well-armed men with dogs are seen working their way across the countryside, methodically shooting zombies in the head. Sheriff McClelland himself is interviewed and seems confident that their mission to destroy all zombies in the area will be successfully completed in a matter of hours. But then the power goes off in the farmhouse, and the undead begin their final assault on Ben and the others. As Ben struggles to beat back the hands and arms that grope and grab through the barricades, he sets the rifle down on the floor. Harry now grabs the gun, trying to reassert his authority, and orders his wife back down to the basement. She refuses, and Ben and Harry then fight over the gun. Ben disarms Harry and shoots him in the chest. Harry falls down into the basement as the living dead break in. Ben turns his attention back to the zombie threat, still trying to fight them off, while Helen is grabbed by undead hands. For some reason, her screams revive Barbra somewhat, who rushes to her aid and manages to free her from the zombies. Helen flees to the basement, where she finds her loathsome husband now dead, his arm being gnawed on by her undead daughter. In a scene whose horror far outstrips that of any previous scene in the movie, the zombie daughter, her mouth still dripping with her father's blood, slowly but inexorably corners her mother and stabs her in the chest fourteen times with a trowel.[21]

Back upstairs, Ben and Barbra continue fighting their losing battle against the zombie invaders. Barbra is confronted by her undead brother, who grabs her and drags her to the heart of the zombie mob to be devoured. Ben retreats back into the basement, tossing the Coopers' zombie daughter out of the way and barricading the door against the zombies, who now have complete control of the upper floor that he had worked so hard to secure. With pounding on the basement door, Ben goes down the stairs to find the Coopers, each of whom he shoots in the head as they reanimate. With undead corpses stomping and moaning above, and regular corpses right next to him—one of them murdered by him, and both of them shot in the head by him while in their zombie state—Ben throws the rifle to the floor in disgust, pauses, then picks it back up and sits down to await his fate.

With the rising of the sun, we again see the situation from the vantage point of the zombie-killing posse, who are grimly but effectively carrying out their work. They pursue the undead across fields and easily pick them off. They proceed toward the farmhouse that had been the scene of such horror just hours before (or, from the perspective of us, the audience, just minutes before), cavalierly dismissing the charred bodies of Tom and Judy with, "Somebody sure had a cookout here!" Back in the farmhouse, Ben hears their gunshots and barking dogs and emerges from his hiding place to peer at them through a window. As he does so, one member of the posse spots him, takes aim, and shoots him in the head. Thus ends our protagonist, not going out fighting, not even the victim of the monstrous zombies, but just someone killed by mistake by careless, trigger-happy humans. A series of grisly frames repeatedly show the meat hooks with which he is picked up and dumped on to a bonfire to be burned with the zombies that he had so bravely fought throughout the movie.

The ending of the first movie shows exactly how skilled Romero is at subverting our expectations. We are aghast at each turn of the movie—the attack in the cemetery, the immolation and devouring of Tom and Judy, the senseless murder of Harry, the savage killing of Helen by her own daughter, the killing of Barbra by her own brother—but in a way those scenes of horror are less shocking narratively than it is to have our hapless and imperfect hero disposed of so meaninglessly and nonchalantly. It is an ending so effective, however, that it has since become a standard part of the horror movie genre: "The unhappy ending now became almost universal in horror movies."[22] More importantly, it is a cinematic statement totally in tune with the horrors of assassination, riots, and war that were going on when it was made.[23] The enormous, worldwide popularity of such a hopeless film shows that its hopelessness struck a chord with people, said something meaningful to people about a world of meaninglessness. Rather than turn away from such a dismal vision, as the well-meaning critics at *Reader's Digest* and elsewhere advocated, it is far better to confront and analyze it, as we shall now attempt.

ANALYSIS

First, we should note the many conventions of the horror movie genre that *Night of the Living Dead* utilizes to create its unrelenting terror, to give homage where it is due at the level of mere craftsmanship and technical proficiency before we move on to analyze its meaning. The beginning sequence of Barbra being chased by one zombie to the farmhouse runs like the primal nightmare every person has had, in which we are being chased and are unable to escape, impeded and moving as if in slow motion.[24] The use of Gothic music and thunderclaps is also as standard as it is effective. The use of black and white film, necessitated by the film's nearly nonexistent budget, has also been frequently noted for its effective evocation of simple, primal fear and greater verisimilitude,[25] without the gaudy distraction of Technicolor "splatter" that both Romero and his imitators would utilize so generously in subsequent films.

It is equally important, however, to note how on this and other points, the movie surprises us on closer inspection and repeated viewing: this sequence is neither filmed in slow motion, nor is it done using a handheld camera from the monster's point of view, as has since become standard practice, but most of us who have seen the film probably remember it this way: it is almost as if the scene so effectively replicates the conventions of our nightmares that we then remember it as if it really were a nightmare and not "just" a film. Such a dynamic is vividly shown by how viewers remember the movie's setting. Several commentators assume the film takes place in the autumn,[26] because in the opening sequence, Johnny and Barbra talk about the time change for daylight savings,[27] and because there can really be no movie better suited in mood to the dying, somber hues of autumn and Halloween than *Night of the Living Dead*. And yet closer attention to the dialogue shows Barbra commenting on how it is still light at eight o'clock at night, so the whole film must really occur in the spring, as inappropriate as that would be to its mood. Romero follows conventions when it suits him, and subverts them when it suits him, constantly throwing even the most observant or experienced viewer off balance.

Once Barbra is in the farmhouse, Romero's favorite device is another standard of the genre, the sudden, frantic cutting between camera angles—"shock cuts" or "jump cuts"—to startle the audience and show the character's rising terror. These are used when Barbra is startled in the trophy room of dead animals' heads, in a fairly predictable scene of momentary shock for us and the character, but which does have some symbolism for its imagery of animals who look disconcertingly both alive and dead, and for its suggestion that the hunters are now the hunted.[28] But in a more interesting way, new characters always appear in the movie from disturbing camera angles. At their first appearances, Ben, Harry, and Tom all lunge out at Barbra (and us) unexpectedly with the camera held at an odd diagonal tilt.[29] The effect of these shots is not just momentary shock, but a deeper disorientation and irony: the living dead can sneak up twice on Barbra at the beginning, and completely harmless taxidermy terrifies her, but living people pose a more disturbing, unexpected threat—both to her and to us, the film implies by the end—because they are so violent and unpredictable.[30] On the other hand, the camera angle can also belie a false sense of stability and security. While the people are shot at disorienting and frightening angles, the television set and the newscasts on it are always shown in perfect symmetry and evenness, implying their solidity and trustworthiness, even while every piece of information and advice spewing out of the television turns out to be fatally in error.[31] Here we have good examples of where mere technique can blend over into a statement about the film's deeper meaning.

Finally, on these points of the film's craftsmanship and technique, there is its careful blending of two horror movie genres. Horror movies often deal with two quite distinct threats—monsters that threaten the entire earth (as in *War of the Worlds* [1953 and 2005]), and those that threaten only an individual or small group (any psycho-killer movie, such as *Psycho* [1960] or *Halloween* [1978]). But *Night of the Living Dead* really presents both sides of the threat, where zombies are over-running a large part of the United States, but we watch a tiny drama of seven people unfold as they fight a few dozen zombies.[32] This will be the formula for the subsequent zombie movies—what has been called the "mass zombie"[33] movie—but has also become a standard feature of many other horror movies, where the threat is global, even though the scope of the drama is minute. As above with camera angles, this is not just a technical change. Part of the increased horror of a mass zombie attack is the complete failure of human institutions to aid survivors, and even the probable culpability of those institutions, either by creating zombies in the first place through some hideous failed experiment, or by providing people with false and inaccurate information that only leads to further deaths.[34] After *Night of the Living Dead*, the formula so often seen in 1950s horror movies of all-knowing scientists directing the actions of a brave and disciplined military, such as in the classic *Them!* (1954), would be regarded as appropriate only in a parody, like *Mars Attacks!* (1996), or a fluffy, escapist, Saturday matinee piece like *Independence Day* (1996). In other words, from now on, both Godzilla and Norman Bates would seem quaint and not really terrifying.[35] After Romero's masterpiece, real horror would be global, and would be partly the fault of our governments and other institutions. Given the deadly effects of and responses to terrorism, global warming, hurricanes, droughts, famines, genocides, and biological, nuclear, and conventional warfare, one would be hard pressed indeed to accuse Romero of exaggerating or being overly pessimistic.

Let us now consider the various failings of human nature in general, and American society in particular, that Romero criticizes in this film. The sin which will become the driving image of *Dawn of the Dead*—materialism or consumerism—is really not present in this first installment.[36] Nowhere is it suggested—as it is in all the later movies—that zombies somehow repeat the behaviors and mistakes of their former, human existence. (After all, if that were the case, why would so many zombies be drawn to this remote farmhouse?) In this first film, zombies are simply and monomaniacally driven to kill and eat humans, which they do so with a gusto seldom repeated in the later installments. The zombies' indulgence in other sins, such as greed, seems to be a later development, to make zombies symbolic of human sin and addiction more generally. In *Night of the Living Dead*, zombies are consumers only in the narrow sense of eaters, and they are sinners only for the specific sin of gluttony.

Likewise, the racism that is so blatant at the beginning of *Dawn of the Dead*, and so undercut by its ending, is treated much more subtly and indirectly in *Night of the Living Dead*. Although the protagonist of the first film is black, nothing is ever made of this. Ben's race is never the subject of approval, disapproval, judgment, innuendo, or even remark.[37] As we saw above with the film's supposed setting in the autumn, it is hard for viewers sometimes not to "read" back into the film a reaction that is not there, for even critics have asserted that Harry Cooper is a racist or bigot,[38] when such is never hinted at in any way in the film itself. And the posse that kills Ben at the end—as destructive and careless as they may be—never remarks on Ben's race before or after shooting him. Nevertheless, while we should give Harry the benefit of the doubt, Romero goes out of his way to surround the posse with imagery that makes it nearly impossible to over-look their similarity to an American lynch mob—a crowd of exclusively white men, only loosely governed by governmental authorities, with guns and barking dogs, killing everything in their path.[39] Moreover, in their role as enforcers and reestablishers of societal order—which is to say, a white, American, capitalist order—against the zombie's chaos, the posse's killing of a black man may be meant to connect him to the zombies as a perceived threat to that order.[40] As above with materialism, racism seems to be an issue that the second and subsequent movies would deal with much more explicitly, but Romero left hints in the first film of how racism appeals to the basest, most violent and uncontrolled urges in all of us, and how perva-sive and subtle it is in our society.

Even more than with materialism and racism, the critique of sexism that will be more prominent in the later films is wholly absent in this first installment. If anything, Barbra's catatonic helplessness,[41] Judy's clinging infatuation, and Helen's middle-aged dissatisfaction are all quite negative female stereotypes in the film. Barbra's caricature of weakness and irra-tionality goes as far as to equate her with the zombies at one point, when she flinches at the sight of a flame, the way a zombie would. But, in a way, if Romero is not interested in critiquing negative female stereotypes this time, it is just because in this film, everyone—male or female—is almost com-pletely unlikable and unappealing. The men, too, are portrayed extremely negatively—Ben, the hot-headed, violent individualist; Harry, the sniveling, hysterical coward; and Tom, the obedient but inept follower. We can really only talk in relative terms, in which the brave but murderous Ben is more appealing than the craven and treacherous Harry.[42] This is brought out vividly in their first encounter with one another, when Ben angrily com-plains why Harry had stayed hidden in the basement when he could hear Barbra's screams, to which Harry responds, "You're telling us we got to risk our lives just because somebody might need help?!" It is the most cowardly abdication of responsibility and humanity, and Ben coldly and with disgust answers, "Yeah, something like that." But with his own will to dominate and quickness to violence, Ben is still, at best, "a compromised hero."[43] He is much more willing to fight and die for another person than Harry ever could be, but he is also much more willing to bully and kill another human being in order to establish his dominance.

The characters' shortcomings—which are presented here as universal and predictable weaknesses due to human nature, and not just character "flaws" unique to these seven people—seriously change the nature of the threat posed to them by their nightlong siege. Part of the power of Romero's film is that the threat is as much within the house as without. It is not bad enough for our band of survivors that they are surrounded by walking corpses who will never go away until they have torn the humans limb from limb and eaten them alive, for on top of this threat, the humans constantly fight amongst themselves.[44] Without heroic qualities or virtues, our human protagonists are as much a threat to one another as the living dead are to them. This is clear as soon as the people emerge from the basement, when Ben promptly declares, "I'm boss up here!" Whoever wants to go back to the basement can do so, but, according to Ben, anyone who stays upstairs will be in his jurisdiction and under his control:[45] "If you stay up here, you take orders from me!" Whereas the increased number of people could be regarded as an asset for the survivors, with more people to build fortifications and defend against the undead, the opposite is the case in this film, where each extra person is perceived as a new threat.[46] As presented here, there is never any possibility of cooperation or even compromise among the humans, but only of competition and conflict.[47] The one brief sequence of cooperation when they try to get to the gas pump ends with Tom and Judy being incinerated, and then quickly degenerates back into violent competition, with Harry trying to kill Ben by locking him out, and Ben retaliating by savagely beating Harry. The utter savagery and brutality of the people in the film are in their own way much more shocking than anything the zombies do. What the film does, essentially, is present a scenario, like *Lord of the Flies* (novel, 1954; films, 1963 and 1990),[48] that takes the idea of original sin seriously, showing how depraved, violent, and predatory people would be to one another if they really were fundamentally sinful. What goes on in the farmhouse in *Night of the Living Dead* is cynical and horrifying, but it is not unorthodox or even surprising.

The negativity of the characters extends, in fact, into every facet of their lives; indeed, the film implies the deepest denial of the goodness or effectiveness of every facet of human life in general. Every kind of human relationship is ridiculed or negated in the film. The Coopers, the only example of a married couple in any of the films, obviously hate each other and have been slowly tormenting and killing each other for years.[49] Tom and Judy, on the other hand, are a sharp contrast and obviously love each other, but their love is so clingy and irrational that it directly contributes to their horrible deaths, and renders them pathetic.[50] With Karen killing her parents and Johnny killing his sister Barbra, we have the complete negation of family and biological ties.[51] As noted, Ben, the only unattached person in the film, is an example of the kind of fierce individualist who would be the hero in a different kind of movie,[52] but here is reduced to being just a violent bully, and finally, to being just dead garbage. Outside of the farmhouse, we have the televised scenes of the complete ineptitude and duplicity of the government, scientists, and the military. All of this has been called a sharp critique of the "viciousness of American society,"[53] and it is that, but it really goes much deeper. This is a rejection of any value for any human relationship, institution, or virtue.[54] According to this most cynical and nihilistic of the films we will be examining, nothing really matters, because the result is always the same—death.[55] It is a vision at which any sane person should cringe, but let us not be too quick to dismiss the contemplation of death as an essential part of religious thought and maturity.

Two of the antidotes most commonly prescribed for these human problems of death and meaninglessness are the exercise of human reason—a natural, human solution, if you will, even if one acknowledges that reason is a gift from God; and the acceptance of faith—a supernatural solution given by and oriented towards God. Since the eighteenth century, these two have often been perceived as competitors or enemies, with many in the modern, western world preferring the solution of human reason to divine revelation and faith. With the same thoroughness and cynicism we have already observed, Romero denies the value of either reason or faith, but in a way which I would suggest is still heuristic and beneficial to faith. This is because Romero proceeds by offering fairly typical, modern critiques of religion throughout the film, but simultaneously undermines the premises of those critiques. In the opening sequence, Johnny mocks his sister for her praying. The fact that he is promptly killed does not discredit his mockery, either, as it would in a simpler film, for Barbra and everyone else die too, and more horribly than with a blow to the head.[56] Later, as the survivors watch the television, a doctor offers a similar dismissal of religion in his advice for how to dispose of dead bodies: "The bereaved will have to forego the dubious comforts that a funeral service will give. They are just dead flesh and dangerous." Again, religion is dismissed by a hard-nosed rational-ist as foolish, irrational, counterproductive superstition and sentimentality. Reason alone can save the day. But as with the official pronouncements that zombies are "misshapen monsters" and "assassins," this description of them as "just dead flesh" is also not accurate. They remain human, and can-not be treated as trash, at least not without serious damage to the humans who do so.[57] If religion cannot protect us from physical death, reason and the detached, unemotional violence dictated by reason cannot protect us from the psychological harm of killing and death. And the failure of reason and human resourcefulness in the film is just as complete as the failure of Barbra's gestures of faith. Ben is, for all his faults, a very rational, purpose-ful, and even brave man, but all of that is as useless against the undead as Barbra's prayers. This is brought out perhaps most graphically with the utter failure of the gun in this movie, especially striking since spectacular head-shots against zombies are so prominent in every other installment. But here, the gun, a tool of human ingenuity and power, is only useful for killing other humans. And even more importantly, Ben's modern, rational-ist virtues are also completely useless against his own inner demons of vio-lence and domination.[58] If the movie's modern, rationalist critique of religion is totally unsurprising in the context of the late twentieth century, its complete rejection or denial of the value of reason is quite shocking,[59] and even, perhaps, a little refreshing.

There are two main reasons that I think the film's dismantling of both reason and faith is ultimately much more damning to reason than it is to faith, and may even be indirectly supportive of faith. First, there are the dif-ferent claims made by faith and reason for what they can and cannot do.

With some exceptions,[60] most modern religions, including most forms of Christianity, do not claim to be able to eradicate physical death, or even to avoid misfortune and suffering before death. Such a limitation is frankly admitted in the biblical book of Job, and in theological works such as *City of God* by St. Augustine (354–430), which makes clear that,[61] exactly as in *Night of the Living Dead*, piety and prayer will not keep the faithful from being killed in war, and even subjected to worse wartime atrocities, such as rape, mutilation, and cannibalism. But reason and human ingenuity, it has often been claimed—as the doctor claims in *Night of the Living Dead*, and as Ben seems to believe—will lead to material prosperity and physical well-being, if not all the way to immortality, then at least to a very long and healthy lifespan on earth. So if this movie claims that neither faith nor reason can physically save your life in a crisis, then it seems as though the claims of reason's proponents have been seriously undermined, while the claims of most believers in faith are unaffected, for the faithful do not claim such a power over physical death and adversity.

More importantly, I think, is the observation made above, that for all its cynicism, *Night of the Living Dead* presents us with a scenario that is not just compatible with the Christian idea of original sin, but a scenario that would have to turn out this way if we really believed in original sin. Here again, the optimistic claims of unaided human reason are far more unrealistic, according to Romero's film, than are the claims of religion. Reason and all the modern movements and concepts that grow out of it—the Enlightenment, modernity, and modern concepts of how people could be made to behave nicely and cooperatively by utilizing a supposed desire like enlightened self-interest—all of these simply ignore human sinfulness. So if one follows only the dictates of reason, one would be powerless and completely taken by surprise when people start behaving in accord with what is called, in Christian theology, the *libido dominandi*, the innate "lust for domination," which the survivors in the farmhouse display with a vengeance.[62] Romero may not think that Christianity has the cure for sin,[63] but he would at least have to admit that it has the diagnosis right, in counterdistinction to its major modern detractors and competitors.[64] And Christians would have to admit that, although they must disagree with

Romero's denial of a cure, he has the diagnosis of sin more right than many modern thinkers and artists, and has compellingly presented it in all its power and horror.

CONCLUSION

In sharp contrast to how he will conclude the later movies, Romero ends *Night of the Living Dead* with the complete defeat of the zombie hordes at the hands of organized, victorious human troops. With the dawn, the world is saved and humanity is once again safe: "Everything appears to be under control," announces the newscaster at the end of the film. And yet, who could feel uplifted at the end of this first movie? It is clearly and overwhelmingly the most hopeless and depressing of all the Romero zombie movies, even though the others end with the total victory of the undead and the complete (or near complete) extinction of the human race.[65] What gives this film its "gluey, bottomless horror"[66] is that at the end, the world has been returned to a normalcy of extremely dubious value or goodness, a world in which thoughtless, unrestrained violence is the only thing to be valued or pursued, and real love, sacrifice, and morality are literally consumed by undead mouths and callous, undiscriminating funereal pyres. But, as with the horrors of Dante's *Inferno*, even in this most cynical installment of the films we will examine, there is something positive to be learned about human life, if not as a reality, then at least as an ideal or hope. The later films are able to hint at some future restoration and improvement in human life, only because the darkness of this first night so thoroughly and terrifyingly shows the limits of human nature, reason, and institutions. *Night of the Living Dead* is a disorienting, unmooring, harrowing statement of hopelessness, but one in which, I think, one can find the hints of a future hope, or, at least, the adamant rejection of an unrealistic optimism or sentimentality that overestimates human abilities and underestimates human depravity. According to this film, there probably is really no hope for a fallen, sinful humanity. But it seems even more clear that we would never be able to escape from or reject sin, unless and until we admitted its hold on us, and stopped looking to our own strength and reason to save us from it. This first part of redemption, at least—the part in which we realize our weakness and insufficiency—this film shows much more vividly, disturbingly, and therefore effectively,[67] than works that are straightforwardly orthodox or pious. For its effectiveness at undermining our human arrogance, supposed self-sufficiency, and resulting complacency, *Night of the Living Dead* is relevant for Christians, or for any humane person who believes in human sinfulness and seeks to limit it.

Chapter 2

DAWN OF THE DEAD (1978)
CONSUMERISM, MATERIALISM, AND THE
FOURTH CIRCLE OF HELL

Ten years after the release of his enormously popular and profitable film *Night of the Living Dead*, Romero finally prepared the sequel that he had been discussing for years. What he came up with is certainly one of the few sequels that lives up to its progenitor. Roger Ebert, whose pronouncements carry about as much weight in modern American film as the Delphic oracle's did in ancient Greece, has hailed *Dawn of the Dead* as "one of the best horror films ever made . . . brilliantly crafted, funny, droll, and savagely merciless in its satiric view of the American consumer society." Although most would admit that *Night of the Living Dead* remains the scarier movie, some critics have noted that *Dawn of the Dead* is more complex and thoughtful. Romero's budget this time, variously reported between $1 and $2 million,[4] was a factor of ten beyond that of the original, but it was still nearly nonexistent by the standards of Hollywood, where the following year the bar would be raised on high budget clunkers with the release of *Heaven's Gate* (1980), a movie reportedly made for $44 million that grossed $1.5 million. For a second time, Romero had taken no money and a group of unknown actors into western Pennsylvania and produced a commercially successful movie that would eventually go on to be deemed a classic of its genre.[5]

The recognized high quality of *Dawn of the Dead* has nothing to do with increased budget, better special effects, or higher production values than its precursor, or other horror movies, for that matter. Rather, what Romero did a second time was hit a raw, frayed nerve about life in the United States in the late '70s, just as he had in the late '60s. The black-and-white zombies of his first movie devoured an America mired in and distraught over race riots, Vietnam, and the assassinations of those men who brought hope; the zombies and humans whose insides are splattered across the screen in gaudy Technicolor in *Dawn of the Dead* inhabit an America of enormous shopping malls, a fuel shortage, grinding urban poverty, abortion on demand (Roe v. Wade having been decided in 1973), and a Cold War and racism still simmering and sickening our society. Considering how our national debates and individual lives are still so strongly influenced by racism, consumerism, poverty, abortion, dependence on foreign oil, and terrorists left over from the Cold War (the Soviet Union invaded Afghanistan the same year *Dawn of the Dead* was released, a war in which the United States would support and arm Islamist terrorists), it is little wonder that Romero's second zombie film is considered by many his most trenchant and timeless classic.

SYNOPSIS

The movie begins in a television studio. People are furiously running around in a state of panic, disorganization, and exhaustion. They are broadcasting some kind of news cast of the unfolding zombie crisis. An "expert" tells an incredulous and argumentative interviewer that all dead bodies must be "exterminated," either by decapitating them or destroying their brains. Each corpse not so treated will rise up as one of "them" and will attack and kill others, who will then go on to attack and kill. Further, the "expert" declares that all citizens must trust the government and submit to martial law, abandoning private homes, the place of refuge in the first movie, to gather at designated rescue stations.[6] Everything the doctor says smacks of staggering arrogance, blinding ignorance, and stifling inhumanity. As the interview goes on, the locations of the supposed rescue stations are run across the bottom of the screen, though the crew admits many of these stations have already been overrun by the undead. With such fatal flaws being knowingly broadcast, the interviewer and the rest of the studio crew refuse to cooperate with the doctor as the purported voice of reason and authority. Instead they shout him down, challenging the accuracy and morality of what he suggests. They are also shown leaving the studio in ones and twos, fleeing the dying city, which we find out is Philadelphia. Government, science, the media, the "experts"—all the authorities of our society who are responsible for keeping barbarism and chaos at bay—are falling apart. As one crew member succinctly diagnoses the situation, "We're losing it."

In this opening scene, our attention focuses on one woman, Fran, who courageously refuses to broadcast inaccurate information, and takes the names of rescue stations off the screen until an accurate list can be made, over the protests of her boss, who is still insanely concerned with their ratings. She is approached by a man in a flight jacket, Steve, who tells her to meet him at nine o' clock to escape with him in the traffic helicopter. Fran hesitates, still feeling a responsibility for others, but she is assured by another worker that the studio will be shut down tonight anyway and be put into the control of the Emergency Broadcast System. As the doctor shouts that people must trust the National Guard to control the situation, the scene cuts abruptly to a SWAT team assaulting an apartment building in the darkness of night. The scene shows graphically, in the most horrible carnage of the film up until the end, how unprepared the authorities are, and how fatally futile the doctor's advice would be if heeded. The police burst into a housing project occupied by blacks and Latinos, killing several, as several police officers are lost to residents who return fire. All of this carnage is committed, we soon find out, because the apartment dwellers have been keeping dead bodies in their building, locked in apartments and in the basement, refusing to "exterminate" their former family members and neighbors. The authorities are here to retake control, as the doctor predicted, but they are not up to the task. In one part of the building, when the police and National Guard find the hiding place of the zombies, they are immediately overwhelmed by the hordes of the undead and are driven back; in another part of the building, officers work their way upstairs unimpeded.

In all of this chaos, we follow one SWAT team member, a blonde-haired young man named Roger. With his eyes stinging from tear gas, he watches the horror unfold. Before the attack even begins, the young rookie next to him is shot between the eyes. Roger then sees one member of his team go berserk on a racist shooting spree, killing blacks and Latinos indiscriminately while shouting racial epithets, until one of his fellow officers finally guns him down. Roger is then forced to fight for his life with a zombie inside an apartment. He shoots it in the head, and then witnesses a fellow officer commit suicide, rather than face more horror. In the hallway, meanwhile, another zombie attacks a woman, apparently his former wife, and he tears massive, bloody chunks from her neck and arm as she screams and writhes in agony. The police are unable to help her because they cannot get a good shot at the zombie with her in the way.

The sickening ordeal drives Roger down to the basement, where he bends over a sink, on the verge of vomiting. He is joined by Peter, a black SWAT team member, who first appears ominously in inhuman form, wearing a gas mask and emerging from the shadows.[7] The two smoke cigarettes together and develop an instant rapport, based on their mutual witnessing of the violence, futility, and horror above.[8] Peter is enlisted in the escape plan for this night with Steve and Fran. Roger and Peter are interrupted by the one-legged, old Puerto Rican priest who oversaw the humane but dangerous action to protect the building's (un)dead and forebodingly warns them, "You are stronger than us, but soon, I think, they be stronger than you."[9] He leads them to where more animate corpses are hidden, this time under some restraints, tied up, or in bags, and Peter and Roger carry out the grim task of shooting each of them in the head. It is perhaps the most horrifying scene in this or any horror movie, for it is not a struggle against some monstrous threat, or even a victimization by such a threat. Instead, it is merely an "extermination," just as the doctor ordered, but a horrible and dehumanizing extermination of quasi-human vermin, squirming around in their own filth, helpless to defend themselves and helpless to be anything other than what they are: bestial, stupid, and deadly.[10] One could rejoice at impaling Dracula, one could even rejoice at shooting a terrorist in the head, but at this execution one can only stare, stupefied, bewildered, and sickened.

Next, the four protagonists—Fran, Steve, Roger, and Peter—get aboard a helicopter to escape. As they lift off, the lights of a skyscraper in the background flicker ominously and go off, floor by floor. The group flies west over Pennsylvania, looking down on civilians and National Guard units in the hinterlands who have organized their own way of dealing with the zombie menace. People in rural areas are, for the time being, faring much better than the city dwellers, gathering in a boisterous group in a field on a cool and beautiful autumn morning, drinking coffee and beer, boasting of their successful zombie kills so far, and easily executing the undead who approach them in ones and twos. Our protagonists fly over, eventually landing to refuel at a rural airport. Here, Romero's social commentary is pretty obvious and concrete: a lack of fuel dogs the protagonists' existence throughout the film, as it did America's at the time, and still does today.[11] At the airport, the four unwisely split up, the oldest and most inviolable of horror movie clichés, and the undead set upon them and nearly kill them all. Steve and Fran, with the least combat experience of the group, are predictably taken by surprise, but Steve does have the prowess to dispatch one zombie with a sledgehammer. But even the experienced Peter is ambushed by two children zombies, and another zombie sneaks up on Roger while he is pumping the fuel, providing one of the most spectacular shots in any of the films. The zombie steps up on a crate while approaching the helicopter and rises into the whirling helicopter blades, which lop off the top two inches of his head. The four eventually escape and keep flying, now more fully aware of the danger posed by the undead.

Even with fuel, Steve cannot keep flying the helicopter without sleep, so the group has to land somewhere. After their first stop, they are understandably wary, and Peter raises a further complication—that the living, like the undead, may not be sympathetic, especially when it comes to two police officers who have abandoned their posts in a crisis, and two other people who have stolen a helicopter: "We're thieves and we're bad guys. . . . We've got to find our own way." Suddenly, an enormous edifice looms up before them, one that would be immediately recognizable to any North American today, but which was sufficiently novel in 1978 so that Roger could believably exclaim, "What the hell is it?!" It is a giant shopping mall.[12] The helicopter lands safely on the roof, though crowds of the undead mill about aimlessly in the parking lot below. Since the zombies cannot get to the roof, it will at least provide a place to sleep, but when the protagonists look down through the skylights, they quickly realize that the mall has much more to offer, despite Fran's protest that "This is exactly what we're trying to get away from!" Fran and the others first notice a number of rooms not directly attached to the mall proper. They can access these from the roof, and they are full of boxes of civil defense supplies. The group occupies these rooms, eats their fill of Spam, and Steve finally gets some sleep.

But Peter and Roger are tempted by the further wonders and treasures that the mall holds. While the parking lot is full of zombies, the mall itself is still fairly deserted, since the zombies cannot really operate the door handles, except by trial and error. The two men, therefore, decide to go down into the mall to get more supplies. They begin this mission with Steve still asleep, but Fran wakes him up when they do not come back. Steve then goes off to "help," or at least to find them. Again, the inviolable horror movie rule of splitting up in order to investigate unknown, and especially dark places is invoked, and, just like at the rural airport, all four protagonists are nearly killed for their mistake as the slow and clumsy undead come out from hiding and attack them. Fran comes especially close to death when a zombie corners her without a gun. In a movie of such sophistication, it is almost as though Romero knows he is sinking to a cliché—as though he is using the cliché to make fun of his characters, two of them professionals highly trained in combat who should know better than to act like the hysterical teenagers in a *Friday the 13th* (1980, with sequels still in production) movie.[13] And, since we identify with those characters, Romero is thereby making fun of us.

Our four protagonists survive, however, and are now better stocked in their "apartment" above the mall, and able to eat something other than Spam (they spread dark goo on crackers, which may be caviar, showing how quickly they move from bare survival to luxury).[14] We learn at this point that Fran is pregnant, which gives the men pause and even causes them callously to suggest that she undergo a coat hanger abortion, but they then accept the pregnancy as simply another part of their existence.

They also accept Fran now as more of an equal, agreeing that she should always carry a gun, and reluctantly, on Steve's part, that she should also learn to pilot the helicopter to ensure the group's ability to escape in an emergency. With a television they have procured, they again watch the continued rantings of "experts" on the zombie crisis. The doctor of the original broadcast has been replaced by an even more pompous and sinister figure, an enormous man with a black eye patch whose only explanation of the zombies is that they are "pure, motorized instinct," and cautions everyone that "We must not be lulled by the concept that these are our family members or friends. They are not." The disintegration of society they witnessed and fled from at the beginning of the movie is clearly continuing, or even accelerating.

With the outside world receding into irrelevance and inaccessibility, the mall continues its seduction of our protagonists, most especially the men. Now they are not content to raid some supplies and retreat to the apartment, with the eventual goal of moving on. Peter suggests, and the other men readily agree, to the idea of taking over the mall completely and staying there permanently. Their plan involves flying the helicopter to a nearby lot where there are numerous tractor trailers, driving the tractor trailers back and parking them as close as possible to the four mall entrances, thereby preventing more zombies from entering. Then they would go inside the mall, arm themselves to the teeth from a gun shop, and shoot what zombies are already inside. Again falling into clichés and formulae—this time of the action movie genre—Romero presents an exhilarating sequence of a complicated and violent plan that our protagonists enact with skill, precision, teamwork, and success.[15] Though, as with everything good in *Dawn of the Dead*, it comes with a terrible price. Roger is twice bitten by zombies, and his death and return as a zombie are inevitable. There is no treatment for his wounds other than morphine and alcohol, and he cries out in delirium, "We did it, didn't we? We whipped 'em, didn't we? We whipped 'em and we got it all!" His enjoyment of the mall's treasures will only last a few days. In a series of short vignettes, we see the four enjoying the pleasures of the mall, picking out expensive clothes and watches, filling up bags of gourmet candy and food, skating on the mall's ice rink, playing basketball and video games. All that Roger's sacrificial death has procured for them is the ability to act like greedy children.[16]

The reality of life and death intrudes back on their childish antics as Roger's death nears. While Fran and Steve watch television, Roger, horribly emaciated and pale from the hellish contagion, expires in the other room, with his friend Peter standing watch over him, ready to perform the necessary but horrible final service of executing his friend when he rises up as a zombie. On the television, the doctor's suggestions have turned from the unhelpful to the outright terrifying and insane. He suggests such plans as feeding recently dead people to the zombies in order to sate their hunger, and dropping nuclear weapons on all large cities to exterminate the zombies. When the television crew understandably objects, the doctor lapses into a strange, almost trance-like state, rubbing his temples, rocking back and forth and chanting a kind of mantra, "We must remain rational . . . logical . . . logical." Clearly, no help will be coming from outside the mall. The most our protagonists can hope for is that no one is "logical" enough to drop a thermonuclear bomb on them.[17] Fran correctly diagnoses their situation with the observation that "It's really all over, isn't it?" A second later, the shot startles them as Peter shoots Roger in the head.[18] In a scene that again combines real pathos with bizarre and humorous parody in the way at which Romero excels, Peter buries his friend in a planter box in the mall. Roger died securing the fun and goods of the mall, and now he is a part of its eternal display—a grim reminder to future shoppers, but one that they will probably overlook or ignore under the fake rhododendrons.

If the scenes in the mall before Roger's death were ones of childishness, the ones afterwards jump immediately to stagnant, jaundiced middle age. Steve and Peter build a fake wall that hides the entrance to their upstairs apartment, just in case anyone, whether zombie or living, should get back into the mall and try to attack them. Their position is now completely secure, but for what? Unless one really is a zombie, one cannot shop all the time, no matter how much fun it seems at first.[19] And if a person is trapped inside the mall, there is really nothing to do with his "purchases" anyway. Once physical needs are met, the usual point of further consumption in our society is that it be conspicuous, a blaring advertisement of status and prestige to show off in front of the neighbors. But when the neighbors are rotting corpses wandering around the parking lot, this surely offers little satisfaction. Steve attempts a romantic evening with Fran to propose marriage to her, but she remains as sullen and unimpressed with him and the mall as when they first landed. What is a marriage proposal when you are the only woman in town who still has a pulse? She rightly and pithily tells Steve that "It wouldn't be real." Everyone kind of just putters around, and occasionally they get into spats over some trivial, stupid detail of their hopelessly circumscribed existence, but life is grindingly boring and pointless, the ultimate parody or degeneration of a domesticity that is useless without a purpose to fulfill or a goal to pursue. Human life requires challenges, and there are none in the mall where everything is free, and therefore worthless. Fran is again the one to diagnose their disease rightly, as she wretchedly utters, "What have we done to ourselves?"

But if a life without challenges can be deadly boring and dull, a life with deadly challenges can be downright fatal, as the following, climactic sequence shows. As Fran finishes her flight training with a successful landing of the helicopter on the roof, we see others watching them through binoculars. The others prove to be a rather large army of motorcyclists, armed with a plethora of medieval and modern weapons, who determine to attack and loot the mall. As they approach, Peter and Steve attempt to raise their defenses, locking the gates on the stores so that the bikers and the zombies will be confined to the hallways of the mall outside the shops, forcing the bikers to move on. The bikers break in and tear about the mall. They decapitate, blow up, set on fire, run over, hack, stab, smash, and shoot countless zombies they have thereby let inside. Exactly mimicking the zombies' tactics of holding a person down and tearing him limb from limb, the bikers hold down one big woman zombie and steal her jewelry. All of this is done with sadistic, cackling glee, before they lapse into complete slapstick, grabbing a bunch of pies, smashing them into the zombies' faces, and hosing off the pie cream with seltzer bottles. They break through the gates of several stores and trash those, indiscriminately grabbing more or less useless items without strategy or restraint. Things too big to carry they just break for no reason, other than that it is enjoyable.[20]

Peter and Steve look on this destruction and carnage from relative safety above, but soon Steve cannot stand to see what he regards as his rightful possessions being stolen or destroyed. He starts shooting at the motorcyclists, insanely exclaiming that "It's ours! We took it!" He thereby gives away his position, and the bikers return fire and begin closing in on him. Peter starts shooting in an attempt to protect Steve, and also draws fire from the bikers. With the humans shooting at each other, the undead begin filling up the mall in even greater numbers. Now they are not so funny at all, and the film enters its final orgy of violence. The bikers retreat from the mall. Any caught off of their motorcycles or wounded are dismembered, disemboweled, and eaten alive by zombies in some of the most sickening moments on film. Steve is also killed by the living dead after being disabled by gunfire from the bikers. But when he revives as a zombie, he heads purposefully back to the hidden entrance to the upstairs apartment, leading other zombies with him. He throws himself at the fake wall, clawing and biting it until he and the other zombies break through. They climb up to the apartment, where Peter and Fran are waiting. Peter shoots Steve in the head, and ushers Fran to the roof to escape in the helicopter. Peter at first intends to commit suicide, staying behind while only Fran escapes. Neither this plan nor his recanting of it are very well explained, but Peter does reconsider and ends up shooting, kicking, and punching his way past the zombies in the apartment and making it to the helicopter. With only a little fuel, Peter and Fran lift off in the helicopter as the sun rises, the dawn of a new life for them.[21]

Their future is uncertain at the end, but as the end credits roll, we are shown the future of the mall—the dawn of the dead's reign. Fully occupied now by the undead, the mall is a much happier place than it has been in the whole movie. As cheerful, infectious Muzak plays, hilariously reprised in the ads for Shaun of the Dead, we see the undead, looking very content and much happier than Roger, Peter, Steve, and Fran when they occupied the mall. Those people were bad mallgoers because they ultimately expected more from life than mallgoing, just as the members of the biker gang were bad mallgoers, because they were shoplifters and vandals who sought to ruin the shopping experience for others. With those bad mallgoers out of the way, the zombies take their rightful place as the ideal mallgoers, never getting bored or bickering or fighting over items. (There is a little tussle over some entrails, but this is in the days before malls had food courts.) Instead, the zombies are shown peacefully shopping, now and forever, for nothing in particular, and content with anything they find. Theirs is the really and unambiguously happy ending of the movie, with zombies and the mall finally and eternally in a state of blissful peace. It is this kind of brilliant image, one that makes us laugh uncontrollably but uncomfortably by show-ing us the level to which human beings can degenerate, that secures *Dawn of the Dead* its place in the history of filmmaking, and makes worthwhile the arduous ordeal of sitting through the nauseating blood bath that imme-diately precedes it.

ANALYSIS

As is obvious from the ending and much of the rest of the film, American consumer culture comes in for a withering, blistering, frightening, and hilar-ious critique in *Dawn of the Dead*. For Romero, it is not the zombie's bite that turns us into monsters, but materialism and consumerism that turn us into zombies,[22] addicted to things that satisfy only the basest, most animal or mechanical urges of our being. This is repeatedly shown throughout the movie in the behavior of both the zombies and the human characters.

For the zombies, the addiction is shown primarily by their monomania-cal obsession with getting into the mall, even if it means their destruction at the hands of Roger and Peter with their deadly accurate, high-powered rifles, or by the more varied and colorful armory of archaic weapons, firearms, and explosives wielded by the biker gang. Sheer tenacity or the search for prey cannot explain why the zombies pick *this* place as the one that they feel they must occupy, over any other, and at any cost or risk. Though we will never know for sure, one can reasonably infer, based on Romero's depiction, that in a zombie-infested world, the former churches, libraries, and classrooms are not nearly as crowded with the undead as are the malls. (Even, one could reasonably suspect, conventionally sinful places like casinos, bars, and broth-els would not be as crowded with the eager undead as shopping malls. Materialism and constant, mindless consumption are not just tolerated, but enthusiastically encouraged in our society, while other sinful behaviors—gambling, drinking, and prostitution—are still regarded as slightly embarrassing and furtive.) Steve interprets the zombies' behavior very accurately when they first land on the roof of the mall. In response to Fran's question, "Why do they come here?" he answers, "Some kind of instinct. Memory. What they used to do. This was an important place in their lives." And, as noted in the introduction, the potency of this image is in how this place that was important in their lives is now going to continue to be important to them, forever. Again, the horror for human beings lies not just in being torn to pieces and eaten alive by zombies, but in becoming one of them, a mindless mallgoer, never again able to conceive of anything higher or more interesting to do than wander about with a vacuous look of contentment, punctuated by longing, lustful stares at windows and racks and displays full of useless, worthless stuff.[23]

Peter will infer this eternal judgment of the zombies and themselves later in the film, as the human survivors again ponder the zombie hordes that are so eagerly and tenaciously trying to break into their fortified mall, even though the humans have just finished slaughtering hundreds of them to secure it: "They don't know why, they just remember they want to be in here," to which Fran asks, "What the hell are they?" and Peter replies, "They're us, that's all. . . . When there's no more room in hell, the dead will walk the earth."[24] It is the most chilling line in a chilling movie, repeated in the remake in a cameo appearance by Ken Foree, who played Peter in the original. With this statement, Peter rightly judges both zombies and humans as damned to repeat their trivialities and mistakes for all eternity, never again with the possibility of learning from them or improving, because such education and improvement were so consistently spurned in life, and such trivial sinfulness was so enthusiastically embraced. Though people usually use the word "Dantean" to describe the horrible grotesquery and torture in a movie like *Dawn of the Dead*, it is really more applicable to a vision like this. For Dante depicts sin as an addiction—just as it is depicted here—one that is willingly embarked on in life, and hopelessly and eternally repeated in death: "I learned that to this place of punishment all those who sin in lust have been condemned, those who make reason slave to appetite."[25] When they had reason and could think of better things to do than go to the mall, the people who would become mall zombies did not. Instead, they enslaved and finally killed their reason with their mundane and trivial appetites, thereby dooming themselves to repeat their sinful actions forever, never able to correct or extricate themselves from their sinful mistake. Exactly like the damned in Dante's hell, the undead zombies, with their reason gone, simply follow the "motorized instinct" of their "appetite," even if it is now more useless, pointless, and insatiable than ever before. If you "shop till you drop," you will drop very far indeed.[26] If you define yourself as a shopper—most likely unconsciously, and therefore all the more insidiously, for probably no one consciously thinks, "I shop, therefore I am,"[27] but we all sometimes act as though we think exactly that—then you really might become only a shopper, and nothing more, forever: "And when there's no more room in hell, the dead will shop on earth."[28] But, of course, Romero has made such a pointed and Dantean critique even more relevant and uncomfortable, for the humans in this film are no less obsessed with getting into and staying in the mall than are the zombies. This is the first of several points on which Romero will equate zombies and humans in the film, and it is the most important: both zombies and humans are insane and insatiable consumers.[29] The plot of the movie is consistently driven by the humans' lust to acquire and possess, which is especially predominant in the male characters. Roger, Steve, and many of the bikers, almost all of whom are, of course, also male, are killed for their mad, foolish lust for possessions, but all the characters succumb to this lust at one point or another. The bikers, comically portrayed as the least thoughtful among the characters, are even more obsessed with possessions and indiscriminate in acquiring them than our protagonists, killing and dying just to grab any old thing in sight.[30] Steve and Peter steal money and then play poker with it, showing how empty and meaningless it is, and how empty and meaningless they have made their own lives. Steve also epitomizes the attitude that possession is nine-tenths of the law and nine-tenths of the value he puts on his life, apparently, when he snarls, "It's ours! We took it!" and madly sacrifices his life to die in his consumerist prison rather than give it up without a fight.

Even more poignantly, earlier in the film, Roger, in his final, dying delirium, must be convinced by Peter that his sacrifice was worth it, but we know that this is simply and pathetically not so. A telling comparison would be to the similar scene in *The Magnificent Seven* (1960). At the end of the movie, the character Harry Luck is dying after the seven gunslingers have successfully saved a Mexican village from the horrible, violent predations of bandits (who look and act very much like the bikers in *Dawn of the Dead*, one of whom even wears a sombrero). Throughout the movie, however, Harry has been convinced entirely that this was a ruse, and that there is really fabulous treasure hidden in the village, which is what they came and fought for. His companions can console him by lying to him about hidden treasure because they know that he died for something noble, even though his own motives were base. But with Roger, the situation is exactly reversed: there really is loot in the mall—plenty of it—but that is all he died for, not to save a village or secure freedom or goodness or anything noble, but just to get stuff, and that makes his death utterly pathetic and pointless. Even Peter, who seems the most enlightened and thoughtful of the men, is in fact the first to utter a cry of delight at what they variously call their newfound "kingdom" and "gold mine." In response to Roger's objection that they are now cut off from Fran and Steve and trapped inside JCPenney's, Peter shouts, "Who the hell cares? Let's go shopping!" From beginning to end, the film is full of men killing themselves and others to get and hold on to things that they do not really need, and which do not even make them happy. It is one of the saddest and most damning critiques of materialism imaginable.

After Roger's death, as noted, their consumerist bliss turns from childish greed and glee to a more somber kind of middle-aged boredom and resignation.[31] As the saying goes, they no longer own their possessions, their possessions own them. This is especially poignant because of how insidiously it poisons their relationships, especially that between Fran and Steve. The scene of Steve's marriage proposal is the most obvious example.[32] Although I strongly suspect that it is another ploy of our consumerist society to persuade men that they *have* to spend two months of their salary on an engagement ring, it would also seem true that all of the romance and attraction is lost if one could just walk into a jewelry store and grab anything one wanted for free, as Steve has done with Fran's ring. Such a "gift" is not real, for it costs nothing. And what would apply to an engagement ring would apply to everything in their mall paradise/hell: Christmas, birthdays, and anniversaries would be meaningless, as would any gift, because everything is simply lying around, worthless and unappreciated. Without the ability of human beings to give gifts or make sacrifices and thereby show that they care about and value one another, caring and intimacy themselves become difficult for our protagonists. At one point, Steve is shown in a fancy bed with silk sheets as the camera pulls back to reveal Fran right next to him, sullen and bored. They could be making love or cuddling or talking or even just playing checkers, but instead they are utterly miserable and alone together in their gilded prison.[33]

Even Fran, although she seems ten times more perceptive and resistant to the mall's supposed charms than her male companions, is shown briefly succumbing to some kind of consumerist fantasy late in the movie. She sits at an enormous vanity mirror, made up with so much make-up that it is clownish and grotesque, not sexy or attractive. She tries to strike seductive or suggestive poses with a pearl handled pistol, like Bonnie in *Bonnie and Clyde* (1967), though it all seems quite unnecessary and absurd. Fran is a very pretty woman, allowing for the clothes and hairstyles of the '70s, and this hideous posturing is clearly no improvement.[34] Her fantasy is going badly enough when the mall loudspeakers issue a call, "Attention shoppers!" Her illusion of glamour and beauty is completely shattered by the loudspeakers' offer of a free bag of cheap candy with every purchase, and Fran seems more disgusted than ever—this time with herself as well.[35] She realizes the mall is hypnotizing them and making them as fake as it is, with its faux foliage in planter boxes, one of which now rather unceremoniously serves as a tomb; its hollow, toyland-like clock tower, chiming hours in a land where time certainly does not matter anymore;[36] and its mannequins with painted tans and grins in a world where there is no sun and very little at which to smile. The mall is also making them as dead and numb as the other zombies that ravenously and impotently paw and slobber at its outside doors. They are trapped outside, and our three survivors are trapped inside. But the movie, like Dante, is not fatalistic, at least not for those still on this side of undeath. Right up until the death rattle or disembowelment that will make someone permanently and irrevocably a zombie, he or she can make choices that matter. Fran takes responsibility for herself, not blaming the situation or others, when she confronts the men in the group: "What have we done to ourselves?"[37] She can see what their base and simplistic urges are doing to them, and she is ready to make different and better choices.[38] If the movie is to have meaning and importance, its audience must be so willing as well.

This consumerism that overtakes the male characters especially is perhaps the most noticeable part of the film's critique of sexism. With all of the protests that some American men make about how they hate to go shopping with their "womenfolk," it is a hilarious parody to have the swaggering, macho male characters as the ones who are immediately enthralled by the lure of eternal shopping, while the female character is the lone, disdainful holdout, insightfully observing, "This is exactly what we're trying to get away from."[39] When Fran is understandably shaken after being cornered by a zombie and nearly killed, Steve's only consolation is that there is so much loot that it must be worth the risk of a horrible death: "You should see all the great stuff we got. . . . This place is terrific, it really is. It's perfect!" And as the images of their shopping spree flash by, most of the images seem designed to cast the men in the worst and most humorous possible light.[40] They either laughably indulge in shopping for stereotypically feminine items, like gourmet food, or effeminately primp before a mirror. In other scenes, they go to the other extreme of rabidly indulging in male fantasies, driving and shooting in the video arcade, or feverishly shopping for the most hyper-masculine items, namely the enormous guns and bullets they load up on in the gun shop, a scene accompanied by faux African music and the screeches of jungle animals, as the men seem to descend into a kind of mad, pagan worship of "the cult of the gun."[41] When they finally look down on the conquered mall, Romero dresses them up in enormous, poofy fur coats in what can only be described as the fashion choice of a pimp: gaudy, tasteless, flamboyant, androgynous, and utterly unnecessary in their climate-controlled fortress/prison.[42] The men seem able to indulge both their feminine and masculine sides, but much to the detriment and parody of either. Unlike the men, except for the one brief scene of cosmetic stupor from which she shakes herself loose, Fran seems unmoved by any of this,[43] skating slowly, gracefully, and sadly on the mall's ice rink. She remains, to the end, the voice of reason, restraint, and introspection in the group, a powerful symbol of how wrong and hypocritical men are when they demean women as vain, shallow, spendthrift "shopaholics," a stereotype and accusation more fittingly directed back at themselves.

Sexism takes a decidedly sinister and deadly turn, however, when the male characters discuss aborting Fran's pregnancy. Here, oddly, it is Peter who first suggests the callous act to Steve, seemingly without any thought that Fran might object or have a say in it. Despite usually being more appealing than the other male characters, Peter is hardly perfect, and is again, as with his shout of "Let's go shopping!" shown to be subject to the same sinful limitations and urges as the other characters. In this case, his sin is to devalue Fran and her autonomy and humanity, to treat her as a voiceless object, and to treat her baby only as a possible inconvenience or impediment to survival, rather than the possibility of future human survival. Here, the original film is much more cold and cynical than the remake, in which almost every positively portrayed character shows how much they value the love of parent and child. Here the male characters show no parental instinct, and Fran herself is silent on the matter. She expresses no maternal affection, but only outrage that her rights have been ignored.

This devaluing of Fran seems momentary, however, especially on Peter's part, for in the next scene, after Fran has thoroughly berated them for their callous treatment of her, Peter readily agrees with her that henceforth she is to have a say in their plans, and is always to carry a gun from now on.[44] Like C. J. in the remake, Peter starts out as the more sexist character, but quickly unlearns this bad attitude, and thereby makes himself more the focus of our admiration and emulation. In both characters, there is a sense in which sexism is presented as essentially unreasonable and unreflective, for both Peter and C. J. seem simply convinced by experience that women are to be respected; they are not swayed by emotion or some moral code, but just factually disproved, as it were. It would be unreasonable and counterproductive to have one member of their group be a helpless burden, so Fran is to be treated like the other members, with responsibilities and rights. On this sin of sexism, at least, Romero seems optimistic in the ability of human reason to tame and conquer our baser instincts.

The sin of racism is handled in various ways in the film, some violent and blatant, some subtle and hopeful. At the very beginning, it is presented in an over-the-top way with the insane, homicidal cop who just starts shooting blacks and Latinos randomly and gleefully in the housing project, flinging racial epithets, including "nigger."[45] (Later in the film, the bikers are also racist, but somewhat more restrained, calling Peter "chocolate man.") Before he starts shooting, he voices the typical white, American complaint, that public housing, or any assistance, for that matter, gives to poor and lazy minorities what whites have had to work hard to get. Of the housing project, he claims, "Shit, man, this is better than I got!" Having him then sadistically and enthusiastically shoot innocent people in the head is Romero's way of saying to anyone who has ever used similar rhetoric that they are unfeeling monsters, and potentially murderous maniacs, if given the chance to act on their racist convictions. Indeed, there is little cause to think that anything has changed much in a quarter of a century, when a U.S. congressman could find a silver lining to the clouds of Hurricane Katrina by suggesting that a storm that had killed hundreds of people, most of them poor and black, had "finally cleaned up public housing in New Orleans."[46]

On a much more positive note, *Dawn of the Dead* depicts a deep interracial friendship between Roger and Peter.[47] Their rapport in the basement of the housing project is striking, for it highlights succinctly but eloquently how the shared experience of suffering and horror brings people together and transcends their differences. This rapport continues throughout the movie, with each of the two men always knowing what the other is thinking, because they think alike and agree on everything.[48] Despite their striking physical differences—Peter towers over Roger in height, and one of the most real and believable scenes is when they kid about this—the two men are kindred spirits with nearly identical minds. When Roger is bitten and doomed to die, the macho and laconic Peter is obviously fighting back tears, as he is throughout the scenes as Roger lies dying. Only Peter ever tries to break through the macho facade that seeks to hide Roger's pain and Peter's grief, when he says awkwardly to Roger, "Look here, man, I'm . . ." and Roger cuts him off: "I know. Shut up." Peter is sorry that his friend is dying, and his friend knows it, and for Roger there's no need to talk about it. Roger also gives Peter the ultimate honor, as well as the most horrible responsibility, by asking him to swear to shoot him before he can come back as a zombie. Once Roger is dead and buried, we see Peter at his grave, drinking a toast to his lost friend. Compared to the usually ridiculous and gratuitous black/white relationships in buddy movies since, epitomized in the *Lethal Weapon* (1987, with three sequels following) franchise, this relationship in *Dawn of the Dead* is a sincere and poignant depiction of two men who care deeply about each other, fight for each other, and, so far as we can tell, never once think of their respective races.

But, as on so many other points, *Dawn of the Dead* is not content to depict only what is safe or expected or uplifting. Black/white friendships, while more rare in movies in 1978, were becoming more frequent, and they remain a safe, affirming way to include black characters in movies to this day. Despite what we might expect though, the love that dare not speak its name in Hollywood is most emphatically not homosexuality. Hollywood represents homosexual relationships on television and movies with increasing frequency and positivity, so long as the participating actors are young, fit, and attractive, and especially if they portray lesbians. Viewers register their approval of such depictions of homosexuality with high ratings and box office returns, both in the supposedly righteous and religious red states, and in the supposedly debauched and atheist blue states. Rather, the forbidden love on screen in 1978 and even in the early twenty-first century is the depiction of heterosexual romance, love, and sex between blacks and whites, especially between a black man and a white woman. And that is precisely where *Dawn of the Dead* leaves us, with a black man and a white woman flying off into the dawn of a new life together.[49]

Whether that future will be happy or not, zombies aside for the moment, we only have a few hints in the film itself. Peter's phallic name may well be Romero's mocking slap at white, American sensibilities. On the other hand, if that is all Peter represents, the film stands in serious jeopardy of lapsing into the other negative stereotype of the oversexed, predatory black man. That is not the impression we get of Peter in the movie in general, and especially in his brief dealings with Fran. As noted, of all the men, he is the most polite and respectful toward her, except for the notable lapse when her pregnancy is discovered. Their first meeting, however, is perhaps the most telling of their possible future relationship. When our four protagonists are boarding the helicopter for their escape at the beginning of the film, it is Fran who objects to Peter coming along, in exactly the hushed asides to Steve that one would expect in such an awkward situation. Once they are in the helicopter, the awkwardness is increased, with Peter sitting next to Fran.

> Peter (nodding toward Steve): "He your man?"
> Fran (laughing nervously): "Most of the time."
> Peter (smiling): "I just like to know who everybody is."
> Fran (smiling): "Me too."

In a film of great depth but very simple dialogue, it stands out as a particularly realistic and revealing exchange. It is exactly the kind of awkward small talk one would make with a stranger, especially someone that one has potentially insulted or inconvenienced. But Peter's evaluation of Fran and Steve's relationship here is quite unexpected: he phrases it as though be believes that Steve belongs to Fran, not that she belongs to Steve. It is an immediate show of respect to her that Peter does not assume she is passive, or another man's property, or, for that matter, potentially his property. Fran seems to welcome this rapport, just as Roger had welcomed the rapport with Peter in the basement. She responds with a joking observation that Steve is, just as she is, his own person, and then agrees with Peter's stated desire that it is important to know and respect the relationships and boundaries within a group. They have in a very few words shown that their skills and expectations in a relationship or community work much better than those of the headstrong, "lone-wolf" Roger, or the envious, irascible, unselfconfident Steve. Nor does it seem too speculative at this point to posit that such a rapport between Peter and Fran stems in part from their similar experiences of being belittled and pushed aside in a racist, sexist America.

Peter is also the only one who welcomes Fran's learning to fly the helicopter, which is the only thing that saves them in the end. When they fly off together, he is much more beholden to her and reliant on her than she on him. She is literally in the driver's seat, and we have some reason to think that Peter is more comfortable with that than Steve ever could have been.[50] And most importantly, we have to remember that Fran is pregnant with Steve's (white) child, not Peter's. Whatever their relationship may develop into, Peter's first role will be as a stepfather to another man's child, a child of another race born to an interracial couple. It is a strange permutation of the Adam and Eve roles that we might expect at the end of such a movie, but oddly hopeful in its own way. Given Peter's kind, generous, and respectful attitude throughout the movie, we have some confidence that he will fulfill such an awkward and demanding role better than most men. It also presents us with a potential future in which the significance of race is seriously undermined, if not totally abolished. As with sexism, Romero seems more optimistic that racism might one day be overcome, that is, if one considers it optimistic to think that racism will only end when zombie hordes force us out of our foolish, sinful hatred and bigotry.

But the little community and loving relationships formed among our protagonists are hardly mirrored in the larger world of *Dawn of the Dead*. The prevailing relations between people in *Dawn of the Dead* are venal, nasty, predatory, and destructive, all in the name of self-defense and self-preservation. This indicates that the more positive relations amongst our protagonists may just be wishful thinking, or a fortuitous happenstance, that could just as easily go the other way—toward violence and predation—if the people involved were different, or if they were pushed just a little bit farther. Even our protagonists are petty and selfish to those outside of their little group, as when they refuse to share cigarettes with other police officers at the beginning, even though they have plenty.[51] That they are so petty and selfish while making their escape from Philadelphia, the city of brotherly love, is another of Romero's mocking jibes at his characters, his society, and at us.[52] As noted above, the male characters in the group are quite obsessed with and enamored of violence, stocking up on guns and ammo and blasting zombies and bikers with sadistic glee.[53] It is probably the most significant and hopeful sign in the movie that Peter leaves the mall without his gun, a zombie having grabbed it as Peter makes for the helicopter,[54] and he lets go of it permanently, rather than casting it down and then picking it back up as Ben had done in *Night of the Living Dead*. Peter is also completely under the care and protection of Fran, the nonviolent, wise, maternal figure who has been throughout the movie immune to most of the sinful temptations of their mall existence, and utterly uninterested in their macho fantasies of violence, potency, domination, and possession. *Dawn of the Dead* ends, therefore, on a hopeful note of the rejection of violence and sin. It may even be a fulfillment of the mysterious prophecy given by the priest in the basement of the housing project at the beginning of the film: "We must stop the killing, or lose the war."[55] But this hopeful ending only comes after a long and harrowing examination of how fundamental these urges are to all humans, less so to our protagonists, who are relatively noble, but especially to the other people, who show little such restraint.

The bikers are the more blatant and extreme example of violence between humans, but they are hardly unique. As the end of *Night of the Living Dead* indicates, roving posses of zombie hunters pose just as great a threat to other human beings, especially dark-skinned human beings in the United States, as do deliberately destructive vandals and the ever-present undead.[56] The posses who join forces with the National Guard near the beginning of *Dawn of the Dead* seem well on their way to becoming a lawless army,[57] and their choice of weapons seems especially telling. As in *Land of the Dead*, they are shown with weapons, artillery, and armored vehicles— of little use against the undead, but perfect for killing other people, and especially for demolishing the fortifications that only people, and not zombies, could build. Like Ben and Harry fighting over the rifle in *Night of the Living Dead*, humans here seem instinctively to arm themselves for prospective sieges and firefights with other humans, rather than primarily prepare for the more immediate threat of the undead. And even more ironically, our nuclear weapons that were built to protect us from the ultimate threat posed by other technologically advanced humans prove utterly useless against the undead; their use may even hasten our destruction, as shown in the bonus features on the DVD of the remake. (There is even more Cold War irony and mockery of technology here, in that the mall, which first protects the protagonists but then turns into a horrible prison from which they must escape, is said to be powered by a nuclear plant.) As the final battle for the mall unfolds, it is clear that the zombies are not the only threat, but that the removal of all restraints and laws have quickly caused people to prey on each other with just as much ferocity, and a great deal more cunning and ingenuity, as the zombie hordes. Again, it is a powerful image of all humans, both the living and the undead, giving themselves over to their sinful, violent urges and descending into a cannibalistic hell, preying on each other eternally without pity or remorse.

In the world of zombie movies, and especially *Dawn of the Dead,* using violence to defeat evil is not all that it is cracked up to be in our fantasies of easy, noble, and satisfying triumph. It is, instead, nasty, crippling, and often fatal, even to those on the winning side, as witnessed by Roger's death after he becomes too enamored of and fascinated by the violence he can inflict on the hapless and only seemingly helpless zombies.[58] It is a grim and accurate reminder along the lines of *Saving Private Ryan* (1998) and other complex and subtle war movies, that violence, war, and sacrifice are never cost-free or "good": they are always, at best, the lesser of two evils. As a bumper sticker I just saw proclaimed, "You can no more win a war than you can win an earthquake." The most one can hope for with wars, earthquakes, or zombies, is to make the best of a bad situation and to emerge with the least number of physical, psychological, emotional, and spiritual scars possible.

Worse even than the violence itself, our protagonists must endure the complete abandonment of rituals for the expedient of sudden, emotionless, lethal violence. Peter understands this loss at the beginning of the movie when he correctly notes why the inhabitants of the housing project have protected the corpses of their neighbors, no matter how great the risk: "They still believe there's respect in dying." But this respect must be abandoned in order to survive, though its loss will haunt and torment the survivors. There can be no last rites for Roger or Steve besides a bullet to the brain, and the anonymous zombies who are perfunctorily or gleefully blown away to secure the mall are treated even more unceremoniously, stacked up by Peter and Steve like cords of wood. Even in a battle with mindless zombies, let alone "normal" battles between humans, there is no truly holy or just war, for the victors are never perfect and sinless, and the defeated are never completely sinful and monstrous. Both groups are sinful and imperfect—they are both human, in short—and can only hope for reconciliation and lasting peace despite their sinfulness, a vision in the zombie world that will not be attained until the final *Land of the Dead*, and which in our real world of interhuman violence is perhaps even further from fulfillment.

The enormous and incurable violence of both humans and zombies is not, however, the only characteristic Romero uses to equate them in this film. The zombies in this film are simply more human than in the previous film, and, though far less intelligent than those in the later installments, they remain more human in some ways. For the most part, the ghastly makeup effects are reserved for the scenes of bloody attacks and cannibalism, while zombies, when seen roaming around in their everyday "life," look like normal people, without the horribly imaginative wounds—cheeks bitten through to expose their teeth, throats torn out, eyes gouged out, limbs torn off—so common in the other films.[56] This invites us constantly throughout the film to see them as more like us, and to realize that we are like them, which is brought out in an exaggerated and graphic way with some camera angles. Many of the camera shots of zombies being killed are taken from the zombie's perspective, with us, the viewers, staring down the barrel of a gun before it fires.[60] We see that zombie "death" is as fearful and final as ours, and we pause to consider how unfair their execution is, as well as the inevitability of our own.

The equation of humans and zombies is also brought out in a gentler, but at the same time, more disturbing way. Often, the human characters are sympathetic to or mesmerized by the seeming humanity of their zombie foes, and therefore also appreciative of their own zombieness—a behavior that is nearly inconceivable in the other films. When moving the trucks to block the mall entrances, Roger is attacked by a female zombie in a long and harrowing scene, with her on top of him, writhing and struggling and moaning, in a way that simply cannot be ignored or accidental for how sexual it looks. In the same sequence, Roger is mesmerized momentarily when another zombie grabs his face, not violently and hungrily, but in the way that a blind person feels someone to identify him, gently and lovingly. And

Fran, the most perceptive and least violent character of the group,[61] seems especially aware of this identification between human and zombie. Twice when she is locked behind the glass doors at JCPenney's, awaiting the completion of the men's killing spree, she stares at zombies and identifies with them and their plight. Apart from the orgy of violence, these are two moments of pure sadness and pity, the closest our human survivors can come to the emotions of a prezombie world. First, Fran stares at a zombie nun that has its habit caught in the door before Fran frees it, and then Fran stares at a zombie Little League coach who stares back at her with what cannot be described as the usual mad, bestial hunger of a zombie, but rather the timid longing of adolescent puppy eyes. Both instances rightly illicit Fran's pity. The most violent character, Roger, and the least violent, Fran, have an epiphany that the zombies' plight is ours, and our hopes and desires still persist in stunted, undead form in the zombies' rotten brains. In this movie, more than in the others, we are asked to put ourselves in the zombies' smelly shoes, and therefore to see ourselves for what we are—prezombies, as it were, temporarily animate corpses, temporarily capable of some free choice, but fast frittering that free choice away on sinful, addictive habits like materialism and violence.

Throughout this analysis, one thing is clear in this film: zombies are not just some deadly threat like sharks or ebola, they are *us*, and we are *them*. This equation of zombies and humans is a theological vision of universal sinfulness, both among the living and the undead, and it gives *Dawn of the Dead* its deep and disturbing horror, and also its relevance and humanity. It forces us to admit and confront our sinful and hypocritical existence of materialism, consumerism, racism, sexism, and predatory, exploitative violence. The grotesquery and monstrousness of sin is by no means confined to the rotting, reeking zombies, but, if anything, is more noticeable, pervasive, and ineradicable among the humans in the film, who are constantly equated or even unfavorably compared with the living dead. It is such a Dantean vision of human existence that allows for the possibility of hope at the end of the film, that Peter and Fran may learn from this and create a world better than the former, or that viewers may leave the film sobered and shocked enough to change their own sinful lives.

CONCLUSION

Dawn of the Dead is rightly hailed as a timeless classic. Exactly like Dante's *Inferno*, the film is ghastly, funny, shocking, but also humane and humanizing. Both works unmask human beings for the selfish, greedy, self-destructive creatures that they are, but thereby, these works seek to shock us out of our sins, especially out of our violence and materialism. As Fran and Peter flee the mall at the end of the movie, and the zombies fully and permanently occupy it, we rejoice just as we do at the end of the *Inferno* when Dante climbs up out of hell. One critic has rightly noted that the ending is "curiously exhilarating," and has even put it in the religious terms that the film suggests "the possibility of moving beyond apocalypse."[62] Like Dante, Fran and Peter have learned and grown and therefore have rejected and climbed up out of their own hell,[63] a hell that sadly claimed two of their friends and numerous enemies and strangers. Similarly, Dante saw both friends and enemies among the damned in hell because unaided human virtue and reason are not enough in the face of sinful human nature. The mall was hell on earth, a hell made all the more seductive and tempting because it seemed so attractive or harmless or safe.[64] As uncertain as their future is at the end, it has to be better than the boring, repetitive hell of their own making into which they were sinking in the middle of the film. And the zombies, as noted above, are as happy as sinful people can be, wandering aimlessly, contentedly, and endlessly in the exact place where they want to be. If people are, as Christians believe, mired in sin and unable to extricate themselves on their own, then Romero's conclusion would be about the closest thing one could expect to a "happy ending." It is, at the very least, a sobering and realistic ending, one that demands that its viewers reject the earthbound, hell-bent "kingdom" of the mall, in which life has been utterly and eternally eclipsed by the dawn of the dead, and instead strive for a higher kingdom in whatever secular or religious terms one conceives of it.

Chapter 3

DAY OF THE DEAD (1985)
VIOLENCE, PERVERTED REASON, AND THE
LOWER CIRCLES OF HELL

Romero's next film was intended as his masterpiece and the conclusion of a trilogy. Though it was made with a bigger budget, $3.5 million, than the previous two films, apparently Romero intended an even larger, more grandiose vision of a zombie-infested world, and was denied more funding when he refused to bring the film in with an R rating.[1] As with *Dawn of the Dead*, he held to his principles or aesthetics and released the film as unrated. But the result was a very small, claustrophobic film,[2] more reminiscent in look and feel, at least, of the first *Night of the Living Dead*, than it was of *Dawn of the Dead*. Despite its title, *Day of the Dead* takes place almost entirely in the dark. The tone, too, had abandoned the playfulness of *Dawn of the Dead* and returned to the oppressive grimness, depravity, and madness of the first film.[3] This time, however, the tone really did not work for most viewers or critics.[4] Perhaps it was the cinematic mistakes throughout the film. Visually, darkness can be very effective for frights, but sometimes just makes it hard to follow what's going on. Acoustically, *Day of the Dead* is a much bigger disaster. Even with a DVD, which allows for repeated listening to a scene, it is impossible to make out much of the dialogue, as everyone in the film is either shouting over one another or mumbling. And such a shortcoming is greatly exacerbated by the fact that, unlike either of the first two extremely laconic films, this one has seemingly endless scenes of people talking, and talking, and then talking some more. It is therefore a very plodding, somber psychological drama that often makes the cinematic mistake of *telling* us rather than *showing* us,— a mistake more egregious and aggravating when we cannot even make out what the people are saying.

Its shortcomings notwithstanding, the film is still an important contribution because of how it develops the themes and ideas of sin and human nature. The wealth of sometimes decipherable dialogue, in fact, gives us a much more detailed and explicit look at Romero's vision of human and zombie nature. If anything, although it is less satisfying as a movie than any of the others, conceptually or intellectually it is much deeper and more complex than the last two films, *Dawn of the Dead* (2004) and *Land of the Dead*, and possibly more so than any other installment.

SYNOPSIS

The movie begins with a dream sequence, in which we see a young woman in a white room with no windows or doors. The only object in the room is a calendar on the wall, open to the October page, and with all the dates crossed out. The woman approaches the calendar, and as she nears it, hands shove through the wall to grab her. She wakes up, startled, in the back seat of a helicopter.

The woman is Sarah, and she is in the helicopter with three men: the pilot, John, a black man with a thick Jamaican accent;[5] McDermott, an electronics expert who drinks constantly; and Miguel, a nervous, young Latino man in a military uniform wearing numerous religious medals, who we also learn is Sarah's lover. They are flying up and down the Florida coast, trying to contact other survivors of the zombie takeover. McDermott signals via radio, asking for anyone to respond. They find a city and land the helicopter despite McDermott's protests and with John's promise to lift off again if there's any trouble. Sarah and Miguel get out and walk a few steps from the helicopter with a bullhorn, calling out to see if there are any human survivors. The only answer is a long, chilling moan as the zombie hordes arise from their stupor and shuffle toward the humans. The zombies here are much more grotesque and mangled than in the previous two films, with hideous wounds from when they died as well as signs of decay. They quickly fill the streets of the dead city, while dollar bills are blown about by the wind, together with an old newspaper with the head-line, "THE DEAD WALK!"

The four humans fly back to their base, a fenced-in area in which there are other men in military uniform, one of them watering marijuana plants. There is also a small graveyard, where the four people returning from their reconnoitering see a new grave, which they are told is that of the former base commander, Major Cooper. Hundreds of zombies press against the cyclone fence, attracted by the signs of human activity, and Sarah urges everyone inside, because the living dead are getting "too riled up" and might eventually break through. The humans descend to an underground bunker, labeled the Seminole Storage Facility, where there are a dozen human survivors. The group consists of Sarah and two other scientists, Drs. Logan and Fisher; the two other civilians, John and McDermott; and seven soldiers. Among the soldiers are their new leader, Captain Rhodes, and Steel, the largest and most sadistic soldier and Rhode's right hand man. We immediately see the tensions in the group, as the scientists and military argue over who is in command and what should be done.

Sarah and Miguel are immediately dispatched with Steel and another soldier to go deeper into the cave to get more "subjects." We see that deeper within the cave, a section is barricaded off from the area where the humans live, and zombies are kept in this other section. The humans can take zombies out of their "corral" by using long poles with lassos at the end, which allow them to grab a zombie around the neck, push it into a box with a gate at either end, close the gate to the corral, and open the gate to the main section of the cave and bring the restrained zombie out. Miguel and Sarah help Steel and the other soldier do this with two zombies, though again there is violent antagonism between the humans. When Miguel loses his grip on the pole, the other soldier is nearly bitten by a zombie, and Steel nearly kills Miguel in retaliation, holding him over the zombie pen and pushing his head down into the reach of the zombies, only relenting when threatened by Sarah with a gun. Rather than showing his gratitude, Miguel later slaps

Sarah, believing she only emasculated him further. After that, the new commander, Rhodes, is shown to be even more cruel and sadistic, threatening Sarah with rape. As in the first film, the violent tensions among the humans are clearly as big a threat to their survival as the living dead.

Sarah visits the chief scientist, Dr. Logan, who is called "Dr. Frankenstein" by everyone else in the film. It is a completely fitting name for the doctor, with his grizzled beard, wild, unkempt hair, and blood-stained lab coat. The doctor is surrounded by human cadavers, some of which are writhing and twitching in their zombie state. Logan claims to have isolated the part of the brain that causes the zombies to attack and eat other humans, showing Sarah a human cadaver with its head removed, and just a tiny bit of its brain remaining at the top of its spinal chord. It lies motionless on the table, while a zombie corpse, with all of its internal organs severed but its brain intact, still flails about and tries to attack. This zombie tries to break free from its restraints, and succeeds in half rising from the table. All of its organs then spill out onto the floor before Logan dispatches it with a drill to the forehead. Both Sarah and the audience almost gag from this spectacle. Logan claims his efforts will eventually lead to the "domestication" of zombies. Sarah sees Major Cooper's uniform and realizes that it is his body on the table with the brain mostly removed. She thereby realizes that the doctor is going as mad in his experiments as the soldiers are going mad with their violent aggression and domineering.

All of the survivors then gather at a meeting in the dining hall and the soldiers hurl insults and accusations at the other team members. They do not understand why McDermott cannot raise anyone on the radio, and they do not understand why the scientists have not yet invented some kind of weapon with which to destroy the zombies. When Sarah gets up to leave in exasperation, Rhodes orders Steel to shoot her. When Steel refuses, Rhodes threatens to shoot him, and the stand off escalates until Sarah sits back down. Logan tries to explain his work to the soldiers, claiming that he will discover a way to make the zombies "behave" by "controlling them," though he cannot offer a definite timetable for success. Rhodes gets more frustrated and threatens to fly off in the helicopter, though Logan calms him down by observing that the undead now outnumber the living 400,000 to 1, and there is nowhere left to go that is safe. Rhodes agrees to let the scientists continue their work, so long as his dominance and control are recognized by all, warning them that "I'm running this monkey farm! . . . Anybody f**ks with my command, they get executed."

Sarah dozes off and has another dream, in which Miguel is lying on a bed, and when he stands up, like the zombie in Logan's lab, all of his guts spill out on to the floor. When she wakes up from this nightmare, she goes to have a drink with John and McDermott, who live in a trailer close to the zombie pen and away from both the soldiers and scientists. She first berates them for not siding with her against the increasingly dangerous soldiers, but John somewhat deflects her criticism, playfully blaming her for her more or less useless scientific work. John and McDermott are also planning on escaping the compound, without Rhodes and his men, of course, and John invites her along. She leaves them without agreeing to this escape plan, though she is obviously tempted by it.

Sarah returns to her own work, and again visits Logan's mad laboratory. Here she meets his favorite project, a zombie he has named "Bub." Sarah is amazed that Bub has undergone so much training that he does not try to attack or even get agitated when Logan enters the room with him. Logan explains somewhat mysteriously that zombies can be trained, like people, to do things with the promise of some "reward." He lays out three objects before Bub: a toothbrush, razor, and Stephen King's novel *Salem's Lot*. Bub knows enough to drag the razor across his face and to flip through the book. The tension and amazement build as Bub performs tasks that require even more cognition: when handed a phone, Bub can be coaxed into saying, "Hello, Aunt Alicia," into the receiver. In all the movies, Bub is the only zombie to speak. And when Rhodes appears to observe the zombie's supposed progress, Bub recognizes the military uniform and salutes him. Then, with much greater coordination, but much more ominously, Bub shows that he knows what to do with a gun. He can cock it, aim it, and pull the trigger. Rhodes, somewhat understandably, is unimpressed with such "progress," and probably even a little more perturbed at the prospect of zombies using guns. He shouts at Logan, "What are we supposed to do, teach him tricks?"

Sarah, Miguel, Steel, and two other soldiers are again dispatched to get more zombies from the holding pen. This time it is no mistake on Miguel's part that causes an accident, but instead the noose on one of the sticks used to restrain the zombies breaks, freeing the zombie. It immediately lunges at one of the soldiers and tears his throat out. As the soldier struggles, his assault rifle goes off, and several shots hit the other soldier in the chest, killing him. As Sarah shoots the one zombie in the head, Miguel lunges at the other, shouting, "I didn't do it!" In the struggle Miguel is bitten in the arm and then runs off as Steel shoots the zombie in the head. Steel also finishes off the one wounded soldier, at his own request, before he can come back as a zombie. In this scene, even Steel seems to appreciate the horror, sadness, and desperation of their situation.

Meanwhile, Sarah catches up with Miguel as he nears the trailer of John and McDermott. In a fairly gratuitous scene that is perhaps more unnerving than when zombies attack, John helps Sarah chop off Miguel's bitten arm with a machete and cauterizes the wound with fire, in the hopes of saving him from the inevitably fatal infection that always follows zombie bites. As they are tending to the wounded Miguel, Steel arrives with the other soldiers, eager to kill Miguel for supposedly causing the deaths of the other two soldiers. The civilians refuse to hand Miguel over, and both sides draw their guns in another standoff between the human characters to determine who is going to be in charge. Since John is the only person who knows how to fly the helicopter, Rhodes must back down, so he and his men leave the four in the trailer near the zombie pen.

Later, Sarah and McDermott leave the trailer in an attempt to sneak in and get supplies from the main compound while the others are asleep, and they stumble upon the remains of Logan's even more hideous experiments. Under a bloody towel, they find the head of the soldier who had just been shot earlier outside the zombie pen, his mouth and eyes still moving. As they retreat from that horror, they see Logan carrying a bucket to another room. He does not see them, so they follow to observe him interacting again with Bub. Bub is now wearing headphones attached to a Walkman, and Logan shows him how to turn the Walkman on and off to listen to music. The tape in the player is Beethoven's Ninth Symphony, "Ode to

Joy," which mesmerizes even a zombie. Significantly, at one point Bub grabs Logan's arm and could obviously bite him, but does not. It is the closest to a "breakthrough" that Logan could hope for in zombie behavior modification, and like his previous observation, it requires positive reinforcement with a "reward." Logan gives his bucket to Bub, and Sarah and McDermott watch in revulsion as Bub gorges on bloody chunks of what is obviously the butchered remains of the dead soldier. What was just a seemingly docile, innocent being mesmerized by music is once more a ghoul, savagely tearing flesh from bones, his mouth dripping with blood.

Unfortunately for Logan, Rhodes shows up right at this point to investigate, discovers the headless corpse in the freezer, and shoots the doctor. He and the other soldiers take Sarah, McDermott, and Dr. Fisher prisoner, and lead them back to the trailer to force John to surrender. In another standoff, Rhodes brutally executes Dr. Fisher, and has McDermott and Sarah thrown into the holding pen with the zombies. Steel beats John into submission, and Rhodes, Steel, and the two remaining soldiers drag him away to fly them out of there in the helicopter. Unfortunately, a delirious Miguel then wanders off, gets up to the surface of the compound, and opens the gates to let the zombies inside. The zombies tear him apart and begin to flood into the underground bunker. In the ensuing pandemonium and carnage, John escapes and goes back to try to save Sarah and McDermott, who are running further and further back into the caves, fighting off zombies as they go. John finds them and they escape to the surface through a back entrance. Bub, meanwhile, has escaped and, finding the murdered body of Logan, also finds a gun and shoots Rhodes. The other zombies then tear Rhodes and the others limb from limb, except Steel, who had the foresight to shoot himself in the head before the undead could reach him. In a trademark sort of sequence, much like the gruesome end of the bikers in *Dawn of the Dead*, there is then a feeding frenzy of zombies feasting on entrails and other body parts. Rather than the garish, well-lit splatters of almost orange blood in *Dawn of the Dead*, however, the scenes in *Day of the Dead* are played out in a ghastly grey, punctuated with spurts of thick, dark blood, making the scene seem more hellish and less like a comic book.

Sarah, John, and McDermott reach the helicopter as more zombies still on the surface close in on them. But as Sarah opens the helicopter door, a zombie grabs her, and she then wakes up on a beach, with John and McDermott fishing in the surf, and a calendar beside her, open to November, on which she marks an X through one day. The movie is deliberately ambiguous whether this is a dream, or the final zombie grabbing her was a nightmare from which she awoke, or, indeed, if everything that happened in the movie was a dream, from which she and the others had escaped earlier and about which she now has nightmares in their island paradise. Romero has insisted that it does not matter what happens at the end,[6] but this ending does not seem nearly as satisfying or exhilarating as the ambiguous ending of *Dawn of the Dead*, where we are not sure what happens to Peter and Fran. The ending of *Day of the Dead* seems more like the cliché now common in horror movies such as *Friday the 13th* (1980, with sequels following) and *A Nightmare on Elm Street* (1984, with sequels following), where the audience is meant to think, "Oh, it was only a dream . . . *or was it?*" As conceptually or intellectually rich as the film is, narratively it disappoints all the way through to the ending.[7]

ANALYSIS

As we shall see, the social criticism so prominent in the other films, especially in the original *Dawn of the Dead*, is much less a part of *Day of the Dead*. But the more abstract consideration of human nature in general is much more pronounced. This is both the film's strength, making it a more thought-provoking and disturbing look at human nature, at the same time as it is the film's weakness, dragging it into endless, plodding soliloquies.

Although social critique is not the film's centerpiece, it is still a noticeable element—sometimes on its own, and sometimes in comparison to the earlier films. First, the materialism and consumerism of *Dawn of the Dead* seem completely absent in this version. Whereas the humans fought over money in *Dawn of the Dead* and will do so again in *Land of the Dead*, in *Day of the Dead* money is only seen blowing about uselessly, ignored by the living and the undead alike.[8] The zombies themselves are also not mall-walkers interested in material goods, but are a throwback to the depiction in the *Night of the Living Dead*. There is no reason to think that they want anything in the bunker other than human flesh, just as the zombies in the first film had no previous connection to the farmhouse. In this film, the zombies are driven by hunger and the humans are driven by a lust for power, but neither group is materialistic.

The lessened prominence of materialism in this film at first makes sense, given that the setting is an underground bunker rather than a shopping mall, but hints of the bunker's contents make this more surprising and lead us to question more about what is going on. As the soldiers drive around in the caves, we see that they are full of autos and RVs. No indication is ever given why the government might be storing such things, but if there are RVs, there must be other things to play with, and yet the occupants do not really seem to do anything besides butcher zombies (and, eventually, other humans) and yell at each other. The only exception is McDermott, who is constantly drunk, and some of the other soldiers who get high on marijuana (the latter would normally be expected to cut down on the bickering, but does not). And even if the occupants lacked diversions or supplies, their mobility with the helicopter would seem to make them capable of foraging elsewhere for supplies, as the humans did in *Dawn of the Dead*, and would do so more aggressively in *Land of the Dead*. The only alternatives in this post-apocalyptic world seem to be argumentation, violence, or anesthetized inebriation.

Such a depiction seems intended to show that there are much darker and more violent, sinful urges of human beings than mere greed. In Dante, greed is punished higher up in hell, with the lesser sins of unrestrained appetite and desire, while violence and deceit are punished much further down in the depths of hell, in the sixth through ninth circles. Physically, the location of *Day of the Dead* in an underground bunker contributes to the impression that we are descending down into deeper depths of sin than we saw in the mall of *Dawn of the Dead*. As in *Night of the Living Dead*, *Day of the Dead* focuses on the worst sins of violence and domination over other people, ignoring more minor sins like materialism and consumerism.

The sin of sexism is treated by Romero somewhat more directly in this installment. First, of all the characters in the films Sarah is probably the strongest female. The story is, in fact, told primarily from her perspective,[9] as the *Dawn of the Dead* remake is mostly seen from the perspective of the female protagonist Ana. Sarah wields a gun against zombie and human attackers with little qualm or hesitation. Indeed, the speed and calm with which she chops off her lover's arm and then sizzles his flesh with a torch is more than a little unnerving,[10] but certainly shows that she seriously undermines the stereotype of females as passive or helpless. More than one reviewer has noted Sarah as part of the new breed of stronger women leads in action, sci-fi, and horror movies, starting with Sigourney Weaver in *Alien* (1979).[11]

As Sarah undermines some sexist stereotypes, however, the violent side of male domination among the other characters is more explicit than before. The violence that is acted out or threatened against Sarah is much more overt than in the previous two films. While Ben hit Barbra to end her hysterics, Miguel only has his wounded male ego to blame for hitting Sarah. The explicit threats of rape against Sarah by the soldiers anticipate the exact same scenario in the remake of *Dawn of the Dead*, or in the related *28 Days Later*, and the threats are in a way more shocking than the bloody violence later in the film.[12] Rhodes's threat to kill Sarah goes even further, for it takes even the pretense or façade of sexuality away and shows that he will use direct, nonsexualized violence against her just because she threatens his dominance and authority.[13] Indeed, it is probably significant that he commands Steel to shoot Sarah, rather than doing it himself, thereby showing his dominance over a "mere" woman through his dominance over the other men; if he can command men to kill against their will, he can certainly command a woman to sit down and shut up. This more violent depiction of how men treat women shows the rising level of realism in these horror movies, despite their fantastical scenario. The later films are more disturbing and honest in suggesting that women would be the constant prey of brutalizing men in a lawless society. If the film world was becoming more accepting of women in the '80s, the world inside the films was becoming more dangerous and violent, a shocking reflection of the real violence perpetrated against women throughout the world, especially during times of war or social upheaval.

The treatment of racism in *Day of the Dead* is also somewhat more pronounced. The evil and sadistic characters are more vocally racist than any other character, besides the insanely murderous cop at the beginning of *Dawn of the Dead*. They call Miguel a "spic" and John a "jungle bunny." Steel cruelly taunts Miguel by nearly feeding him to the zombies, then later brutally beats John, the black character who is several times shown to be the wisest and most articulate of the group. All of this makes the humans much more vulnerable to attack from the zombies, who are once again a racially mixed mob that moves and attacks with more or less complete cooperation and no internal dissent. But in distinction from the earlier films and in anticipation of both the *Dawn of the Dead* remake and *Land of the Dead*, we have several sadistic human characters whose deaths seem much more deserved and less inevitable or random. Unlike the deaths of Roger and Steve, Steel and especially Rhodes appear to get what they deserve, and probably could have avoided their fate if they had not been such violent racists.

On the other hand, we see the more sympathetic characters—people of real character and wisdom—totally overlook race.[14] For example, Miguel and Sarah represent, for the first time in these films, an interracial couple whose relationship is established and not implied, again anticipating the similar scenario in the *Dawn of the Dead* remake. The relationships between the main characters exactly replicate those in the original *Dawn of the Dead*, with McDermott and John sharing an interracial friendship like Roger and Peter—even going so far this time as to have them set up house together—and with Sarah and John as the interracial, heterosexual couple surviving at the end, like Fran and Peter.[15] Significantly and perhaps more hopefully than in the previous film, both the interracial friends and potential mates survive this time, and presumably in such a way that their triadic relationship will not degenerate into competition or jealousy, as it surely would if any of the other characters had been the ones to survive. On this one point, the film is perhaps the most optimistic of any of the films we are considering, foreseeing a future in which racism is completely overcome, though only at the expense and destruction of the entire previously existing human civilization.

As in the prior films, especially *Dawn of the Dead*, the humans and zombies are often equated in *Day of the Dead*, most often in a way in which the humans come off as the less edified or less forgivable creatures. Logan makes the zombie/human equivalence explicit, expressing it in biological terms and without the supernatural or theological overtones of Peter's speech in *Dawn of the Dead*, by observing of zombies, "They are *us*! The same animal, simply functioning less perfectly," and wondering outloud about Bub, "Is he alive, or dead?" Indeed, the idea of zombies "simply functioning less perfectly" seems highly debatable in this film, as Bub is one of the most likable characters in the movie, definitely behaving more humanely than either Rhodes or Logan, who have sold or lost their souls. Romero, meanwhile, has described Bub as a "zombie with a soul."[16] Unlike the two human monsters in the film, Bub is shown to be capable of mercy, restraint, contemplation, and enjoying things other than shouting at or killing people. Perhaps most significantly, in the climactic sequence, Bub finds Logan's murdered body and lets out a wail of anguish and grief over it, then takes up a gun to avenge his beloved master.[17] In both of these gestures, he totally anticipates the Big Daddy character in *Land of the Dead*. Also like Big Daddy, during the final feeding frenzy, having mortally wounded Rhodes and chased him into the eager arms of the rest of the zombie horde, Bub shuffles off without partaking in the ghoulish feast. Bub at least seems able to stop eating human flesh, but the human characters show no signs of ceasing their self-destructive preying on one another.

The division of the human characters into the two groups of scientists and soldiers allows Romero a more detailed analysis of human sinfulness and shortcomings by essentially splitting the characteristics of Ben from *Night of the Living Dead* into two opposing camps: the scientists, who are men (and one woman) of reason, and the soldiers, who are men of action—especially of violence.[18] Once again, neither side fares too well in this examination. Among the scientists, their ability to inflict torture on the zombies—who, it must be remembered, look and basically act exactly like human beings—is revolting.[19] (Sarah is spared this negative portrayal in the film, as we only see her looking at x-rays and spinning vials of blood in a centrifuge, not dissecting zombies.) The props in the laboratory are designed to maximize this effect, for although the zombies are chained by the neck like dogs and not bound by the wrists, their chains are nonetheless attached to a series of crosses along the one wall of the laboratory. Even for unbelievers, few images evoke senseless, evil torture and innocent, undeserved suffering more than the Christian symbol of the cross. And even if the zombies cannot understand that they are being crucified, the scientists, if they had not lost every last vestige of humanity, should be able to recognize what they are doing and suffer enough in their conscience to stop themselves.

Not only do the scientists not stop torturing zombies, by the end of the film, Logan also takes the next logical step and moves on from the butchery of zombies who look like people to the actual butchery of real people. The physical makeup and behavior of zombies makes this clear and horrifying, for zombies only eat human flesh, and any human who dies will become a zombie, and therefore his flesh will be inedible. So for Logan to be feeding pieces of the dead soldier to Bub at the end must mean that the soldier was still alive when Logan decapitated him, before he could become a zombie. The figure of Logan, like his namesake Frankenstein or real-life monsters like Dr. Mengele, is in fact able to rationalize everything he does in the name of science, expediency, or survival.[20] It is a depressing but altogether realistic indictment of science and rationality, showing not only how they cannot provide people with a new morality to replace that previously supplied by religion, but also that science will even devolve humanity further by undermining morality and deadening conscience, thereby causing evil to grow, not diminish.

We are shown in the film that Logan does have some sense of morality, but it is a very disturbing and dangerous one. To counter Rhodes's constant brutishness, Logan claims that it is "social behavior that enables us to communicate, to go about things in an orderly fashion without attacking each other like beasts in the wild." This may sound like a (slight) improvement over Rhodes's behavior, which seems to be rapidly degenerating from a brutal social contract of "the strong rule the weak" to the complete anarchy of "every man for himself" (exactly how he and the three remaining soldiers act once the zombies break in, thereby hastening their destruction). But

Logan's further elaboration on what he means by "social behavior" makes it clear that his vision is, if anything, only a more deceitful, cunning version of Rhodes's "might makes right": "They [the zombies] can be fooled, don't you see? They can be tricked into being good little girls and boys, the same way we were tricked into it, with a promise of some reward to come." Ethics are not a matter of doing something good and beneficial for oneself and one's fellows, but of being "tricked" into doing something against one's own interests by being bribed with some future recompense to make up for being "tricked" in the present. Morality is not "natural" to humans, but only an unnatural "trick" they can be trained to do, the way a dog can be taught to walk on its hind feet, or a chimp can be made to wear human clothes and ride a tricycle.[21] No dog or chimp would act this way if they did not get treats; therefore, according to this theory, anyone who lived an ethical life without being "paid" for it would be a silly or misguided dupe. Anyone who saw ethics as this kind of comical charade would seek to maximize the amount he "tricked" others and minimize the amount that he himself would be "tricked" into doing silly good deeds. Logan's immoral, criminal behavior shows that he embraces and pursues this perverted definition of ethics in his cruel and murderous experiments.

Because the scientists espouse such a horrible, mechanical, dehumanizing view of human nature, *Day of the Dead* presents the evil posed by science as much deeper than science's frightening lack of morals. The problem would seem to be at the core of the scientific method and enterprise itself, even when practiced by a relatively humane and sensitive person like Sarah.[22] John makes this clear in one of the long soliloquies in the film:

> "We don't believe in what you're doing here. . . . You ain't never gonna figure it out, just like they never figured out why the stars are where they're at. It ain't mankind's job to figure that stuff out. . . . We've been punished by the Creator. He visited a curse on us, so we might get a look at what hell was like. Maybe he didn't want to see us blow ourselves up and put a big hole in his sky. Maybe he just wanted to show us he was still the boss man. Maybe he figured we was getting too big for our britches, trying to figure his shit out."

In *Night of the Living Dead*, it was speculated that the horrible rising of zombies was the result of human science gone awry, through radiation brought back to earth from a space probe, while in *Dawn of the Dead*, the "scientific" explanation was abandoned for a theological one—judgment from an angry God on a sinful humanity. *Day of the Dead* rather brilliantly combines these two "explanations": scientific hubris and encroachment on the prerogatives of an inscrutable and jealous God are precisely what has brought down the divine judgment on a proud, sinful humanity. Zombies are not just a disaster or even a mistake; they are a very potent, to say the least, reminder from God of human limitation, mortality, and ignorance. Or, as John's diagnosis also considers, since humans have so often and so vigorously pursued an agenda of creating a hell on earth—frequently with the eager collaboration of scientists, as vividly shown in Logan's mad experiments, and in real-life, man-made hells like Auschwitz—then eventually God will lose patience and give us a taste of the real thing.

Rhodes's abiding sin, on the other hand, is more purely and overtly the *libido dominandi*, the "lust for domination" observed in the previous movies, and such an integral part of the Christian idea of original sin. He has no interest in hubristically pursuing knowledge about God's ways; he wants only to usurp and then hold onto power and domination over the other humans, and is willing to kill anyone in order to maintain his dominance, no matter if it further risks his survival. Sarah expresses disbelief that Rhodes could have followed through on his threat to shoot her with the optimistic speculation, "He can't be that inhuman." John corrects her by saying, "No, he's human. That's what scares me." John then diagnoses the problem with humans: "That's the trouble with the world . . . people got different ideas concerning what they want out of life." But it is not just human subjectivity or disagreement that is the problem, it is the almost inevitable tendency of people to impose their "different ideas concerning what they want out of life" onto other people, using either violence, like Rhodes, or deception and rationalization, like Logan. Using, tricking, dominating, and bullying others is not inhuman or monstrous, but utterly human and predictable, and therefore it should be expected and guarded against.[23] Spending a half hour in any boardroom, playground, or senate would show that this evaluation is totally accurate. The fact that our protagonists are trapped in a bunker with armed men and surrounded by walking corpses only raises the stakes from abuse and exploitation all the way up to rape and murder. It also means that they will have to participate, to some extent, in such violence, as John observes during one standoff: "We're getting to make this a habit, man, pointing guns at each other."

John also gives a fuller and more pessimistic evaluation of human nature when he tells Sarah of their plans to escape. John describes the contents of the storage facility, and apparently it contains vast records of human history—tax returns, government budget reports, census tallies, copies of every movie ever made, and records of every war and disaster that has ever occurred. He calls it one vast "tombstone" to the dead human society. His list of items is very telling, indeed. Besides the movies, which seems a self-deprecating reference on Romero's part to his own craft, it is just a list of the records of nearly infinite pain and/or pettiness.[24] John does not mention, and the storage facility apparently does not contain, great works of art, literature, philosophy, or religion, but just a vast amount of useless information and chronicles of human suffering from either man-made depredations in war or from natural disasters. John urges Sarah to abandon and reject her feeble attempts at salvaging something from this world through her useless scientific investigations, suggesting instead, "We could start over, start fresh. Get some babies and teach them never to come over here and dig these records out." According to this, human society thus far, dominated by the Rhodeses and Logans (Frankensteins) of the world, has amounted to nothing but human misery and petty grubbing for power and knowledge—a long, pathetic history that God has rightfully and almost happily put to an end, a realm better left to the mindless zombies who now fully occupy it.

With all of this dismal evaluation of human reason and human history, *Day of the Dead* takes us back to an evaluation of human nature very much like that of *Night of the Living Dead*, in which there is little or nothing noble or salvageable in the human beast. The humans have perverted reason, the faculty that they still have that the zombies lack, and they have succumbed to the sin of pride and to the "lust for domination," a sinful urge which the zombies also lack. This is exactly how Dante categorizes the sins in the sixth and lower circles of hell. These are sins—such as murder, robbery, and, especially, treachery and betrayal—in which people seek to hurt and dominate others through violence, which is then made worse by the perverted use of reason to perpetrate injustice and falsehood, rather than justice and truth: "All malice has injustice as its end, / an end achieved by violence or by fraud; / while both are sins that earn the hate of Heaven, / since fraud belongs exclusively to man, / God hates it more and, therefore, far below, / the fraudulent are placed and suffer most."[25] While Bub seems capable of becoming more human, listening to Beethoven and refraining briefly from biting the hand that feeds him, most of the human characters have sunk deeper and deeper into self-destructive, sinful, bestial violence than ever before.

The fact that John can nonetheless suggest escaping from the tomb in which they have trapped themselves shows that, as with the depiction of racism and its possible end, there are several points on which this film is more optimistic than its predecessors. First, each of the survivors seems to have learned from or rejected some part of the now dead human society, the society that caused the zombie outbreak and incurred divine wrath. John, though he is able and willing to use violence when it is necessary against Rhodes, symbolically rejects it at the end. Exactly like Peter in *Dawn of the Dead*, he throws away his gun in the final moments of the film, and without even the exigency of having it grabbed by a zombie, thereby more unambiguously rejecting the violence and domination represented by Rhodes and the other soldiers. His name, like Sarah's, is also biblical, and even more suggestively, carries with it the note of apocalypse. Romero's John—like the biblical John of the Book of Revelation (also known as the Apocalypse of John) and very much like Romero himself—has condemned and rejected the current world, and announced God's apocalyptic judgment of it.[26]

McDermott, on the other hand, is an even more explicitly, if somewhat humorously, religious character. He is so in a way different than Miguel, who dies clutching his religious medallions and succumbing to God's judgment rather than trying to overcome his own sinfulness.

McDermott's religiosity is less overt, but also less morbid and suicidal. He constantly mutters "Jesus, Mary, Joseph!" At one point, he seems to cross himself (the gesture is not complete, from head to chest, but an ambiguous motion across the forehead), anticipating the unambiguous gesture by Ken from the new *Dawn of the Dead*. He has hung a needlepoint that says "God Bless Our Home" in the trailer where he and John "indulge in verbose and alcohol-fueled philosophizing,"[27] which, while not exactly prayer or sober philosophizing, is still a good deal more humane and noble than the bickering and threats of the soldiers and scientists. None of this need indicate a real religious commitment, but seems more like the trappings and nostalgia of an upbringing in Christianity. And, certainly, the one character who is outwardly religious and also a rip-roaring drunk is mocking Christianity. Nonetheless, whether because of his adult preoccupation with liquor, or because of the vestiges of a childhood faith, McDermott seems to have no attraction toward either the scientists' hubris—although he is an electronics expert, and therefore more in line with them professionally and intellectually—or the soldiers' violence. If anything, he is the character who combines and moderates reason, emotion, and decisiveness: he is a loyal friend to John, and he effectively defends Sarah as they fight their way past the zombies in the cave.

Sarah, finally, seems to be the human character who is on a journey to learn and change and take on some new role by the end of the film. Her three dreams in the course of the film are part of this journey. Significantly, Dante, as he journeys up the mount of purgatory, also has three dreams, one of them a horrible nightmare like Sarah's dreams here. And as Dante's dreams push him to continue his journey toward a new life, Sarah's dreams seem to convince her, by showing her the horrors of their life in the bunker, to abandon it and attempt a new life. Her name, too, seems more symbolic than those of the women in the first two films: Romero is, thankfully, not so heavy-handed as to name her "Eve," since she is destined to develop a new human world, but the biblical Sarah was to be the "mother of nations" (Gen. 17:16), and she comes to this only after much wandering and doubt. Through her dreams and her name, Romero's Sarah also seems to learn to leave behind her old life—the "tomb-

stone" that John warned her about, and the sinful drives of her fellow scientists—and try for something new, a life-changing and life-challenging
"leap of faith," in explicitly Christian terms.

If one interprets the ending as an escape to a deserted island, then we
have three characters who have survived, the most of any of the first three
films. More importantly, these three seem specially suited to founding a
new society: each in his or her own way has demonstrated a rejection or a
simple lack of interest in any of the sinful urges displayed by the other characters. They are loyal, unselfish, nonviolent, and noncompetitive, and
would seem to stand a good chance of continuing their lives without the
fear of zombies, other human predators, or, most importantly, internal dissent and violence amongst themselves, which has been the undoing of the
humans in every other movie. Despite its most pessimistic evaluation of
human nature, *Day of the Dead* would therefore offer us the most optimistic ending to any of the first three films.[28]

CONCLUSION

With its glimpses of a slightly better human destiny, *Day of the Dead*
acknowledges in a small way that it might be possible to reject the human
sins of arrogance and pride, epitomized by Logan, and the sins of violence
and domination, epitomized by Rhodes.[29] As in the other films, however,
this will come about only with the complete abandonment and destruction
of the preexisting human society by the hungry zombie hordes and a wrathful God. Indeed, it is part of Romero's symbolism that the characters who
do reject the sinful perversions of reason and violence are once again people who, because of their gender, race, or socially unacceptable behavior,
stand outside the power structure of the "normal," pre-zombie, prejudg-
ment America—a woman, a black man, and a drunken (nominal)
Christian.[30] Bub, too, falls into this category, for he is the ultimate "outsider" to human society—a rotting corpse—and even he finally shows himself to be a better neighbor and more loyal friend than the sinful, selfish
scientists and soldiers. And more than any other character, Bub shows himself capable of moral improvement, shuffling off at the end, apparently no
longer interested in killing or eating humans, while the three surviving

humans apparently found a better human community that has learned from the mistakes of the past. These images will be played out much more fully and hopefully at the end of the final film, *Land of the Dead*, in which smart zombies and virtuous humans, such as those in *Day of the Dead*, finally topple the last vestiges of the old, sinful, human regime.

Chapter 4

DAWN OF THE DEAD (2004)
LIMBO AND THE PARTIAL VICTORY OF
REASON AND VIRTUE

In March 2004, the remake of Romero's classic *Dawn of the Dead* was released after a bombardment of television ads, the volume of which was staggering to me as I eagerly awaited the movie's debut. For three weeks it seemed that I could not watch a *Law and Order* rerun without seeing the *Dawn of the Dead* trailer several times, and it was particularly effective, showing just enough to make it interesting, but hiding enough that you felt you had to go see the movie, because there must be plenty more.[1] Apparently I was not alone—in its opening weekend, *Dawn* edged Mel Gibson's *The Passion of the Christ* out of the number one spot at the box office. Though it did not keep up the pace after opening weekend, *Dawn* achieved solid box office ratings, domestic and worldwide, followed by large sales of home videos, and catapulted its director, Zack Snyder, into the big league. It was Snyder's first theatrical release after a successful career of making television commercials, and he is now slated to direct the film version of Tom Clancy's *Rainbow Six* (scheduled for 2007).

For a first-time director who had previously worked in the fast-paced medium of television commercials, Snyder nonetheless brought an impeccable sense of pacing to the film, alternating between scenes of frenetic action and violence, and slower, more thoughtful scenes of conversation that allowed the actors some room in which to develop their characters, but without making the movie seem "talky" or dragging. He also made the most of his (relatively) low budget, variously reported between $27 and $45 million. Besides the much better makeup effects and more spectacular explosions he could afford (and which horror and action film aficionados appreciate so much), the acting is the main cinematic improvement over the original. For the first time in the movies we have examinined, most of the actors in the new *Dawn of the Dead* are at least recognizable, if not bankable or big-name, and they did an excellent job conveying the characters' fear, tension, and hope. The contribution of Snyder and the screenplay writer, James Gunn, to the series of films is striking, for they give us probably the best-acted movie in the series, especially noteworthy in the horror genre, which is known for abysmal or nonexistent acting. And for our theological analysis, the film's vision is also noteworthy, for it addresses even more social concerns than earlier films, and is one of the most optimistic in its depiction of human nature, softening Romero's cynical edge, and perhaps even influencing Romero's own more hopeful final installment, *Land of the Dead* (2005). In this *Dawn of the Dead*, human community and reason are shown as more effective and resilient at surviving the zombie hordes and at providing some amount of human happiness and fulfillment.

SYNOPSIS

The film takes place in the fictitious town of Everett, Wisconsin. It was actually filmed in Canada, like many low-budget movies, and experts with a good freeze-frame on their DVD players can find numerous visual giveaways (license plates, signs, etc.) of the Canadian provenance. It begins with a young nurse, Ana (played by Sarah Polley, known from many childhood roles, such as in *The Adventures of Baron Munchausen* [1988], and *One Magic Christmas* [1985]), ending her shift at a hospital, just as there are reports of a mysterious, incurable infection in a patient who has been bitten by another man. As she drives home, there are more ominous reports on the radio, but she keeps flipping past them to listen to music. When she arrives home, she first talks to her neighbor's daughter, Vivian, saying that she'll see her tomorrow to go Rollerblading. All the shots are well-designed to give a sense of suburban calm, but with an unusual (by modern American standards) feeling that people really care and interact with each other in a neighborly way, which is overladen for the audience with a heavy, oppressive dread of the disaster that we know must be approaching quickly. Ana and her boyfriend, Luis (they could be married, but there's nothing to indicate this), make love in the shower, and therefore miss the television reports that are now urging people to lock themselves in their homes because of the increasing danger from some mysterious outbreak of mass violence.

The next scene is early the next morning. Luis awakens first, surprised to see Vivian standing in their hallway. He immediately notices that she's covered in blood, and he runs to help her. As Ana is just waking up, Vivian snarls like a beast and tears out Luis' throat with her teeth. Ana manages to pull the child off of Luis, who falls backwards on the bed, blood spurting from his mortal wound. Ana hurls the tiny girl zombie down the hall, but in the first harrowing scene to show us the power and speed of zombies in this version, Vivian springs up with impossible speed from a prone position, to a crouching one, and then flies down the hall towards Ana with the swiftness and roaring of a jaguar. Ana closes the bedroom door just in time, which shudders from the zombie's blows as Ana calls for help on the phone. "All circuits are busy" is the only reply she gets, as we see Luis stand up, covered in his own blood, his face ashen, and his eyes glowing unnaturally. As soon as he sees Ana, he attacks her, and she again barely manages to get away, locking herself in the bathroom. She escapes out the bathroom window and makes it to her car, narrowly avoiding a panicked, gun-waving neighbor. Ana tears off, again escaping from Luis, who comes out the front door and runs after her, and is able to keep up with her speeding car until he is distracted by another neighbor to kill and eat.

Ana drives through the devastated city, past numerous wrecked vehicles, buildings and cars in flames, and scenes of zombies tearing people limb from limb. As she is mesmerized by one such scene of carnage, a man opens her car door and tries to pull her out, but she steps on the gas, lurching off the road, down a hill, and into a tree. As she is slumped over the steering wheel, unconscious, the director uses the interlude to run the opening credits, while newsreel footage plays in the background, accompanied by Johnny

Cash's haunting and apocalyptic song, "The Man Comes Around." The news footage gives us most of the information about zombies that is known from the other movies: all over the world, some unknown disease is causing corpses to get up and kill and eat the living, who go on to kill and eat others. Together with the preceding two scenes, it is an amazingly harrowing and effective opening sequence, showing us the complete breakdown of society and of our heroine's life, all with just a few carefully chosen and shockingly presented scenes of horror and violence.[2] It also introduces Ana as a very calm and capable heroine. Though she is clearly and understandably shaken by the ordeal thus far—she is shown crying in the car and later in the movie— she never shows any signs of panic, hysteria, or even hesitation.

When Ana awakens, she is confronted by an enormous, hulking police officer, Kenneth (played by Ving Rhames, of countless "tough guy" roles, often playing villains, presently in the new version of television's *Kojak*). He does not offer to help her, but does not turn her away, either, and the two wander off. They are soon joined by another small band of survivors: the calm, kind, and self-effacing Michael (played by character actor Jake Weber, now on NBC's *Medium*, with remarkable understatement and affability); the hotheaded, streetwise, gun-wielding Andre (played by Mekhi Phifer, best known as Dr. Pratt on television's *ER*, though here also reminiscent of his character in *8 Mile* [2002]); and Andre's beautiful and pregnant wife, Luda (played by a relatively unknown actress, Inna Korobkina). Kenneth seems uninterested in joining their group, but with their report of hordes of zombies all around the area, he accompanies them to the nearby, seemingly deserted mall, hotly pursued by more zombies before they reach the relative safety of the mall and lock themselves inside.

Once inside, they unwisely split up to investigate the place. Despite its effectiveness and freshness, the movie does obey many of the conventions of the horror movie genre, and splitting up to investigate dark places is one of the most inviolable of horror movie clichés. Michael is nearly killed by one zombie before driving a pointed stick through its head, while Luda and Kenneth are simultaneously attacked by another before Ana takes Kenneth's shotgun and shoots it in the head. They try to flee to the upper floors of the mall, where they hope there are no zombies, when they are confronted by three armed mall security guards, the leader, C. J., with his underlings, Terry and Bart (played by Michael Kelly, Kevin Zegers, and Michael Barry, respectively, all relatively new to feature films). C. J. is at first unwilling to help them, but relents and lets them stay, though he insists on disarming them and effectively making them prisoners. We find out at this point that Luda was bitten during the attack in the mall (again, just barely discernible on DVD with freeze-frame), though she is keeping it hidden from everyone but her husband. Michael further convinces C. J. to help them secure their position by barricading the doors, killing whatever zombies are already inside, and painting "HELP" on the roof, so that military or police helicopters can see them and possibly rescue them. While on the roof, they see another survivor on a roof across the street, Andy, barricaded in his gun shop, who communicates with them by holding up a dry-erase board. Their first day of siege ends with the security guards locking the others together in one store, C. J. sneering at them, "I don't want anyone sneaking around, stealing shit." C. J. then watches the final television broadcasts, with more scenes of mayhem and destruction, as in the opening credits, before the anchorman announces that they are going off the air permanently, and a minister (played in a cameo by Ken Foree, who played Peter in the original *Dawn of the Dead*) pronounces that this is all God's judgment on a sinful humanity.

The next day begins with Terry releasing the prisoners to use the bathroom. As he waits for them, Terry watches a mall surveillance camera and sees a large panel truck careening around the parking lot, pursued by increasing hordes of zombies as the people inside the truck desperately shoot at them and try to find some escape. Terry and all the prisoners go up to the roof, where C. J. and Bart are already watching the truck. An argument begins over whether or not they should help the people in the truck, and C. J. and Bart grow increasingly belligerent, waving their guns at the others. Terry wavers in his allegiance as he sees his colleagues turn heartless and violent. Michael and Kenneth simultaneously attack and disarm C. J. and Bart and reverse the situation, imprisoning the two bellicose security guards. The truck backs up to a loading dock, where those inside the mall are able to unload the occupants safely, after another harrowing confrontation with zombies, many of whom are shot or run over with the truck.

The new band of survivors consists of the driver of the truck, Norma; the guy who was shooting at the zombies, Tucker; a father, Frank, who is bitten; his teenage daughter, Nicole; a quiet, nervous, older man named Glen; a gorgeous blonde, Monica, who immediately starts complaining; an obnoxious yuppie, Steve (the only one of the group played by a well-known actor, Ty Burrell), who immediately begins insulting his rescuers; and an anonymous woman who has been severely bitten and is transported inside with a wheelbarrow. Kenneth foolishly and callously wants to take this opportunity to leave the group by driving off in the truck. Though he can see the impracticality of his plan, since the truck is now swarming with zombies, and because the new survivors tell him that the military base to which people were supposed to flee has now been overrun by them as well, he stalks off, snarling "F**k y'all" at the rest of the group. Only when he goes to the roof and uses the dry-erase board to "talk" with Andy—a fellow "tough guy" with lots of guns—does he begin to relent and see that he now has responsibilities to the group.

Ana, meanwhile, is tending to the wounded. The bitten woman promptly dies and reanimates seconds later, attacking Ana, who dispatches her spectacularly with a fireplace poker through the eye. Ana then realizes that zombie bites are always fatal, and always result in the victim rising up as a zombie to attack and kill others. She shares this information with the others, who realize that Frank is therefore doomed, though the survivors here are humane enough to wait for him to die and reanimate before shooting him. Andre is also now weighed down with the burden of knowing that Luda will become a zombie, though he keeps this information from her and the others.

Following Frank's execution, we see a montage of scenes of relative happiness for the survivors in the mall: each brief vignette gives us information about the characters and their relationships. Michael and Ana watch old comedies on television, and are clearly growing fond of each other; Terry and Nicole go up to the roof to look at the stars and are also falling in love; Kenneth and Andy play chess long-distance and are developing a friendship; while Monica and Steve, clearly the less sentimental and more vain members of the group, engage in voyeuristic sex in front of a video camera and big screen television. Other than the last pair mentioned, the survivors' enjoyments seem much less indulgent and sinful than in the original movie, as they are based on real human relationships of love and trust. C. J. and Bart, meanwhile, are not part of the group, but C. J. wiles away the time reading women's magazines and is especially fascinated by an article declaring that "trust is the number one ingredient in a successful relationship." Not being able to wave around a gun and bark orders seems to be mollifying and improving his character, enabling him to reenter better the community that is growing among the other survivors.

As the group is enjoying dinner together, however, the power goes off, which begins two horrific action sequences. First, Michael and Kenneth release C. J. and Bart so that they can help them go down to the underground parking garage and start up an auxiliary generator to restore power. When they reach their destination they find a cute dog, another horror movie cliché. They are also, of course, attacked by zombies, and Bart is killed. In the fight with the zombies, it is also clear that there is now some trust between C. J. and the others, as they fight side-by-side to save themselves from the undead. Luda, meanwhile, is going into labor. We see that Andre has isolated her away from the rest of the group in a maternity and baby's clothing store. He has also prepared for her transformation into a zombie by tying her down with a harness that will restrain her and keep her from attacking him. In a scene that is both poignant and extremely horrific, Luda dies, reanimates, and gives birth in her new, undead state, all the while trying to break free and kill Andre. Norma unfortunately stumbles on them at this point and shoots Luda, the new zombie, between the eyes. Andre, holding his "baby," crazed and distraught, shoots Norma to death. She also returns fire, killing him. The other survivors respond to the shots and see the ghastly scene of a blood-spattered nursery and three dead bodies. Norma and Andre do not reanimate, however, as Ana correctly diagnoses that they did not die from infection and therefore will not become zombies (in this version). Ana uncovers the further horror of a zombie baby in Andre's dead embrace, levels her gun at it, and the camera cuts away before we hear the bang.

These nightmarish scenes are enough to shock the human characters, unlike their counterparts in the original film, out of their lethargy and growing addiction to material possessions and trivial enjoyments. Kenneth is the first to suggest that they try to break out of their consumerist prison, rightly diagnosing that "Some things are worse than death. And one of them is sitting here, waiting to die." Steve, of course, is the only one who is dismissive and mocking of the idea, but his sarcastic remark that they should just hop on his boat and sail off on Lake Michigan causes both Ana and Michael to formulate what becomes the group's plan: to take two buses from the parking garage, armor them as best they can, drive through the zombie hordes to the marina, and escape on Steve's boat to some relatively uninhabited island on Lake Michigan.

Their plan, however, barely feasible as it is, is further complicated by the fact that they are loyal enough to their neighbor Andy across the street to include him in their escape; they are also being practical, in that they need to pick up more guns from Andy's store if they are to survive. They will have to pick Andy up, but he is on the brink of passing out from starvation, so they first have to contrive a way to get food to him. They fill a doggy-backpack with food and a walkie-talkie and put it on the dog they found, to which Nicole has become very attached, and send it across the parking lot. When the dog gets to Andy, zombies push in behind it and attack Andy, who shoots them all, but not before he is severely bitten. Nicole, fearing for the dog's safety, takes the truck and also gets inside Andy's store. She retrieves the dog, but has to barricade herself inside a closet when Andy turns into a zombie and attacks. The group, still at the mall, now has to formulate a plan to save her as well.

Kenneth, Michael, C. J., Terry, and Tucker all go through the sewers to get as close as possible to Andy's store before climbing up and shooting their way past the zombies and into the gun shop. Kenneth then has to shoot his friend Andy, tersely but sincerely apologizing as he does so: "I'm sorry, brother." They retrieve Nicole and the dog and load up on weapons, fighting their way back to the mall, though Tucker is killed. And because Steve has foolishly and cowardly locked the door on them (reminiscent of Harry Cooper doing the same to Ben in *Night of the Living Dead*), when they finally get back inside the mall, the zombies are pursuing so closely that they too break in, so the survivors have to go directly to the buses to try to make their escape. In one of the more spectacular shots, the two buses must fight their way out of the parking lot through a throng of literally thousands of (computer-generated) zombies, at one point having to blast hundreds of them with an exploding propane tank. In the ruined downtown, one of the buses crashes, killing Glen and Monica, and Steve tries to escape from the wreck, refusing to help the others, only to be killed by a zombie. The other bus stops to help the survivors, and Ana shoots the undead Steve in the face to retrieve the keys to the boat. The remaining survivors arrive at the marina, with zombies in hot pursuit. C. J. is killed in the ensuing melee, spectacularly sacrificing himself by detonating a propane tank to slow down the zombie onslaught while the others escape. As the boat shoves off, Michael reveals that he was bitten back at the bus crash, and therefore cannot escape with them. Kenneth, Ana, Terry, and Nicole sail off on the boat, and the movie proper ends with the sound of a single shot, as Michael commits suicide, standing on the dock as the sun rises. It is dawn, both of the undead, who now totally control the city, and the dawn of a new day for the human survivors, who have hopefully escaped the zombie hordes and their own sinful selfishness to found a new colony.

As the end credits roll, the director provides a sort of alternative ending, however. The survivors on the boat find a video camera, and document their voyage, which ends with them arriving at an island, only to be attacked and presumably killed there by zombies. Even with this parting shot that undoes the relatively happy ending, however, the movie is one of the most optimistic of the series. Regardless of whether or not they survive to the very end, most of the human characters in this version have shown themselves to be noble, loyal, and loving to one another, and this has made their community, as limited and circumscribed and mortal as it is, as successful and happy as it can be, under the circumstances. In this they are exactly like the inhabitants of limbo in Dante's *Inferno*. For Dante, the first circle of hell, limbo, is inhabited by those who were virtuous in life, but who did not have faith: "Now you should know before we go on farther, they have not sinned. But their great worth alone was not enough."[3] They are therefore condemned not to enter heaven, but the limbo they live in is not unpleasant: unlike the rest of hell, it is a community of people who love each other, and who converse, philosophize, and play music together.[4] They live the best that people can, without God, exactly as do most of the survivors in *Dawn of the Dead*. In that way, both works show the real, but ultimately very limited victory of unaided human reason and community over the forces of sin and destruction.

ANALYSIS

The new *Dawn of the Dead* shows many of the familiar elements of social criticism and reflection on human nature that we have seen in the other films. Racism and materialism are again prominent themes, though this version criticizes sexism more than the other films, and adds homophobia to its list of social ills. Besides social criticism, it also considers several important aspects of human life neglected in the other films.

As noted, the materialism in the film is much more subdued than in the original. The characters for the most part do not seem indulgent or extravagant. They smoke cigarettes and drink espressos, but most of the time when we see them without zombies trying to eat them alive, the humans are laughing or building friendships or romances with one another, and the latter are, for the most part, remarkably chaste by Hollywood standards. The only exception is Steve and, as far as we can tell with a minor character, Monica. Monica is the only one we see dressing up in extravagant clothes, as the characters did in the original. One of the most ghastly, haunting shots in the original, that of a tennis ball rolling off the roof to bounce past a rotting corpse, is reprised by Steve, more for laughs than shock: he stands up on the roof, hitting golf balls that whack the zombies below in their heads. In either version, the shot is one that shows sinful, myopic humans engaged in trivial games while stinking, rotting death swarms all around them. It is a graphic and chilling image of how far we will go in our diversions to distract ourselves from the obvious facts of our mortality, limitedness, and frailty. It also shows, more than that humans are consumptive or greedy, that they are just wasteful as they carelessly discard things over the side of their haven into the sea of undead. (More chilling examples of that same image are also shown in the movie when the mall survivors dispose of bodies by throwing them off the roof of the mall, and in *Land of the Dead*, when they take their trash to a dump inhabited by the undead.) But only Steve seems so wasteful and shallow; the other characters seem to enjoy each other's company more than they enjoy the "loot" of the shopping mall.

This softened or lessened criticism of materialism is also seen in the depiction of the zombies in this film, for they are both more bestial and sub-human, but also therefore less odious and sinful. Here the zombies are almost never shown eating someone—the nauseating scenes of cannibalism that are the hallmark of the genre. They seem quite intent just on killing people with a quick, savage attack and moving on to their next victim. Also, all the comical scenes from the original *Dawn of the Dead* that showed zombies addicted to "shopping" are absent in this version. Zombies no longer appear as mocking parodies of living people who stagger around the mall with blank expressions on their faces. Here the zombies act more like wild animals; they even sound and move like them. They only mill around outside the mall and at the doors of Andy's gun shop because they know there is human prey inside. The zombies are therefore less symbolic of gluttony and greed and other human sinfulness, and are instead more purely and consistently just a deadly threat to the human characters.[5] By removing much of the humor and horror of the living dead, this version focuses much more intently on the psychological drama of the human survivors and their sinfulness and virtue.

What materialism there is in the new *Dawn of the Dead*, however, is shown to be just as corrosive of human relationships as ever. Steve cannot get along with the other characters right from the start, because he is so materialistic and selfish, and especially because he is so dismissive and mocking of anyone who is not materialistic. His own base behavior begets a cynicism that alienates him from others even more than his selfishness. His first exchange with the other characters, after being saved from a certain and horrible death, is to say to Michael and Norma, "Excuse me, but when you two are done blowing each other, maybe Davy Crockett here can tell us what the deal is?" He assumes that there's some "deal," some hierarchy of command and domination, or some price to be paid for assistance. All his comments are similarly sarcastic, cynical, and divisive. Monica is also briefly shown sniping at Nicole, who is never presented as anything other than a sweet, innocent girl. Steve predictably uses up food supplies without any concern for the others, being more picky and voracious than the pregnant Luda with her understandable cravings, and he never helps with the preparations for their breakout. The movie is also quite clear that his death, unique among any shown in the film, is both deserved, and a direct consequence of his selfishness. If he had not locked the others out of the mall, they all would have stood a much better chance of survival, and if he had not abandoned the others in the crashed bus, he probably would not have been killed by a lone zombie, as there would have been other people to watch his back. That is perhaps the clearest message of the film, or of Dante's analysis of sin: being selfish turns out to be ironically the most self-destructive kind of behavior in the long run, as it angers and pushes away other people until there is no one left to help you when you need it.

Steve's status as the most unlikable character in the film points to its critique of class and wealth, for he is the only character who is identifiably wealthy, a "yuppie." All the other characters are described as solidly blue-collar—a nurse, cop, security guard, retail clerk, musician, and even a sometimes criminal[6]—while most of the characters in *Night of the Living Dead* seemed middle class, possibly white-collar, as were Fran and Steve in the original *Dawn of the Dead*. And other than the one rich person in their midst, all of the blue-collar characters in the new *Dawn of the Dead* are portrayed as virtuous in the extreme, a significant nod to the class or status reversal in this version. In a humorous take on this, the male characters in this version of *Dawn of the Dead* stand on the roof of the mall and hold up a dry-erase board with a celebrity's name on it, so that Andy can then spot the zombie celebrity look-alike with his high-powered scope and blow its head off. We are treated to the spectacle of Jay Leno and Burt Reynolds being disposed of in this way. (Steve whacking hapless zombies in the head with golf balls seems a less violent version of the same game.) Their game is a violent parody of class envy and warfare, where the rich and famous—now reduced to rotting, slavering imbeciles—are blown away by the lower classes, who show themselves to be more resourceful, talented, and intelligent than their former oppressors and now would-be cannibalistic murderers. The portrayal of both Steve and the celebrity zombies seems a caricature of the rich as unproductive parasites who drag society down into selfishness, greed, and chaos.

The treatment of racism begins on a note similar to the original *Dawn of the Dead*, with C. J. being cast as a much milder version of the homicidal, racist cop at the beginning of the original. But C. J. does not kill anyone: he just is not too eager to help other people, especially if those other people are black. Even then he can be reasoned with and persuaded to help, although he rolls his eyes and makes sarcastic remarks while doing so. Andre and Luda are an interracial couple, and their tragedy, as noted, is treated with real and effective emotion; it is also treated with little reference to their race, one of the ultimate ways that modern art, especially film, uses to defuse and undermine racism. And Andre is portrayed as especially courageous, if foolhardy and misguided, to hope against hope that their baby will be born normal, and to take such elaborate steps to attempt to bring the birth about. His final, mad shooting spree, while tragic, is also presented as understandable and forgivable.

But it is the relationship, or lack of it, between the two black characters, Kenneth and Andre, that is the most interesting new dynamic in the film's treatment of racism. Several times early on in the film, Kenneth makes it clear that he does not want to have anything to do with Andre. When Andre belittles Michael for his job as a television salesman, and turns to Kenneth for approval, Kenneth snarls back that he prefers a guy who sells televisions to a "guy who steals them." Later, when Andre expresses regret that the apocalypse has come right when he was beginning to straighten his life out, Kenneth is again hostile and dismissive toward him. The casting of Phifer was especially apt, as it puts him exactly on the opposite end of the spectrum from his role on *ER*. Both Kenneth and Dr. Pratt are very uncomfortable and judgmental towards fellow blacks whom they deem to be criminal, drug-addicted, or just plain lazy or irresponsible. They would say that such blacks are not deserving of their respect and are an embarrassment to them. However, since Andre is such an admirable character in the movie, it would seem that Kenneth's judgment of him is unfair and unfortunate, a strange kind of racism directed at a member of one's own race, and cutting one off from the friendship and trust that make life possible or enjoyable.

Sexism is more prominent in this version than in the original *Dawn of the Dead*. The less admirable male characters, Bart, Steve, and C. J., constantly put Ana down. Sometimes it happens in trivial ways, through dismissive, derogatory terms, like "sweetheart" or "lady." Sometimes it occurs in more important ways, as in dismissing her opinions because she is "only" a woman. But in the case of Bart, especially, it takes on the much more sinister and violent edge of threatening her with rape. When he and C. J. are still the only ones with guns, and they are waving them around, Bart says, "Somebody should show her how to use it [her mouth]." As in the case of the obnoxious and selfish Steve, we feel little sympathy when the vulgar, abusive, and cowardly Bart is torn to pieces by zombies. It is an indication of C. J.'s greater virtue and redeemability that he seems capable of outgrowing his prejudice against women, partly through his slightly comical reading of women's magazines while he is incarcerated. Getting in touch with his feminine side, if you will, makes him a better member of the community, teaching him that "trust" is more important than power or intimidation. Even though it is mostly Ana's idea to break out of the mall, and even though C. J. acknowledges that it stands a very low probability of success, he willingly goes along with the plan, enthusiastically throws himself into the preparations, and even sacrifices himself for the group at the end. If Michael and Ana are the more consistently virtuous characters in the movie, C. J. elicits more of our interest and sympathy because he is capable of change and improvement. Michael and Ana seem good almost by nature, while C. J., like most of the rest of us, has to work at it, a task he fulfills admirably by the end of the movie.

The issue of homophobia is raised explicitly several times in the film. As C. J. watches the final television broadcast, the Christian minister interprets the end of the world as God's judgment on a sinful humanity, and he singles out homosexuality as the main sin that is being punished. For those of us who lived during the beginning of the AIDS epidemic in the '80s and had to hear such rhetoric constantly, we surely shake our heads again at such an explanation. First, because it seems rather unlikely that God would stand by for thousands of years while humans commit a nearly infinite cat-alog of sins and atrocities, only to destroy the whole human race (the vast majority of it heterosexual) because of homosexuality. But the explanation elicits more exasperation from us, because it seems almost certain that in such a situation as depicted in *Dawn of the Dead*, many Christians would eagerly grasp on to such a diagnosis. It was even discussed after the recent tsunami and Hurricane Katrina, when some Christians speculated that the cataclysmic floods had been targeted by God against southeast Asia and New Orleans, so as to punish them for allowing prostitution (never mind how many children and other innocents died in the catastrophe). Such an explanation is so convincing and acceptable to many Christians because it makes no judgment of them, it accuses them of no sin, but conveniently blames the whole disaster on some alien group that many Christians are inclined to dislike in the first place. It is convenient and cost-free scapegoat-ing, and many Christians seem eager to accept it, no matter how vengeful and unfair it makes our God seem, and *Dawn of the Dead* holds up such ignorance for the ridicule it deserves.

Later in the movie, Glen reveals that he is gay, and here again, it is the other characters' reaction to him that shows they are ignorant and not weighing the situation correctly. C. J. and Bart are at that point incarcerated by the rest of the group, and they have to listen to Glen describe his homo-sexual feelings, in terms that are polite and not lewd or graphic. He does not at any time express an interest in C. J. or Bart or make advances or sug-gestions, but like many vain, homophobic men, that seems to be what frightens and disgusts them—that they might be the object of homosexual attraction, and somehow thereby implicated as homosexual themselves. C. J. protests against this supposed torment, crying out, "I'm in hell!" It is another hilarious, ironic scene at the expense of the human survivors, for it shows how their values are skewed. C. J. and the others are, in fact, in a place very much like the first circle of hell, surrounded by walking cannibal corpses who will never relent or go away. They are trapped, unable to escape, with dwindling supplies, and about to be torn to pieces and eaten alive at any moment. In that overall context, why would one cry out that lis-tening to a gay man describe his feelings was "hell"? One would think that a world with horrors as deadly and pervasive as armies of the insatiable undead might help people to see that the other things they find distasteful or inconvenient are fairly easy to tolerate, but instead they lash out at other people's idiosyncrasies even more vehemently. As with the preacher who deems homosexuality more horrible than any of the myriad of human sins, C. J. and Bart are so homophobic that they humorously regard even the thought of homosexuality as worse than the constant threat of death and dismemberment under which they live. Both these scenes effectively use humor to satirize homophobia and show how little sense it makes, and how overcoming it might free us up to worry about more important issues, like fighting zombies, or cleaning up our own sinful lives and building loving, trusting relationships with other people, whatever our sexual orientation.

It is the loving relationships among the human survivors that are the most touching and hopeful aspects of the new *Dawn of the Dead*. The original was content to show only the briefest hints of a deep friendship between Peter and Roger, and the love between Steve and Fran seemed quite restrained, probably even waning. And the original *Night of the Living Dead* gave only the most jaundiced and utterly negative view of the ineffectiveness and emptiness of either romantic or married love.[7] Except for the crass pair, Steve and Monica, all the romantic couples in this version—Luis and Ana, Michael and Ana, Andre and Luda, Terry and Nicole—are shown being consistently kind to one another. They are always giving, generous, hopeful, and self-sacrificing. Loving seems also a quality that can be improved upon with practice, and which does not just affect the two people involved, but improves their relations with others as well. Michael reveals in one conversation that he has been married unsuccessfully several times, and yet we cannot imagine how when we see how kind and gentle he is to Ana, and indeed to everyone in their group. The love between the human survivors seems to feed off of itself; the more they love, the more they are capable of love.

The converse, however, is true of the more vicious characters, as it is of the sinners in Dante's *Inferno*. Unable to love in the first place and thereby to ascend to higher and better acts of love, there is nowhere for them to go but to spiral downward into more and more despicable acts of selfishness and self-love, each of which makes them even more incapable of loving others. This is clearest with Steve, as we have noted, who goes from being merely annoying by greedily drinking up all the booze in the mall, to locking the others out of the mall and abandoning them in the crashed bus. Bart also makes his incapacity to love clear at the beginning of the film in another exchange that is both funny and chilling. With the world as they know it at an end and death, torture, and misery all around, the only thing he expresses regret over is that he will now not get a chance to have sex with a girl who worked at the Dairy Queen in the mall; his exact vulgar phrasing is that it "sucks" that he will not get to "tap that shit." The more sensitive Terry tries to shock him out of this ridiculous attitude by noting, "Bart, dude, everybody's dead, okay? Your mom's dead, brother's dead. That fat chick at Dairy Queen, dead!" To which Bart can only respond, "Yeah, that sucks, too." The world has been reduced to a cannibalistic hell on earth, and all he cares about is having sex with a woman he admits he neither likes nor finds attractive. As with homophobia, the skewing of values here is so insanely imbalanced that it is funny: Bart's attitudes are so debased that lust is all he can conceive of or value. When he lewdly suggests raping Ana in the next scene, we are not surprised, nor are we disappointed when the community is rid of his loathsome presence.

But *Dawn of the Dead* is not dualistic or deterministic, as though people were irredeemably or implacably placed in the good or the evil camp and could never change sides. Bad habits are hard to break, but not impossible, and we see this with the characters who change in the course of the film: especially C. J., but also Kenneth and Terry. Kenneth, who was initially dismissive of other people and pushed them away as much as possible, builds a strong friendship with Andy and insists on trying to save him as well, at great risk to himself. We also learn that he is close to his brother and the reason he wants to leave is to try to find him. These deep friendships slowly encourage a change in Kenneth that makes him more caring towards the rest of the group, as he learns to generalize and broaden his love. Early in the film, Terry is shown using the surveillance cameras to watch Ana disrobe; he is slipping into the kind of voyeurism and violation of others in which Bart or Steve would eagerly indulge. But the movie "saves" Terry from this temptation with the sudden crisis of the truck crashing into the mall parking lot, yanking his attention away. Later, when he sees Nicole crying on the surveillance camera, he seems to know that to watch her would be a violation of something sacred—her private pain at her father's death. And C. J.'s evolution is the most dramatic, for he goes from waving a gun around and threatening to kill anyone who disagrees with him—exactly like Rhodes in *Day of the Dead*—to dying for the group. In these characters, virtue is not just a comfortable state; it is a struggle and exercise. Vice is not just an alien quality "out there" in other, bad people; it is a constant temptation against which one must struggle. Their moral improvement, therefore, is all the more relevant and moving to us as we watch the story unfold.

Besides romance and friendship, *Dawn of the Dead* considers another fundamental loving relationship: that of parents and children, which is also touchingly depicted in the recent *28 Days Later*. This fundamental relationship was absent in the original *Dawn of the Dead*, except prospectively with Fran's pregnancy,[8] but it was a powerful and horrible dynamic in *Night of the Living Dead*. The constant and consistently positive consideration of the parent/child relationship is overwhelming in the new *Dawn of the Dead*. The most graphic and horrific example is, of course, with Andre and Luda, wherein Andre goes so far as to kill to protect his child, no matter whether the baby is human or "alive" or not. But practically every character, again, excepting the sinfully selfish Steve and Monica and the vulgar Bart, is shown to be deeply loving and selflessly dedicated toward their children. Not yet having children of their own, Ana and Luis are both loving and caring toward their neighbor's child, Vivian, at the beginning of the film. When Michael reveals that he was a less than exemplary husband, his main regret seems to be that this shortcoming therefore interfered with his ability to be a good "dad" to his children. In the extra material on the DVD, we find out the same information about Andy across the street. As he is starving to death in his prison, the only thing he worries about is whether his divorced wife escaped to safety with their daughter. As Frank is dying, he gasps out his love for his daughter twice as his final words, first to her, and then to Kenneth, his executioner, after she has left the room. All of these scenes are done with amazingly sincere and convincing emotion by actors who should be praised for their work. Exactly the opposite from Steve or Bart—who only regret the end of the world because it curtails their sinful abuse of things and people—most of the characters here only regret that their children will suffer as a result of what has happened, and they feel guilt and pain because they have been unable to protect their children, never minding about themselves. Bearing children can be a powerful corrective to the materialism critiqued in the film, for it is an act of creation, not consumption, and it creates beings whom one then has to love and care for and put before one's own well-being. The inclusion of this dynamic in the film deepens its emotional and psychological analysis and effect tremendously.

Another important human activity that the film considers is outward acts of religiosity or worship, which are almost wholly absent in the other films. The people in this version seem intuitively aware of the sacred, and especially aware of how their present horrific situation violates or keeps them from the sacred and reduces them to an animal existence. Near the beginning of the film, right after the bitten woman brought in from the truck dies, they all feel special unease and disorientation when they cannot pronounce something over her or about her because they just do not know her name. As trivial as it may seem at first, they sense that a special, dehumanizing dishonor has been done to her that is somehow more fundamental and unfixable than even biological death. This unease is repeated after the horrific scene in which Andre, Luda, and Norma are killed, and the survivors feel as though they must perform a funeral, but do not know how to go about it. As with their emotions, all of this is a huge expansion on what was treated very perfunctorily and in an entirely secular way in the original *Dawn of the Dead*, which only showed Peter standing over Roger's grave and drinking a toast to his dead comrade. Here the characters long for something overtly and explicitly religious. They turn to Glen, who was an organist in a church, but he declines, describing his work in the church as just a job, with no feeling or faith behind it. Organized religion in this movie is implicitly on the same level of ineffectiveness and corruption as the government, military, and the media—a mixture of lies and platitudes to cover up inequities, power struggles, and ignorance. The identity of all such useless human entities seems to coalesce into the name of the military installation to which the television tells them they are supposed to go, but which has already been overrun and devoured by the undead, when Ken holds up the dry-erase board: "FORT PASTOR GONE <u>NO HELP</u> COMING."[9] There is no pastor, reverend, father, priest, or pope to help them, but they still desperately long for a direct and personal relationship with God.[10]

This tearing conflict between the irrelevance of religion, the seeming absence of God during their horrible ordeal, and their desperate longing and need for something divine and/or religious, comes to a dramatic head with Glen's statement, "I don't believe in God. I don't see how anyone could!" But then Kenneth steps forward, briefly but clearly and significantly crossing himself, and gives a sermon of sorts, diagnosing their problem: in the normal world, the living are glad to be alive, and afraid of dying, but in their sick, upside-down world, the living envy the dead, who at least have gone on to some kind of peace and no longer need fear being torn to pieces and eaten alive, or just dying of boredom and starvation. Kenneth's speech begins their plans to break out of the mall. It does not seem too speculative to connect the characters' greater level of religiosity with their ability, unlike the characters in the original *Dawn of the Dead*, to pull themselves away from their materialistic prison in the mall and strike out on their own. They long for something more than "stuff," and even if we put a nonreligious label on what they desire—"freedom," or "meaning," or "transcendence"—it remains an inchoately religious and explicitly anti-materialistic longing. This movie is hardly pious, but it is adamant that the consumerist, egoist alternative to religion is a deadly lie, and for that truth the film is to be admired.

In all of this, it is also important and refreshing to note that the film avoids two of the most prevalent stereotypes in horror movies, or in Hollywood films in general, for that matter, the sanctimonious, outwardly religious hypocrite who is secretly a sinner of the worst kind (usually a pedophile, or at least an adulterer or rapist); and his opposite, the outwardly atheistic and cynical sinner who is secretly an intensely moral, upright character. For all their faults, none of the vicious characters in

Dawn of the Dead could be accused of sanctimony or hypocrisy. And as noted, practically everyone in the movie expresses some need for religiosity, even if they are inept and inarticulate about their need. Kenneth was apparently a regular churchgoer, if somewhat flippant in his description of his habits. When Andre says, "You seem like the kind of cat who goes to church and all that kind of shit," Kenneth responds, "Yeah, I do all that kind of shit." As with Glen's bitter regret, one can hardly blame Kenneth for calling his church attendance "all that kind of shit," when faced with the world turned into a cannibalistic hell. Rather than presenting us with the simple stereotypes of the religious hypocrite and righteous sinner, *Dawn of the Dead* gives us a cast that looks much more like our modern world: unchurched people who would probably describe themselves as "spiritual, but not religious," together with people who go to church out of habit, but have deep and frequent doubts and misgivings. Both groups are composed of people who have enough innate goodness to reject materialism and pursue something above and beyond their own physical needs, often by loving and sacrificing themselves for others. While it may not be the image we might like to conjure up of America as a "Christian nation," it is also a powerful denial that America is only a greedy, consumerist, selfish, lazy nation of individualists and hypocrites who would not lift a finger to help one another in a crisis. As on so many other points, the film's presentation is nuanced and complicated, and therefore more interesting and accurate.

For a final indication of the movie's outlook on human destiny, consider the brilliant choice of the Johnny Cash song, "The Man Comes Around," for the opening credits.[11] On the one hand, it is the most brutally and universally apocalyptic song imaginable; it ends with death and hellfire engulfing the entire earth at God's instigation. It is the perfect choice for the movie, as ultimately all the characters are horribly killed. But in apocalypse, whether it is the Bible's or Cash's or *Dawn of the Dead's* interpretation of it, there is always some sense that choices still matter, that how we live our lives is important, even if the same horrible, inevitable, and leveling death awaits each of us. In the song this is expressed in several lines, especially in the assurance that "Everybody won't be treated all the same." Assigning such value to choices is seriously undermined in *Night of the*

Living Dead, but here it is again affirmed. Even in a world of zombies, or in our regular world, where death is no less inevitable, if easier to postpone temporarily, there are noble ways to live and die, and also base, ignoble ways to do so, and which we choose finally makes a very real difference. We shrug when Bart dies, we practically cheer when Steve dies, but we are in awe of the courageous self-sacrifice of C. J. and Michael.[12] The strength and compelling nature of the new *Dawn of the Dead* is that it focuses on people who pursue noble lives, even while it remains starkly and frighteningly realistic about their limitations, shortcomings, and their earthly, physical fates.

As in the original *Dawn of the Dead,* criticism of modern American society is prominent in the remake, especially in its criticism of materialism, racism, sexism, and homophobia, but this criticism is more balanced and less stark. In its consideration of important human activities such as romantic love, friendship, the love of children, and religious worship, it also offers a more general analysis of human nature, one that is about as hopeful as the genre will allow, and one that is much more insightful than the average Hollywood movie, let alone a horror movie.

CONCLUSION

With the new *Dawn of the Dead,* we have a great example of how good a remake can be, and of how meaningful and humane a zombie movie can be. The movie takes the fundamental premise of the original, but alters it wherever necessary to make it more dramatically compelling, or to include new insights. The basic idea of the movie is still the chilling presentation that all humans are just one step away from descending into a frozen, static hell, either as oblivious, mindless zombie mallgoers, or as conniving, grasping human mall-defenders, the greedy, self-absorbed haves, and the envious, slavering, undead have-nots, we might say. Stated this way, one need not posit the existence of a virus that kills people and then reanimates their corpses in order to see the relevance of the film's vision. But on to this pessimistic and all-too-accurate estimation of the human condition, the film has added a touching and optimistic tale of human life right on the edge of the abyss, like the city of limbo right on the precipice of the fiery, stinking maw of hell in Dante's *Inferno.* In both Dante's limbo and in *Dawn of the*

Dead's Crossroads Mall, we find people who use their love and reason to build up a community that is as happy and satisfying as one can be through only human means.[13] Both tales are therefore at the same time uplifting, showing people defeating the sinful destructiveness of both themselves and the zombie hordes, but also sobering, showing just how fragile and limited such a happiness and a community would be without God. It would include charity or love, but would lack faith and hope, as Virgil describes the fate of himself and the others in limbo: "In this alone we suffer: cut off from hope, we live on in desire."[14] Without faith and hope, even love fails, because God, the only real and eternal object of all love, is not there to draw it upwards and complete it.

Chapter 5

LAND OF THE DEAD (2005)
THE DEEPEST ABYSS OF HELL
AND THE FINAL HOPE

In a recent two-year span there was a spate of commercially successful, Romero-inspired zombie films—*28 Days Later* (2002), *Resident Evil* (2002 and 2004), *Dawn of the Dead* (2004), and *Shaun of the Dead* (2004). This culminated with Romero returning in 2005 to the genre he practically created with a new film, *Land of the Dead*. Romero had a bigger budget than ever before—$17 million—but it was still paltry by industry standards, and to get it he would have to produce a film with an R rating.[1] (The unrated "director's cut" DVD has no such limitations, of course, and delivers several more extended scenes of cannibalistic gore similar to the endings of *Dawn of the Dead* and *Day of the Dead*.) Although not as philosophical as *Day of the Dead*, or as scary as the original *Night of the Living Dead*, or as satirical as *Dawn of the Dead*, *Land of the Dead* does present us (together with the usual assortment of thrills and gross-outs native to the genre) with a surprising and revealing development in zombies. If the original *Dawn of the Dead* put us in the zombies' shoes, then *Land of the Dead* surprisingly and consistently puts the zombies in our shoes, making them more human than any of the other films, and therefore no longer the objects of our revulsion and fear, but of strange sympathy and respect. Alongside these greatly improved and much more sympathetic zombies we are presented with another cast of sinful, repugnant humans who tear each other apart. The result is a movie in which the audience might actually find itself rooting for the zombies,[2] as they bring about the end of the racist, capitalist, exploitative, parasitic human society.[3] At the same time, the ambiguous endings of *Dawn of the Dead* and *Day of the Dead*, and the utterly hopeless ending of *Night of the Living Dead*, are replaced here with the only unambiguously hopeful ending in any of the films, in which humans and zombies will finally live—or, more properly, coexist—in peace with one another. The film shows that even in Romero's world of brutal cynicism about sinful human nature, there is still the possibility of some hope for our race.

SYNOPSIS

Land of the Dead begins with a quick montage of newscasts that inform us of the zombie menace and takeover as seen in the previous movies. One new piece of information is the garbled report that some people have formed armed enclaves in cities and are raiding nearby towns for supplies. Our view is then taken to a nighttime scene in the zombie-infested village square of some place called Uniontown. But unlike the Florida city taken over by zombies at the beginning of *Day of the Dead*, this is far from a scene of horror. For the first time in the films, the zombies are behaving in a strangely peaceful way. A band of zombie musicians at the bandstand makes noise with their instruments, to which other zombies seem to listen with enjoyment, teenage zombies who were lovers in life hold hands, and a large, black zombie whose name tag says "Big Daddy" (actor Eugene Clark, known primarily for his work on television) tries to pump gas at the gas station where he used to work in life. Spying on this scene of relative zombie bliss are two armed men, a younger soldier who is clearly new to such a mission, and the main character of the movie, Riley (Australian-born actor Simon Baker, best known from television's *The Guardian*). When they see that the zombies sense their presence, they retreat.

We next see the other major character, Cholo (actor and comedian John Leguizamo, now doing a stint on television's *ER*) with other men, throwing garbage off a truck into a huge garbage dump, in which some zombies still writhe. They heave one last big box into the dump, and we see blood dripping from it.

Riley and Cholo, together with other armed men on motorcycles and other vehicles, converge on an enormous armored vehicle named Dead Reckoning. Riley gives a report of his reconnoitering, that there are lots of "walkers" and "stenches" in Uniontown, and they seem to be acting with more intelligence and organization than ever seen before. Riley is therefore apprehensive about raiding the town for supplies, but they do so anyway. Riley is joined by his sidekick, Charlie (character actor Robert Joy), whose face is horribly disfigured—from a fire, we find out later—and who is mentally challenged. The human raiders head back to Uniontown, Riley reminding his men that they need to get antibiotics. Cholo invites the rookie to join him and others as they attack the town separately, while Dead Reckoning fires off a constant barrage of fireworks into the night sky. In a reference back to the opening sequence of *Night of the Living Dead*, Riley calls shooting off the fireworks "putting flowers in the graveyard." As the raiders tear into town, we see the reason for the fireworks: all the zombies stare up at them, mesmerized, thereby rendering them utterly helpless, and the humans gun them down and run them over. The violence this time seems especially gratuitous, as the humans gleefully shoot, hack, and impale the zombies for no reason other than sheer enjoyment. Big Daddy seems impervious to the fireworks' mesmerizing effect, however, and he tries to warn his fellow zombies, grunting, growling, and even courageously pushing zombies out of the way to save them from the humans' attack, a poignant and humane gesture because one of the zombies is a little girl. (Throughout the film, Clark displays an impressive and uncanny ability to convey emotions and communicate without the use of any words, using only growls and grunts that are about halfway between the sounds of *Young Frankenstein* [1974] and Chewbacca in *Star Wars* [1977].)

During the attack, the barrage of fireworks suddenly stops due to a mechanical failure, and Riley orders his men to pull out, as the zombies are now not nearly so harmless. Dead Reckoning tears into town to provide some covering fire as the zombies turn from hapless, frozen targets into a serious threat. Cholo and his men, however, are in a different part of town, raiding a liquor store for its unessential but very desirable and valuable liquor, champagne, and cigars. While inside the store they are attacked by zombies, and the rookie is bitten. Cholo prepares to shoot the rookie in the head when Riley arrives. Riley objects and is appalled at this scene of senseless greed and carnage, more so when the wounded young man grabs Riley's gun and commits suicide to avoid becoming a zombie himself. The humans leave Uniontown, but Big Daddy watches them drive off toward a huge, eerily lit skyscraper in the distance, and he leads the other zombies out of town, slowly shuffling in pursuit of their human tormentors.

The humans arrive at a fenced-in area surrounded by towers and machine guns. Here they park their vehicles and continue towards the skyscraper via a tunnel under a huge river. (The geography of the surviving human city corresponds roughly to that of Romero's hometown of Pittsburgh, though the movie was filmed in Toronto, for the same financial reasons as Dawn of the Dead [2004].) As they reenter the city, a television advertisement informs us of some of the social arrangements in this post-zombie world. The tower is Fiddler's Green, an exclusive high-riser that seems to be part Las Vegas hotel, part galleria shopping mall, part gated community.[4] It is situated in a city on a peninsula, with water on all sides but one; an electrified fence seals off the last side from the zombie-infested mainland. The television ad extols the Green as the place where "Life goes on!" the way it once did. But the rest of the city is not nearly as pleasant as the Green. It is full of squalor and poverty and crime, though, significantly, it is also where we see children laughing and playing for the only time in any of the movies.

Cholo and Riley go their separate ways in this city, each of them vowing that this has been his last raid and he is now quitting for good. Cholo claims he has saved up enough money finally to buy a place in the Green, and we see him enter the tower. On the DVD version of the film, there follows a scene that was not shown in the theatrical release. It certainly is dispensable, as it does not really advance the plot, but it does show a more humane and heroic side of Cholo, as well as showing some of the unexpected horrors of life in the Green. Outside an apartment, Cholo is accosted by a panicked servant and told there is trouble in the apartment across the hall. Cholo kicks down the door of the other apartment and sees that the owner has hanged himself, and the man's wife and son seem unaware of the danger this poses, once the man reanimates as a zombie (also making clear that in Romero's version, it is not just zombie bites that cause reanimation, but any death). Since Cholo has been required to surrender his weapons before entering the tower, the situation is made more difficult, as he has no effective way to deal with a zombie. He tries to get the woman away from the body, but she is hysterical. Cholo is thereby distracted while the man reanimates and attacks his own son, tearing his throat out in typical zombie attack fashion. Cholo picks up a large, heavy objet d'art to use as a bludgeon and beats the zombie to death. The official security guard finally arrives and Cholo leaves the scene, disgusted and saddened.

Riley, meanwhile, has different plans to end his career as a mercenary zombie-killer. In the streets he first sees a rabble-rouser named Mulligan who is trying to incite the crowds against the injustices of their city: that some live in the comfort of the Green, while most live in the surrounding squalid slum. Riley declines Mulligan's invitation to join the revolutionary uprising, but gives him antibiotics for his sick son. Riley then takes Charlie and goes in search of a car he had contracted to buy so they can escape from the city entirely. He has been cheated, however, and the car is no longer available. Riley and Charlie descend into a strange nightclub where there is alcohol, gambling, topless dancers, prostitution, and odd entertainments involving zombies—having your picture taken with a zombie (the photo-zombies are played in a cameo by Simon Pegg and Edgar Wright, who wrote and directed *Shaun of the Dead*), shooting paint balls at zombies, and caged fighting matches between zombies. Riley finds the nightclub owner, who had agreed to sell him the car, and threatens him. At the same time, Riley notices that a young woman has been thrown into the cage with the zombies and is fighting for her life as part of the sick entertainment. He intervenes and shoots the two zombies, setting off a gun battle in which Charlie and Riley kill the nightclub owner and his henchmen. The police arrive and arrest Riley, Charlie, and the woman they saved from the zombie cage, Slack (actress Asia Argento, daughter of famed Italian horror movie director Dario Argento, who produced the original *Dawn of the Dead*).

Big Daddy and the other zombies, meanwhile, are nearing the city. They encounter a barricade, and Big Daddy possesses the intellect and leadership necessary to break through it. He directs one zombie, who is carrying a cleaver, to chop at the plywood wall until he makes a hole. Big Daddy tears the opening wider and looks through to see zombies cruelly hung upside down by their ankles, with bull's-eye targets taped to them. Further in the distance, the tower of Fiddler's Green again draws his attention as the source of all this suffering and injustice. He lets out a roar and leads the zombies around to find a way to cross the river, the final barrier between them and the tower.

Next we see Cholo at Fiddler's Green, continuing on the errand he began before having to intervene in the suicide and zombie attack. He enters the apartment of Kaufman (veteran actor Dennis Hopper, whose classic *Easy Rider* [1969] was released the year after the original *Night of the Living Dead*), a wealthy businessman who seems to run Fiddler's Green and the whole city. Cholo offers Kaufman the champagne and cigars for which the rookie soldier died, and he asks if now he can move into the Green. Though Kaufman feigns great appreciation for Cholo's work for him, he denies Cholo's request. As Cholo grows angry, Kaufman instructs a security guard to remove him, insinuating that Cholo should be eliminated. When the guard attacks Cholo on the way out, Cholo disarms him, beats him, and leaves.

As revenge against Kaufman, Cholo now plans to steal Dead Reckoning and use the threat of its weapons to extort money from Kaufman (what use money would have for them outside of Fiddler's Green is left unexplained throughout the movie, though there is vague talk that there are other human outposts left). He and his men arrive at the base on the other side of the river to take the vehicle, but the guards refuse to let them. At the same time, Big Daddy and the zombies begin their attack on the base, thereby distracting the guards, so that Cholo and his men can tear off in Dead Reckoning. The zombies succeed in battering down the fence and overwhelming the guards, devouring them and partly destroying the base when a propane tank explodes.

Cholo calls Kaufman and tells him to send money, or the missiles of Dead Reckoning will be fired at the city. He gives Kaufman until midnight, only a few hours away. Kaufman calls Riley into his office and tells him that

Dead Reckoning, which he says Riley designed, has been stolen by Cholo. He offers to let Riley go and give him the car he wants if he can get back Dead Reckoning and save the city from its weapons. Riley agrees, if Charlie and Slack will also be released and allowed to go with him, to which Kaufman agrees. The three arm themselves and prepare to leave, but at the last moment, they are forced to take along three soldiers more loyal to Kaufman—Manolete, Monica, and Pillsbury (all rather cartoonish characters, as they are all played as stereotypical "badasses" with stereotypically juvenile dialogue). The six go across the river and arrive at the destroyed, burning base from which Cholo took Dead Reckoning. They split up to look for weapons, ammunition, and most importantly, a vehicle. Splitting up, of course, allows for several frights when zombies jump out at them while they are separated. Manolete and Riley find a roomful of zombies gorging on soldiers' body parts and proceed to execute them in a scene exactly like the basement scene at the beginning of *Dawn of the Dead.* They all get into a jeep that Monica hotwired, though at the last moment a zombie attacks and bites Manolete. They drive off in search of Dead Reckoning, which Riley reveals he can find with a tracking device. He also reveals that he had to kill his own brother after he was bitten by a zombie, because the infection is inevitably fatal, so Slack rather inhumanely shoots Manolete before he can turn into a zombie.

We next see Cholo's man, who was assigned to pick up the blackmail money, under attack and eventually devoured by zombies while he waited for the money. The zombies led by Big Daddy have now reached the banks of the river opposite the city. They pause there, then Big Daddy steps off the edge and splashes into the water below. One by one the other zombies follow him into the icy waters.

Riley and the others arrive at a hill overlooking the city. Riley is sure this is where Cholo will take Dead Reckoning in order to bombard the city. They lie in wait for Cholo, and when he arrives, Riley and Charlie talk their way inside Dead Reckoning and try to dissuade Cholo from firing on Fiddler's Green, because it will result in such a great loss of innocent life in the city below. Cholo is bent on destruction, however, as he reveals the depths of Kaufman's crimes and his own involvement, including killing and disposing of Kaufman's enemies, such as, presumably, a person in the bleeding trash box at the beginning of the film. (We had earlier heard from Slack that it was by Kaufman's command that she had been thrown into the cage with the zombies.) Cholo orders the missiles to be armed and launched.

Meanwhile, in one of the most memorable shots in the movie, we see Big Daddy and his zombies slowly rising from the river's misty waters. They proceed into the city and begin attacking people in the streets in various horrible ways. Besides engaging in usual zombie attacks, biting and tearing people apart with their hands, these zombies are unusually adept with a variety of regular and impromptu weapons, hacking and stabbing people with various implements. At one point Big Daddy even shows another zombie how to squeeze the trigger on an assault rifle and use it to kill a man. The zombies are quickly taking control of the city's streets and moving toward Fiddler's Green.

Back onboard Dead Reckoning, Riley disarms the missiles via remote control, and Cholo is ready to shoot him. Monica shoots Cholo just as a zombie attacks and bites her. In the pandemonium, Riley and Charlie take control of the situation as Slack and Pillsbury shoot Monica and the zombie that bit her. Riley then lets Cholo and one of his men go free, and they go off in search of another vehicle to use, while Riley and the others take Dead Reckoning. When Riley calls Kaufman to tell him that Dead Reckoning is back under their control, however, Kaufman hears explosions outside his office as the zombies continue their rampage within the city. Riley decides not to return Dead Reckoning to Kaufman, but to use it to try to save the city from the zombie attack. At the same time, Cholo is bitten by a zombie while trying to find another vehicle. Doomed by the bite, he decides to go back and kill Kaufman rather than commit suicide, saying in a great double entendre, "I always wanted to see how the other half lives," leaving it unclear whether he means the privileged class in Fiddler's Green or the undead. Either way, he will wreak vengeance on Kaufman, alive or undead.

The final rollercoaster ride of this climactic confrontation begins with all three groups converging on Fiddler's Green—Big Daddy and his irate zombies destroying everyone in their path, Cholo slowly turning into a zombie and seeking revenge on Kaufman, and Riley and Dead Reckoning trying to save as many innocent residents as possible. Riley has to lower a drawbridge to get Dead Reckoning into the city, since its base was originally outside the city limits on the other side of the river. This involves a harrowing scene, with a single zombie attacking him outside of the vehicle while a horde of zombies attacks the vehicle itself. Meanwhile, a feeding frenzy reminiscent of *Dawn of the Dead* and *Day of the Dead* goes into high gear as the zombie mob breaks into Fiddler's Green and starts tearing people apart in more and more creative ways: one attack involving a belly button ring is especially gruesome and memorable, as are shots of blood spurting onto expensive store windows. Out in the streets, a further setback for the human survivors is that the electrified fence is still turned on, and therefore they cannot escape out of the city, making Riley's earlier observation of the fence all the more prescient and chilling: "I can't help but think we're all locked in." We see a crowd of people trapped at the fence, with zombies closing in on them. Riley anticipates this problem, and as he drives Dead Reckoning toward the fence, he shoots off fireworks to try to save the trapped people, but now it is to no avail, as the zombies are no longer distracted by them.

Kaufman meanwhile makes it down to the underground parking garage in an attempt to escape. On the way, though, he shoots Big Daddy, who follows him down to the garage. Big Daddy traps Kaufman inside his limousine, then sees the gas pump right next to the car, pours gasoline all over the car, and even punches the spigot through the windshield to pour gasoline inside the car. Big Daddy then inexplicably wanders away and up the garage ramp, and a relieved Kaufman gets out of the car, only to be confronted by Cholo. He shoots Cholo several times, but Cholo continues inexorably towards him out of the shadows, until we see that Cholo is now a zombie. As he goes to bite Kaufman, Big Daddy rolls a burning propane tank down the garage ramp, igniting all the gasoline in a huge explosion that destroys both Cholo and Kaufman.

Riley and Dead Reckoning finally arrive at the electrified fence, only to see a crowd of zombies feasting on dead people. In disgust, Riley fires the missiles at the zombies anyway, even though he thinks it can do no good at this point. But after the spectacular explosions that blast the zombies to pieces, and after the fire and smoke clear, some surviving people do emerge from nearby buildings, including Mulligan and his revolutionaries (the DVD bonuses include a few brief shots which were left out of the final theatrical or DVD release, showing Mulligan and his men escaping from jail and arming themselves to fight both the zombies and the authorities). Riley, Slack, Pillsbury, and the remnants of Cholo's crew agree to take Dead Reckoning away to the north and start a new life there, while Mulligan and his revolutionaries vow to rebuild the city there without the corruption and evil of Kaufman and his ilk. Riley and Big Daddy look at each other from a distance, and both seem to acknowledge that the bloody battles between zombies and humans are now over. Big Daddy and his zombies will be left alone by the humans, and vice versa. It is surely the most hopeful and uplifting ending to any Romero zombie film, for both humans and zombies seem to have learned and improved in the course of the film, and both are thereby winners. Unlike the previous films, it was not about whether zombies would "take over" the world, but rather about how, without the Kaufmans of the world trying to "take over," the world could be a place where both living and undead exist together in peace.

ANALYSIS

Land of the Dead continues Romero's social criticism from earlier films, though it does so with more humor and action than previous films. Romero goes for a lot of laughs and a lot of explosions, but by the end, the uncomfortable equation between zombies and humans is as unmistakable and meaningful as in any previous installment, so much so that one reviewer opined that, "It is mind-boggling that this film was released as a big summer blockbuster, for it may be one of the most contestational Hollywood studio films made in several years. Land of the Dead is a film about breaking down the barricades, fences, and walls that offer false security to the powerful."[5] Another ties it in with the political pretensions of other supposedly trite or vapid summer flicks: "Whatever else you think about these films, whether you believe them to be sincere or cynical, authentic expressions of defiance or just empty posturing, it is rather remarkable that these so-called popcorn movies have gone where few American films outside the realm of documentary, including most so-called independents, dare to go."[6] Let us examine the walls that are being broken down, and the places this film dares to go.

Racism and sexism are both in the film as more or less part of the background. The human villain, Kaufman, is somewhat reflexively also guilty of racism, calling Cholo a "f**king spic" at one point. Three of the "tough guys" in the film are women—Slack, Monica, and a crew member of Dead Reckoning—and this passes without comment by any characters in the film. (There may once again be some implied gallantry on the part of Riley in saving Slack, but we can see from his relationship with Charlie that he would have saved anyone in a similar life-threatening situation.) But the race of the zombie leader, Big Daddy, seems far less coincidental; it is, in fact, part of the film's most provocative message decrying class and race in modern America (or the human world in general). Big Daddy is no longer victimized by racist America, like Ben in *Night of the Living Dead*, nor does he simply flee it like Peter and John in *Dawn of the Dead* and *Day of the Dead*, respectively. He actively brings about the final destruction of the old order of racist violence and ushers in a new age of peace, justice, and equality.

Land of the Dead flashes back to *Dawn of the Dead* to continue its scathing denouncement of modern American materialism and consumerism, and this time adds class stratification as a closely related social ill. If *Day of the Dead* gave us two memorable villains, Logan and Rhodes, to stand-in as perverted practitioners of science and the military, *Land of the Dead* gives us the darkest villain of all in Kaufman, a character who seems to be a combination of capitalist robber baron, mad Roman emperor, and organized crime kingpin.[7] His name means "trader" or "merchant" as though that were the essence of his character. To have the new ruler of the only remaining human society be named "merchant," shows how Romero believes that the highest form of power in the old human society is commerce. In this chilling, cynical, but uncomfortably realistic view, it is not the military, government, or church that exercises real power, but the wealthy, who may use these other institutions as proxies or fronts for their selfish machinations. According to Romero, the White House, the Pentagon, and the Vatican do not run or exploit the world—Wall Street does.

Played by Hopper with more restraint than he often exercises, and therefore much more effectively, Kaufman is positively Satanic in the absurd and sadistic lengths to which he will go in order to perpetuate his reign, as the reviewer for *The New York Times* noted: "With this new movie, we jump straight to the ninth circle, where Satan is a guy in a suit and tie who feasts on the misery of others, much as the dead feast on the living."[8] Kaufman is one of the few, perhaps the only one of the characters in any of the films, to note how the zombie menace fundamentally changes all human interactions, and does so to his advantage. When informed that he's in "trouble," Kaufman quite correctly responds, "In a world where the dead are returning to life, the word 'trouble' loses much of its meaning." Only the raiders in *Dawn of the Dead* would perhaps share Kaufman's preference for life in a world overrun by zombies, but the raiders were crude, disorganized, and comical amateurs compared to Kaufman. Again, *Land of the Dead* teases us with the idea that it is not the leather-clad, tattooed biker, or the big, scary black man who will do us harm, but the sinister and well-organized banker and businessman who is the real threat to us.

While others long to return to "normal" life—and this is exactly what the ads for Fiddler's Green falsely promise—or to escape to Canada or a desert isle, or simply to "raise hell" like the bikers in *Dawn of the Dead*, Kaufman sees how "good" life can be in a zombie-infested world, for not only does it remove all restraints on him, but it also lets him set up a hellish society based on his values of greed, envy, vice, and cruelty.[9] We see this when he explains his own version of "civic duty" at one point. According to him, he has a great and noble "responsibility" for his fellow citizens, because he "kept people off the streets by giving them games and vices." Like Milton's (1608–1674) Satan more than Dante's, Kaufman believes that it is "Better to reign in Hell, than serve in Heav'n."[10] And while he is mixing in various classic depictions of Satan, Romero is, of course, not above the burlesque version of Goethe's (1749–1832) Mephistopheles, having Kaufman say, as probably only Hopper could, while picking his nose (!), "Zombies, man, creep me out!"

The fantasy of what Satan/Kaufman tempts us with is graphically shown in the ads and reality of Fiddler's Green. It is a place where "Life goes on!" as before, undisturbed by the miseries of others or by the inevitable specter of (un)death. The ground floor of Fiddler's Green resembles a much more upscale mall than that depicted in the original *Dawn of the Dead*,[11] now made more horrible and wretched by its opulence, and by the fact that it is not just zombies and biker gangs that are kept out, but sick and starving children. All attempt to dress the fantasy up as anything other than crass and cannibalistic consumption has finally been stripped away by the exigencies of a zombie-infested world. The inner sanctum of consumption and exclusion is not named something bellicose like The Citadel, or patriotic, like Freedom Tower; instead, it's got one of those generically happy-sounding names like the $1.5 million condos with 24-hour fitness centers, climate control, and security, cocooned in shining glass and steel towers and advertised in the back of in-flight magazines. It is an image of privileged irresponsibility in the face of suffering, like "fiddling while Rome burns."[12] Apparently, the name even comes from an old Irish legend of where happy fishermen go when they die, a place where "There's pubs and there's clubs and there's lassies there too. And the girls are all pretty and the beer is all free. And there's bottles of rum growing on every tree."[13] It is an adult version of Pleasure Island in *Pinocchio* or Neverland in *Peter Pan*, but it is no more mature, and no more real. The added scene of a suicide in the DVD version makes the fantastical and unsatisfying aspect of such an existence painfully clear. Surrounded by comfort and ease, some people find their life so empty and meaningless that they kill themselves and become zombies, who at least have a lot more drive and ambition. And even if they do not avail themselves of suicide, zombiehood is where they are all headed anyway, but before they get there, they have the added damnation of being the docile and cooperating thralls of Kaufman/Satan.

The reality of the hellish kingdom over which Kaufman rules is indelibly impressed on our imaginations by the view from his office, which is as Dantean as anything else presented in the films. As far as the eye can see is a grey, blighted, lifeless urban moonscape that might as well be Hiroshima or Auschwitz, it is so dead and demoralizing, yet it represents the best view in Fiddler's Green, one which Kaufman is eager to kill to protect and keep to himself from the "common" folk like Cholo or Mulligan, or from the hungry undead. Kaufman first refuses Cholo's request for entrance into Fiddler's Green, then tries to have him killed. As we later find out, he has had many innocent people murdered. When Cholo responds with the threat of violence, Kaufman suddenly invokes the rule of law by hypocritically and hilariously screaming the Reaganesque line that "We do not negotiate with terrorists!" Twice as the zombies are attacking his kingdom, he cries out, "You have no right!" when, of course, Kaufman based his entire kingdom on ignoring others' rights and acting like a terrorist and a criminal. His evil reign is over once Cholo and the zombies realize that Kaufman can make no legitimate appeal to laws and rights, that he has ruled only by violence and deception—or "might makes right"—and now should rightfully perish by his own rules. Since Cholo and the zombies together represent all the disenfranchised and exploited in Kaufman's kingdom, they are also a potent and uncomfortable indictment of the United States, for all the disenfranchised and exploited on which we base our affluent and wasteful lifestyle.[14]

But Romero is not so simplistic as to make the disenfranchised the unambiguous "heroes" of his film. He has, after all, consistently undermined our desire for a hero since the first film, *Night of the Living Dead*. Even if Big Daddy is intelligent and human enough to realize that he is wreaking a more or less righteous vengeance on Kaufman—if anyone could legitimately be said to be waging a "jihad" it is Big Daddy, though Cholo is the one who claims to be doing so—the other zombies are still pretty much mindless, instinctual killers who just respond to his leadership.[15] And on the human side, Cholo is presented as the quintessential aspiring yuppie, willing to climb and claw over anyone in his path in order to live in the "right" neighborhood with the "right" people. His defense of what he is doing is most revealing of how he regards wealth and status. As he is onboard Dead Reckoning after stealing it, he looks outside and sees a zombie peacefully mowing the grass. Cholo claims that without money, he would be just like the zombie—a useless, worthless, nameless subhuman. To drive his point home, Cholo opens the door and rather gratuitously shoots a spike through the zombie's brain, lashing out at the undead parody or indictment of himself, just as he is enviously lashing out at his cruel and unjust master. Cholo has internalized the viciousness and degradation heaped on him by Kaufman (and presumably many others before the zombies rose), and has also unfortunately embraced Kaufman's own values. Once Cholo is bitten, he seems at least partly to realize his mistake, as he mocks himself with the comment that he "always wanted to see how the other half lives." When the two of them die together at the end of the film, Romero surrounds them with an exploding fireball of burning dollar bills from Kaufman's suitcases. It is a fitting and satisfying end—if, in the case of Cholo, somewhat regrettable—to their worthless, sinful dreams of domination.

It is Riley and Big Daddy who are the real heroes of the story—one human, one zombie—precisely because they rise above the sinfulness of either living or undead humans. One reviewer rightly noted that Big Daddy and Riley are the only two sympathetic characters in the film, and even went as far as to say that Big Daddy is Riley's "zombie alter ego."[16] Not only do they informally call a truce at the end of the movie, but Riley has shown throughout that he is ready to accept and befriend others. He is a loyal and protective friend to Charlie, whose disfigured face is shown repeatedly in shocking close-ups, so as to make him look very much like a zombie. And in the opening dialogue with the rookie soldier, Riley shows that he understands and sympathizes with the humanity of the zombies:

> Rookie: [They're] trying to be us.
> Riley: They used to be us, learning to be us again.
> Rookie: There's a big difference between us and them. They're dead. It's like they're pretending to be alive.
> Riley: Isn't that what we're doing—pretending to be alive?

Riley is not one to imagine himself better than other people (or zombies) and can show sympathy and respect even to the lowest "class" in his world.

Despite everything he has seen, including his having to kill his own brother, Riley is probably the most hopeful and optimistic character in any of the movies we have examined. When Charlie innocently calls the fireworks at the beginning "flowers way up in heaven," Riley affectionately tells him, "That's why I love you, Charlie, because you still believe in heaven." And when faced with the horror of the rookie soldier having killed himself, Riley does not accept the simple excuse offered by Charlie that "shit happens," but corrects him, saying, "Only if you let it, Charlie." Riley sympathizes with and loves others, and he takes responsibility for everything going on around himself and tries to improve it.

Riley is also continuous in his rejection of violence, which is the culminating, symbolic act in every one of Romero's films we have examined. If it were up to Riley, they would fire off fireworks and quickly take food and medicine without ever killing a zombie in their raids. The bloodbath in Uniontown sickens him, because, for the first time in the movies, the violence done to the zombies not only seems mindless and grotesque, but downright cruel, as the zombies pose no threat and really are minding their own business. In this scene, the zombies are also at their most disturbingly human, with lovers still hand-in-hand, a cheerleader still with pom-poms, a mother still with her daughter, and yet the orgy of violence continues as though it really were just a video game or target practice on so many cardboard cutouts.[17] When Riley is forced to shoot a zombie in self-defense, Charlie tells him, "Nice shooting," and Riley corrects him by saying, "Good shooting, Charlie. There's no such thing as nice shooting." Much more than most stars of action films, Riley acknowledges violence as, at best, a necessary evil, to be finished as quickly and efficiently as possible, with no enjoyment or celebration.

This time, the zombies show themselves also capable of nonviolence and even something akin to virtue or goodness. Having conquered the earth, they no longer go in search of prey until they are provoked by foolish, greedy humans. Rather, they live in the significantly named Uniontown, a name that is about as rich symbolically as Romero could ask for. It sets the zombie town in ironic opposition to the society created by Kaufman, who murderously seeks to keep his enemies disorganized and fractured among themselves, making Fiddler's Green into the ultimate symbol of disunion and disharmony.[18] There are also the meanings of "union" as organized labor, and as the name for the North in the American Civil War, casting Kaufman as a continuation of union-busting corporate

America and Southern slavery, class warfare, and racial strife. (This would again make Big Daddy's race of obvious, blatant significance to the film's meaning.) The zombies' crossing of the river to destroy Kaufman even has visual overtones of the Israelites escaping from slavery by crossing the Red Sea,[19] eventually to destroy the Canaanites, inveterate idol-worshipers known for the especially horrific practice of child sacrifice, again casting Kaufman as the most inhumane of monsters. A simple white church is also prominent in Uniontown, as is an apocalyptic street preacher in the slum at the base of Fiddler's Green: apparently the zombies and the slum-dwellers have not completely lost touch with God, even as Kaufman has impiously set himself up as the ruler of his own hell/paradise. While "living" in Uniontown, the zombies listen to music, like Bub in *Day of the Dead*, do their "jobs," show affection to one another, and in general behave themselves much better than the human characters. And at the end of the film, they seem to wander off, no longer interested in killing or devouring humans, but content to "live" as best they can, no longer tormented by humans or by their own bestial hunger. The tagline of the movie makes this clear: "The dead shall inherit the earth." Since the biblical original is "The meek shall inherit the earth" (Matt. 5:5 [KJV]), then we are left to believe that the living dead have learned to be meek. And, with the end of Kaufman's evil empire, perhaps the living human beings have, too.

CONCLUSION

With the destruction of Kaufman and Cholo at each others' hands, there is every reason to hope at the end that the world of both zombies and humans will not degenerate back into the cannibalistic hell of Kaufman's Fiddler's Green. Instead, it may turn into something better even than the prezombie world of which Kaufman's version was just an exaggerated, diabolical parody. As Mulligan puts it, "We'll turn this place into what we always wanted it to be!" He has in mind, perhaps, the kind of social reversal and egalitarian paradise also implied in the name of Fiddler's Green, where, supposedly, "You lie at your leisure, there's no work to do. And the skipper's below making tea for the crew."[20] (Hard to imagine Kaufman, Donald Trump, or W. making tea for anyone, and certainly not for an underling.)

For those less socially inclined, like Riley and the crew of Dead Reckoning, there's always the more individualistic and hardy Canada. And for the zombies, "life" can return to what it was at the beginning in Uniontown, a place of unity, simplicity, and peace, where zombies learn to be human, rather than killing, shopping, or preying on others. And, with each of the three groups going off to a more positive and edifying future, we are left with the question, unlike any of the previous episodes, that if zombies can learn to be human and humane, then perhaps we can, too? It is the most bemused, waggishly funny, and uplifting ending of any of the movies, and Romero leaves us looking up at the fireworks exploding against the night sky, much as Dante ended his *Inferno:* "We climbed . . . until, through a small round opening ahead of us I saw the lovely things the heavens hold, and we came out to see once more the stars." The night of living death that Romero began nearly forty years before has finally become a night of life, light, loveliness, and hope.

Conclusion

THE MEANING AND FUTURE OF ZOMBIE MOVIES

It will probably come as no surprise to readers that I remain optimistic about the future of zombie movies, perhaps more optimistic than I am about any other aspect of our government, society, culture, or religion. In just the versions we have been discussing, zombie movies have kept their edge and relevance for nearly forty years, outliving the Cold War, Soviet communism, "free love," the reactionary regimes of Reagan and Thatcher, and any number of other useless, ugly, inhumane things that people have foolishly created and invested with value. Zombie movies are not a fad, and they are not sheer escapism. The analysis in this book has attempted to show that they have engaged in social criticism and an examination of human nature at the deepest and most humanizing of levels. They are, in short, a chilling moan from our conscience, one that very effectively illuminates and lays bare a ghastly side of our consciousness, the side that believers call sin, but which can certainly be relabeled in purely secular terms for those so inclined—hubris, ignorance, selfishness, violence, or hatred.

Like any cultural phenomenon, however, no matter how relevant its message may be, and no matter how compelling its aesthetics, zombie movies will constantly have to change and adapt if they are to remain a powerful and popular force in the future. There is good reason to believe that zombie movies will continue to grow, with Romero recently returning to the genre he practically created, but with new twists, and also with new directors still being interested in the genre. With the recent remake of *Dawn of the Dead*, Romero's new *Land of the Dead*, as well as related films like *28 Days Later* and *Shaun of the Dead*, we see how the basic contours of the zombie genre have adapted to changes in society. In these newer films, the threats of terrorism, anthrax, and AIDS have been incorporated into the depiction of the zombie menace, with the preferred explanation for zombies now being an infectious disease, or a biological weapon gotten out of hand, and with the heartless execution of the "infected" in the name of self-defense. It is surely just a matter of time before a movie depicts zombies as the result of a terrorist attack gone horribly awry, or even a movie with zombies rising from the flood waters of the tsunami or Hurricane Katrina, and this is to be expected. Just as Romero updated the earlier nuclear and voodoo zombies, which had played on the fears of an earlier generation, the genre has adapted to new rationalizations for zombies that fit the changing situations of their audiences.

Such changes can go much deeper than just the mechanics of the nature of zombies. As we saw in the remake of *Dawn of the Dead*, the writer and director can change the basic story to explore other aspects of human nature, or to be more optimistic in their message. If there are social ills that have not been dealt with in earlier versions, such as homophobia, zombie movies have proved they can still provide an effective forum for exploring such issues. It is this kind of flexibility, if it proves lasting and adaptive enough, that will keep zombie movies fresh and will make them attractive to new directors and writers. No one would want to make a zombie movie if it meant offering the same social critique that has already been offered, and looking at people in the same cynical way. The new *Dawn of the Dead*, and even the more hopeful endings of *Land of the Dead* and *28 Days Later*, show that the genre is not frozen and committed to one outlook or one critique. Zombie movies—or, at least, good ones—seem by their very nature to offer social critique and a critical, moralizing look at human beings. The exact target of the critique, however, and the exact content of the moralizing are still negotiable and subject to interpretation in ways that will keep the genre vital and relevant. With new technologies, new threats, and new controversies constantly besetting us, any movie genre that has social criticism and moralizing as part of its basic nature will always have new challenges to reinvent and refocus itself, but it will also always have new material and new relevancy, if it rises to the challenge. The living dead seem more than resilient enough to answer this challenge for decades to come.

But becoming popular and remaining popular for a long time always come with a price tag, whether it is in music, art, film, or any other medium. The risk is that by achieving fame, the given art form will become too mainstream, too status quo, too predictable, and no longer edgy, threatening, critical, and exciting. As well-founded as this anxiety is, it is hard to imagine it happening with zombie movies. While it is true that the newer movies examined here have had budgets a factor of ten beyond the previous, this is probably just a matter of there being a twenty-year gap between *Day of the Dead* and *Land of the Dead*. The budgets of these "mainstream" zombie movies are still around one-tenth to one-fifth of what a major Hollywood release would cost—never mind that really low-budget zombie movies continue to be made for much less.[1] Even with Romero's great success, zombie movies can hardly be considered mainstream economically. Though their low budgets give them great potential for a good return on investment, the place of zombie movies at the margin of Hollywood will probably continue forever, because their subject matter is so controversial by its very nature. Perhaps the mainstream of Hollywood could absorb and tame a genre that contains extensive, graphic depictions of dismemberment and cannibalism. Perhaps Hollywood could tolerate and domesticate a genre that always engages in uncomfortable social criticism of life in the United States, though given the American public's aversion to being mocked and criticized, this seems even less likely than graphic cannibalism becoming an accepted, normal part of American movies. But it seems fairly unlikely that movies depicting unspeakable violence and depravity that simultaneously criticize American culture could ever become mainstream and stale. Zombie movies, in short, just offend too many people on too many levels to be conventional and part of the status quo.

Zombie movies will in all likelihood survive, and perhaps, thrive more than ever, though they will continue to change in many ways. There has just been too much to them beyond their entertainment value for them to fade or become commonplace. They are terrifying and enlightening, slapstick humorous and unnervingly serious. Besides the ubiquitous scenes of nauseating grotesquery, most every installment also includes images that are hauntingly beautiful—the Johnny Cash song "The Man Comes Around" at the beginning of *Dawn of the Dead* (2004), and in *Land of the Dead*, the zombie bride in full wedding garb and veil, backlit to make her look like a horrible angel—to name two notable instances in the most recent films.[2] All of this has made zombie movies morally, theologically, and aesthetically more complex than the usual Hollywood fare, especially more so than competing movies in the horror genre, and it assures their continued popularity and relevance. Unlike some claims of the government or the Pentagon, these movies really do shock and awe us. They do so with their cynical presentation of what humans can degenerate into, and their hopeful outlook that we might eventually reject or reverse such degeneration. If Dante were alive today to see these films with their wicked satire and pointed indictment of sin, he would probably smile and nod at his unsavory, and more purely secular, descendants. He would probably also join us in hoping that zombie movies always remain alive, or, rather, undead, right at the edge of our consciousness and culture—waiting, lurking, and nagging us in the disturbing and sinful shadows that we like to deny and ignore, but which only grow deeper and darker if we do. Zombies will always be the nightmare that we love to hate, and the painful wake-up call from our sinful reveries, one that we dread as much as we need.[3]

NOTES

Introduction

1 Cf. J. Russell, *Book of the Dead: The Complete History of Zombie Cinema* (Surrey, UK: FAB Press, 2005), whose analysis is much more comprehensive than mine—it is, in fact, an exhaustive, loving, and lavishly illustrated look at every zombie movie ever made, no matter how bad the author admits each individual entry is—but who often credits Romero with single handedly defining or saving the genre: "If trash films like *The Incredibly Strange Creatures Who Stopped Living and Became Mixed-Up Zombies!!?* or *The Astro-Zombies* had continued unchecked, it's quite possible that the zombie genre might have completely disappeared. Fortunately, in deepest Pennsylvania, one low-budget film-maker was about to change the course of the zombie movie forever. . . . The result was *Dawn of the Dead*, a film that would have an irrevocable impact on the zombie's cinematic status. Indeed, it's almost impossible to overestimate the film's importance. . . . *Land of the Dead* is likely to become the yardstick by which the millennial zombie genre revival is measured" (65, 91, 190).

2 Interestingly, the use of unknown actors may increase the terror, as observed by J. Fraser, "Watching Horror Movies," *Michigan Quarterly Review* 24, no. 1 (1990): 39–54, esp. 47: "Really horrible things could

happen to *anyone*. And the general loosening and destabilizing was made easier by the fact that the actors and actresses were largely unknown. . . . They were looking, rather, at *people*, relatively ordinary people, people very like themselves" (emphasis in original).

3   As in Ebert's review of *Shaun of the Dead* at http://www.rogerebert.com, or in the analysis of Russell, *Book of the Dead*, 183.

4   Fans will recognize the antecedent for Romero's zombies in the vampires of Richard Matheson's novel *I Am Legend*, which was also officially adapted in *The Last Man on Earth* (1964) and *Omega Man* (1971), films far less memorable than Romero's. See G. A. Waller, *The Living and the Undead: From Stoker's "Dracula" to Romero's "Dawn of the Dead"* (Urbana: University of Illinois Press, 1986), 275: "But by far the most important antecedent for *Night of the Living Dead* is *I Am Legend*. On various occasions Romero has acknowledged that the original idea for his film was 'inspired' by Richard Matheson's novel, and the resemblance between the two works is striking." P. R. Gagne, *The Zombies That Ate Pittsburgh: The Films of George A. Romero* (New York: Dodd, Mead, 1987), 24; J. Hoberman and J. Rosenbaum, *Midnight Movies* (Harper & Row, 1983), 120; and D. Pirie, *The Vampire Cinema* (New York: Crescent Books, 1977), 141; also note *I Am Legend* as the inspiration for Romero. See also S. Shaviro, "Contagious Allegories: George Romero," in *The Cinematic Body* (University of Minnesota Press, 1998), 83–105, esp. 84, where he quotes G. Deleuze and F. Guattari, *Anti-Oedipus: Capitalism and Schizophrenia*, trans. R. Hurley, M. Seem, and H. R. Lane (Minneapolis: University of Minnesota, 1983), 335, on the newness of the zombie myth: "Deleuze and Guattari (1983) aptly remark that 'the only modern myth is the myth of zombies—mortified schizos, good for work, brought back to reason.'"

5   As he is reported saying in Gagne, *Zombies That Ate Pittsburgh*, passim.

6   This is what most fans would want to claim, I think, including Fraser, "Watching Horror Movies," 52, in a moment of hilarious candor for all of us who are professors: "I was also thinking of the fact that, by and large, when I myself have fled to a horror movie in a state of tense and explosive desperation after some faculty power struggle in which I have been on the losing side, I have emerged more relaxed and closer to my normal

self." See also Shaviro, "Contagious Allegories," 104–5: "My intense enjoyment of this spectacle, my thrilling, pornographic realization that mankind 'can experience its own destruction as an aesthetic pleasure of the first order' (Benjamin 1969, 242), is not something to moralize against, but something to be savored. In the postmodern age of manipulative microtechnologies and infectious mass communication, such a pleasure marks the demoralization and collapse of the fascist exaltation Benjamin was warning against, and the birth instead of a politics of mimetic debasement, a subtle and never-completed opening to abjection" (quoting W. Benjamin, *Illuminations*, ed. H. Arendt, trans. H. Zohn [Schocken Books, 1969]).

7 Cf. the similar conclusions found several times in Fraser, "Watching Horror Movies," e.g. 47–48: "But it soon became apparent that I was in a familiar and conventionally moralistic terrain presided over by the spirit of Poe, in which murdered men came back to take horrible revenge on their murderers, and hubristic experiments by scientists always went dreadfully wrong, and there were no short cuts to money and power, let alone happiness"; ibid., 50: "The nearest 'serious' contemporary parallel to the openness of horror movies is the magic-realist fiction of Latin America, in which anything can happen and usually does"; ibid., 51: "And that kind of anxiety is part of most of our literary experiences that really matter, whether we are venturing for the first time (unchaperoned) into *Moby Dick*, or Kafka, or Sade, or *Story of O*, or *Journey to the End of the Night.*"

8 On the uselessness of explanations, cf. Shaviro, "Contagious Allegories," 84: "Of course, the whole point is that the sheer exorbitance of the zombies defies causal explanation, or even simple categorization"; Waller, *Living and the Undead*, 275–76: "To assert that 'mysterious radiation' in some unexplained way causes the dead to roam the land in search of human flesh is finally little better than no explanation at all (especially since this is a quasi-official explanation and therefore likely in *Night of the Living Dead* to be a lie, distortion, or cover-up). . . . Ben and the other people trapped in the isolated house do not have the time to search for explanations, which would make little difference in any case." Romero himself

has dismissed the importance of any explanation, as recounted in Gagne, *Zombies That Ate Pittsburgh*, 27.

9   The special relevance of zombies in a post-9/11 world is noted by Russell, *Book of the Dead*, 192: "The spectre of several millennial anxieties, from SARS to terrorism, hangs over many of these films. . . . As the West braces itself for another terrorist 'spectacular,' could the zombie be read as a response to our current anxieties about this increasingly dangerous world? . . . Whatever the answer, it's apparent that the revival of the genre has coincided with a historical moment that the zombie seems more suited to than vampires, werewolves, serial killers or any of the other usual horror monsters. The genre's traditional use of biochemical warfare and toxic spills as the starting point for its living dead apocalypses have an added impetus today after anthrax scares, concerns about weapons of mass destruction and fears about a 'dirty bomb' being released in a major metropolitan centre."

10   Scott Field also notes (e-mail correspondence, November 15, 2005) a similar dynamic in the genesis of Spiderman, who was originally bitten by a radioactive spider, but in the new movies (2002 and 2004) the spider has been tampered with by genetic engineering.

11   On the latter explanation and origin for zombies, see W. Davis, *The Serpent and the Rainbow* (New York: Simon & Schuster, 1985); ibid., *Passage of Darkness: The Ethnobiology of the Haitian Zombie* (Chapel Hill: University of North Carolina Press, 1988). On voodoo zombie movies, see E. Aizenberg, "'I Walked with a Zombie': The Pleasures and Perils of Postcolonial Hybridity," *World Literature Today* 73, no. 3 (1999): 461–66; and A. Loudermilk, "Eating *Dawn* in the Dark: Zombie Desire and Commodified Identity in George A. Romero's *Dawn of the Dead*," *Journal of Consumer Culture* 3, no. 1 (2003): 83–108, esp. 86–87. For a comparison of Romero's zombies with these earlier ones, see S. Beard, "No Particular Place to Go," *Sight and Sound* 3, no. 4 (1993): 30–31. esp. 30: "Romero completely transformed the zombie mythology he inherited from the voodoo movies of the 30s and early 40s. . . . these gothic shockers all used the same formula. Typically, Bela Lugosi would be the evil sorcerer who ran a Caribbean sugar plantation, while the zombies would be the workforce of resurrected corpses he controlled with his 'devil doll.'"

12 Cf. Russell, *Book of the Dead*, 67–68, 69: "Romero brought an uncompromising realism to the genre and added a previously unheard of dimension to the zombie myth: cannibalism. Before *Night of the Living Dead*, zombies had been content to scare, strangle or bludgeon their victims. Romero upped the ante by giving them a taste for warm, human flesh. . . . Making the body into the site of Otherness, *Night of the Living Dead* offers a vision of the world in which our own flesh is made to seem strange, disgusting and gross. The cannibalism that Romero adds to the zombie mythology wasn't simply a spectacular ploy to drum up controversy and boost ticket sales, but central to the film's provocative vision of individuals being consumed/subsumed into the larger group."

13 P. Hutchings (*The Horror Film* [New York: Pearson Longman, 2004], 161) notes that even in the original *Night of the Living Dead*, the zombies' agility varies greatly, usually being slow and clumsy, but sometimes being quick and "animalistic."

14 Cf. Waller, *Living and the Undead*, 284: "He uses this torch to ward off the living dead, and he even sets fire to an overstuffed armchair for the same purpose. (Like wild animals, these creatures back away from the fire man controls.)"

15 On corpses, see R. H. W. Dillard, "*Night of the Living Dead*: It's Not Like Just a Wind That's Passing Through," in *American Horrors: Essays on the Modern American Horror Film*, ed. G. A. Waller (Urbana: University of Illinois Press, 1988), 14–29, esp. 15: "But the film takes the source of its horrors from another desire and a fear that lies certainly as deep in the human consciousness, if not deeper. This is a fear of the dead and particularly of the known dead, of dead kindred"; also Waller, *Living and the Undead*, 277: "Primitive taboos concerning the dead, Freud argues, are rooted in the '*unconscious* hostility' and 'evil impulses' that the living project onto the dead" (emphasis in original).

16 Cf. Russell, *Book of the Dead*, 190: "What's striking is the fluidity of Romero's living dead metaphor. Previously styled in the series as the dead of Vietnam, the silent majority of the Nixon era, vapid consumers and now an oppressed (ethnic) underclass, Romero's zombies have a symbolic potential unmatched by any other horror movie monster."

17 See N. Carroll, *The Philosophy of Horror, or, Paradoxes of the Heart* (New York: Routledge, 1990), 168: "But, then again, the zombies in *Night of the Living Dead* are not seductive, nor is their unavoidable power—only the numbers are on their side—a source of admiration"; Shaviro, "Contagious Allegories," 85: "These walking corpses are neither majestic and uncanny nor exactly sad and pitiable. . . . They are blank, terrifying, and ludicrous in equal measure, without any of these mitigating the others."

18 Hutchings, *Horror Film*, 97, and J. B. Twitchell, *Dreadful Pleasures: An Anatomy of Modern Horror* (New York: Oxford University Press, 1985), 296–301, both note the prevalence of killer children in horror movies in general, citing *Night of the Living Dead*.

19 Cf. Twitchell, *Dreadful Pleasures*, 268: "In other words, safely protected as monsters, they proceed to do what they could never do in real life, and their 'victims,' instead of reacting with inhibition and trepidation, allow the unthinkable to occur."

20 On the comparison with vampires, cf. Waller, *Living and the Undead*, 275: "Romero's living dead cannot transform themselves into mist or animal form, for they are not one-of-a-kind, supernatural beings. . . . Most important, while the undead as depicted by Matheson and Romero are undeniably threatening, they are not Evil in the sense that the vampires in *Salem's Lot* and most Hammer films are Evil. The living dead . . . belong to our world. They are our fellow citizens who, with no leader and no motive besides hunger, have returned to feed on us, and, with no malice and no grand design, to reach out and pull us into their ranks"; also Twitchell, *Dreadful Pleasures*, 267: "But for me the most important development is what Romero did to the monster; he bred the zombie with the vampire, and what he got was the hybrid vigor of a ghoulish plague monster. . . . Romero's other innovation is that, while he made his zombies into vampires, he subtracted, rather than added to, their physical power, so that they are now pathetic weaklings able to be destroyed by bashing their heads."

21 Cf. Waller, *Living and the Undead*, 306: "*Dawn of the Dead* is, for instance, the antithesis of deadly serious stories that show people at war with killer bees, sharks, or some other form of 'natural' threat that is, in some important ways, superior to human beings."

22 Cf. Waller, *Living and the Undead*, 276–77: "The first of the living dead that we see in the film is a man before he is a thing; he is one of *us* before we realize that he is one of *them*. He and all the rest of the living dead retain the physical appearance of human beings. They do not suddenly bare over-sized canine teeth or stare with blood-red eyes. Even when they are eating the remains of the two teenagers, the living dead never cease to look like— and therefore in some fashion to be?—human beings. . . . The living dead, as Romero told an interviewer, are 'the neighbors'" (emphasis in original).

23 Cf. Russell, *Book of the Dead*, 67: "Lewis [another director] and his imita-tors offered lashings of gore simply for its own sake, with scenes of dismem-berment and mutilation framed by plots that were perfunctory at best, incoherent at worst. Romero displayed a far lighter touch, only pushing the boundaries of good taste in a handful of *Night of the Living Dead*'s scenes."

24 I owe this cinematic point to Waller, *Living and the Undead*, 307, 312–13.

25 I would like to thank my colleague at Iona College, Chris Perricone, for his excellent website that linked to the enormous discussion and bibliography of the question at http://consc.net/biblio/1.html#1.3b (accessed July 25, 2005).

26 Cf. Russell, *Book of the Dead*, 69: "By challenging the distinction between the living and the dead, the normal and the monstrous, *Night of the Living Dead* brings terror into the American home, hearth and family"; Shaviro, "Contagious Allegories," 98: "The dread that the zombies occa-sion is based more on a fear of infection that on one of annihilation. The living characters are concerned less about the prospect of being killed than they are about being swept away by mimesis—of returning to existence, after death, transformed into zombies themselves."

27 On the strain of executing loved ones, cf. Waller, *Living and the Undead*, 313: "As in most of the retellings of *Dracula*, as well as in *I Am Legend*, *Salem's Lot*, and many other stories of the living and the undead, one of the most disturbing requirements in the struggle for survival is that a human being can and will be called upon to kill an undead creature who in life was his closest friend, his fiancée, or his lover."

28 On the loss of funeral rites due to the zombie threat, cf. Waller, *Living and the Undead*, 297: ". . . the bonfire in *Night of the Living Dead* is not a fire

of purification or just punishment. It is less like a funeral pyre for a fallen hero than a pile of flammable rubbish."

29 On the adverse effect of such violence, cf. Gagne, *Zombies That Ate Pittsburgh*, 88: "Further, Romero's protagonists lose something of their own morality as they gun down the zombies remaining in the mall with a zealous cruelty motivated by material greed"; Waller, *Living and the Undead*, 302: "All that will be altered are the hunters themselves, who may come to take extermination as a type of sport or may themselves become emotionless zombies as they carry out their work."

30 Cf. Shaviro, "Contagious Allegories," 83: "Their vision of a humanity over-run by flesh-eating zombies is violently apocalyptic; at the same time, they remain disconcertingly close to the habitual surfaces and mundane realities of everyday life."

31 On zombies' liminality, see M. Dargis, "Not Just Roaming, Zombies Rise Up: Review of *Land of the Dead*," *The New York Times*, June 24, 2005, online at http://www.nytimes.com/pages/movies/index.html (accessed November 13, 2005): "Neither fully alive nor dead, zombies exist between the margins, in a twilight state that makes them among the most unsettling of all man-made creatures. That's the essential paradox of all zombie movies, but it's a paradox that has taken on increasing complexity in Mr. Romero's zombie quartet"; Loudermilk, "Eating *Dawn* in the Dark," 85–86: "Romero's postmodern zombie rises from a variety of tombs, a hybrid of corporeal and ideological monsters. Voodoo zombie, mummy and pod person, all play into Romero's conception of the postmodern zombie in *bodies* that tread the liminal position between human and inhuman (or life and death)" (emphasis in original); Shaviro, "Contagious Allegories," 104: "There is no possibility of evasion, just as there is none of mastery, and none of firm and stable identification, for the zombies always come in between: they insinuate themselves within the uncanny, interstitial space that separates (but thereby also connects) inside and outside, the private and the public, life and death. In this liminal position, they are the obscene objects of voyeuristic fascination."

32 Cf. Fraser, "Watching Horror Movies," 46, who generalizes this: "All good horror movies are funny at times."

33 Cf. Fraser, "Watching Horror Movies," 49–50, who draws such parallels more broadly: "And there are obvious parallels to what obtained in Renaissance drama: the abundance of productions, the accepted roughnesses, loosenesses, and implausibilities, the special effects, the enthusiastic borrowings and appropriations, the violence and eroticism, the exotic locales, the wide range of type-figures; the inclusion, often in transmuted forms, of serious contemporary concerns—in horror movies, ecological hubris, medical experimentation, space travel, changing relationships between the sexes, and so on."

34 On the symbolism, see Loudermilk, "Eating *Dawn* in the Dark," 83–108, esp. 92: "Conversely, the zombies at this point get 'scored' with the mall's Muzak and for the first time seem non-threatening, slapstick-ish, and more like mindless shoppers. They are victims of escalators, fascinated with mannequins, and when one zombie falls into a wishing-well fountain—his hands full of worthless pennies—Romero's satire really aims for the brain of the capitalist identity."

35 On the class identity of zombies, cf. Beard, "No Particular Place to Go," 30, quoting Romero: "Zombies are the real lower-class citizens of the monster world"; J. Caputi, "Films of the Nuclear Age," *Journal of Popular Film and Television* 16, no. 3 (1988): 100–107, esp. 103, who calls them "mass, ordinary, and interchangeable"; Waller, *Living and the Undead*, 278: "Though the creatures in Romero's film do not emerge from any one specific social class, perhaps the living dead are our version of what in the past was called the 'rabble.'"

36 Cf. Waller, *Living and the Undead*, 275, who refers to vampires as "aristocratic."

37 Cf. K. Newman, *Nightmare Movies: A Critical Guide to Contemporary Horror Films* (New York: Harmony, 1988), 5: "*Night of the Living Dead* was the first horror film to be overtly subversive. Previously, all social criticism was veiled or half-hearted"; Russell, *Book of the Dead*, 70, 189: "By collapsing the boundaries between the normal and the monstrous, the living and the dead, Romero signaled a new stage in the zombie's development. Zombie filmmakers no longer had to hide behind half-baked plots and silly special effects. Instead they could approach serious issues with a grim, apocalyptic

nihilism that was shocking and exhilarating in equal measure. . . . Romero may have done more to popularize socio-political readings of film among horror fans than any other director living today." Such social criticism may be the foundation of "great" horror movies in general: see A. Britton, "The Devil, Probably: The Symbolism of Evil," in *American Nightmare: Essays on the Horror Film*, eds. R. Wood and R. Lippe (Toronto: Festival of Festivals, 1979), 34–42, esp. 41: "The great American horror movies . . . seem to me to be characterised not so much by ambivalence—a phenomenon discernible in such eminently mediocre and objectionable works as *The Texas Chainsaw Massacre*—as by the use of the monster as the focus, or the catalyst, for the critical analysis of everything that 'normality' represents." Anti-authority is part of this anti-normalcy, and is a big part of the genre's appeal, as observed by Fraser, "Watching Horror Movies," 48–49: "And beyond that there is the pleased feeling in the air that someone—the moviemaker—is successfully putting something over on 'them'—on the schoolteachers, parents, city fathers, priggish movie critics who if they really knew what was going on there would be doing their best to prevent it. . . . The correspondence columns of the splatter-movie magazines testify amply to the anti-authority enthusiasms of such movies."

38 On American society in zombie movies, cf. Beard, "No Particular Place to Go," 30: "Less the lower-class citizens of the monster world and more the disenfranchised underclass of the material world, they are a projection of postmodern capitalism's worst anxieties about *itself*" (emphasis in original); J. Maddrey, *Nightmares in Red, White, and Blue: The Evolution of the American Horror Film* (Jefferson, NC: McFarland, 2004), 123: "There is no mention of other countries in any of the *Dead* films, with one significant exception in *Day of the Dead*. The zombie disease seems to be symptomatic of American life"; Waller, *Living and the Undead*, 280: "Perhaps the monstrous creatures in *Night of the Living Dead*, the 'things' that are somehow still men, are the projection of our desire to destroy, to challenge the fundamental values of America, and to bring the institutions of our modern society to a halt"; T. Williams, *The Cinema of George A. Romero: Knight of the Living Dead* (London: Wallflower Press, 2003), 21, 32: "[*Night of the Living Dead* is] a devastating critique upon the deformations of human per-

sonality operating within a ruthless capitalist society. . . . *Night of the Living Dead* does thematically interrogate the dysfunctional mechanisms of a deeply disturbed society. It explicitly presented the image of an America in which the old values were now harmful and obsolete, leading to a chaos very few would survive unless some drastic personal, political and social change would follow."

39 As noted by Hoberman and Rosenbaum, *Midnight Movies*, 121, and by R. Wood, "Apocalypse Now: Notes on the Living Dead," in *American Nightmare: Essays on the Horror Film*, eds. R. Wood and R. Lippe (Toronto: Festival of Festivals, 1979) 91–98, esp. 91–93: "Brother and sister visit a remote country graveyard (over which flies the stars-and-stripes: the metaphor of America-as-graveyard is central to Romero's work)." See also S. Higashi, "*Night of the Living Dead*: A Horror Film about the Horrors of the Vietnam War," in *From Hanoi to Hollywood: The Vietnam War in American Film*, eds. L. Dittmar and G. Michaud (New Brunswick, NJ: Rutgers University Press, 1990), 175–88, esp. 182: "At the end of the credits, Romero's name is superimposed over the American flag waving symbolically in the foreground as the couple finally arrive at the cemetery"; Newman, *Nightmare Movies*, 1: "In a carefully composed shot, George A. Romero's director credit is offset by stars and stripes"; Williams, *Cinema of George A. Romero*, 23: "One shot reveals . . . an American flag as the camera pans right. Romero's director credit appears superimposed over this shot. It not only signifies cinematic authorship but also alerts the viewer to *Night of the Living Dead*'s examination of a culture characterized by death as well as life: 'Old Glory' will soon become an American landscape of 'Old Gory.'"

40 E.g., on Steve's boat at the end of the new *Dawn of the Dead*, and on one of the raiders' motorcycles in *Land of the Dead*.

41 Cf. Russell, *Book of the Dead*, 69: "*Night of the Living Dead* suggests that the whole of society is rotten to the core."

42 Cf. Carroll, *Philosophy of Horror*, 198, who discerns social critiques in many works of horror, including zombie movies: "George Romero's *Night of the Living Dead* cycle is explicitly anti-racist as well as critical of the consumerism and viciousness of American society." See also Shaviro, "Contagious Allegories," 87: "The zombies do not (in the familiar manner

of 1950s horror film monsters) stand for a threat to social order from without. Rather, they resonate with, and refigure, the very processes that produce and enforce social order. That is to say, they do not mirror or represent social forces; they are directly animated and possessed, even in their allegorical distance from beyond the grave, by such forces."

43 P. Engall, "George A. Romero's Fears for Horror and Hollywood: The Underbelly of the Monster," *Metro Magazine* 133 (2002): 158-63, esp. 160-61: ". . . most controversial of all for the time, a black man is the group's leader."

44 The observation is well-nigh universal: see Higashi, "Horrors of the Vietnam War," 184: "During the final moments of the film, now in grainy still shots, his body is dragged with meat hooks to a burning pyre as the chopper is heard on the soundtrack. We need hardly be reminded that black men were lynched and burned in our recent past"; Hutchings, *Horror Film*, 112: "More than one critic has seen references here to lynching"; Waller, *Living and the Undead*, 295: "Though the posse cannot see that Ben is a black man, this murder evokes American racism at its deadliest and most virulent, a topic Romero will return to in the opening sequences of *Dawn of the Dead*."

45 Cf. Russell, *Book of the Dead*, 68: "In many respects, it is the living's failure to cooperate and put aside their petty differences that invites the chaos. Fascinated by how quickly the social order can crumble—a theme he would return to in the next two installments of his living dead series . . . Romero shows us that it's the territorial bickering of the living that's the real threat to civilization."

46 On this multi-ethnic, "rainbow coalition" of zombies, see Beard, "No Particular Place to Go," 30, who notes their heterogeneity: "They are lean, fat, old, young, male, female; they are dressed in suits, jeans, pajamas, slips, nightgowns and, in one case, nothing at all; they are the rural, metropolitan, suburban. The implication—one that has become more transparent to more people since 1968—is that nobody is immune from the social restructuring of post-Fordism. Everybody's job is potentially at risk." Waller, *Living and the Undead*, 305, on the other hand, notes their homogeneity as contributing to this "everyman" quality: "When the living dead are seen

from a distance (as in many of Romero's long shots), these shared characteristics tend to cancel out individual distinctions and to make the creatures—inner city blacks as well as suburban whites—all part of one
homogeneous mass." Pirie, *Vampire Cinema*, 143, similarly notes how the
zombies are "a cross-section of the dead community." Williams, *Cinema of
George A. Romero*, 26, notes how this increases in the later films to be an
"ironically . . . idyllic vision of a multi-cultural and multi-ethnic society that
1960s radicals promoted."

47 This is a marked development between Romero's movies, and also in the
remake of *Night of the Living Dead*, as observed by B. K. Grant, "Taking
Back the *Night of the Living Dead*: George Romero, Feminism and the
Horror Film," *Wide Angle: A Film Quarterly of Theory, Criticism, and
Practice* 14, no. 1 (1992): 64–76 (repr. in *The Dread of Difference*,
200–212, ed. B. K. Grant [Austin: University of Texas Press, 1996]). On
strong women in the horror movie genre more generally, see C. J. Clover,
Men, Women, and Chain Saws: Gender in the Modern Horror Film
(Princeton: Princeton University Press, 1993); for a critique of Clover's
work, see Shaviro, "Contagious Allegories," 89–90.

48 Romero's mild sexism is also noted by Waller, *Living and the Undead*, 283:
"That Barbara is a woman would seem to support certain sexist assump-
tions about female passivity, irrationality, and emotional vulnerability."

49 In this they are again very different from vampires, who are hyper-
sexualized: see Caputi, "Films of the Nuclear Age," 103: ". . . the disturbance at the heart of the vampire myth is one of emotion, sexuality,
desire"; also Waller, *Living and the Undead*, 276: "The feeding habits of
the living dead have nothing in common with the sexually charged, mutu-
ally pleasurable act of bloodsucking. . . . Quite unlike the experienced,
masterful vampires who seduce their victims and unlike even the hissing,
possessed brides of Dracula, Romero's living dead tear at their food and
devour it like starving animals." This would also distinguish zombies from
the aliens in the movie *Alien* (1979) and its sequels, who appear to devour
their human victims, but are really impregnating them, presumably in a
way that brings sexual gratification to the alien. On the other hand, cf.
Higashi, "Horrors of the Vietnam War," 179–80, who sees the zombies'

cannibalism as a perverted kind of sexuality, and Shaviro, "Contagious Allegories," 96–97: "Everything comes back to the zombies' weird attractiveness: they exercise a perverse, insidious fascination that undermines our nominal involvement with the films' active protagonists. . . . We cannot in a conventional sense 'identify' with the zombies, but we are increasingly seduced by them."

50 Cf. D. J. Skal, *The Monster Show: A Cultural History of Horror*, rev. ed. (New York: Faber & Faber, 2001), 357, who pushes this all the way back even to the first movie, which seems unlikely, but certainly applies to the later installments in the series.

51 Cf. Shaviro, "Contagious Allegories," 89: "The macho, paternalistic traits of typical Hollywood action heroes are repeatedly exposed as stupid and dysfunctional."

52 Often observed of Romero's work, as recently by Dargis, "Not Just Roaming, Zombies Rise Up": "The fourth installment in Mr. Romero's vaunted zombie cycle (which began with his 1968 masterpiece, "Night of the Living Dead"), the new film is also the latest chapter in what increasingly seems like an extended riff on Dante's 'Inferno.'"

53 Dante, *The Divine Comedy: Inferno*, trans. M. Musa (New York: Penguin Books, 1971), 3.17–18.

54 Cf. Newman, *Nightmare Movies*, 209: "A rotten social order suffers its just desserts in the shape of the Living Dead, who at once epitomize and chastise any number of vices: conservative complacency, consumerist frenzy, mindlessly instinctive political positions, random violence, pointless greed."

55 Dante, *Inferno*, 11.25–27.

56 Cf. Shaviro, "Contagious Allegories," 85: "Romero's zombies could almost be said to be quintessential media images, since they are vacuous, mimetic replications of the human beings they once were. They are dead people who are not content to remain dead, but who have brought their deaths with them back into the realm of the living."

Chapter 1

1 Gagne, *Zombies That Ate Pittsburgh*, 31; Hoberman and Rosenbaum, *Midnight Movies*, 125; Russell, *Book of the Dead*, 66; Twitchell, *Dreadful*

Pleasures, 267; and G. A. Waller, "Introduction," in *American Horrors: Essays on the Modern American Horror Film*, ed. G. A. Waller (Urbana: University of Illinois Press, 1987), 4, all give the budget as $114,000, with $60,000 as the initial start-up capital. Dillard, "Not Like Just a Wind," 14, gives it as "$125,000 to $150,000."

2   On the comparison of the two scenes, see Russell, *Book of the Dead*, 69: "The Coopers' traditional nuclear family can't offer any hope; mother and father both hate each other and their daughter ends up turning on them when she becomes one of the zombies, hacking her mother to death with a garden trowel in a scene that's an eerie but poignant echo of *Psycho*'s shower murder"; Waller, *Living and the Undead*, 292: "The staccato rhythms of the music and editing in this sequence clearly recall the murder of Marion Crane in *Psycho*, though the differences between these two scenes are telling indeed. Romero, like Hitchcock, focuses on the eyes of the helpless victim, eyes that in *Night of the Living Dead* see not a psychotic stranger . . . but a beloved child armed with a weapon more mundane and—we could say—more 'unweaponly' than a butcher knife." Hoberman and Rosenbaum, *Midnight Movies*, 120, 122, also note the Hitchcock influence.

3   Quoted at length in, e.g., Gagne, *Zombies That Ate Pittsburgh*, 36; and Russell, *Book of the Dead*, 66.

4   As quoted in Russell, *Book of the Dead*, 65; see also Dillard, "Not Like Just a Wind," 15; Higashi, "Horrors of the Vietnam War," 184; and Hoberman and Rosenbaum, *Midnight Movies*, 110.

5   On the film's commercial success, see Dillard, "Not Like Just a Wind," 14-15; Gagne, *Zombies That Ate Pittsburgh*, 36-39; Hoberman and Rosenbaum, *Midnight Movies*, 125-26; Russell, *Book of the Dead*, 71; Skal, *Monster Show*, 357.

6   The list is online at http://www.afi.com/tvevents/100years/thrills.aspx (accessed September 22, 2005).

7   Wood, "Apocalypse Now," 91. See also Hoberman and Rosenbaum, *Midnight Movies*, 112-13, on the film's recognition by critics.

8   The division given in, e.g., Waller, *American Horrors*, 2; and Hutchings, *Horror Film*, 28, 172 (with discussion and bibliography). See also M. A. Arnzen, "Who's Laughing Now? The Postmodern Splatter Film," *Journal*

of Popular Film and Television 21, no. 4 (1994): 176–84, who traces the influence of Romero's *Night* on subsequent horror films, and C. Balun, "I Spit in Your Face: Films That Bite," in *Splatterpunks: Extreme Horror*, ed. P. Sammon (New York: St. Martin's Press, 1990), 167–83, esp. 167, where he lists *Night of the Living Dead* as one of the films of "seminal 'moist' cinema" that "obviously, and irrevocably, influenced the parameters of splat fiction." See also Russell, *Book of the Dead*, 65, who puts *Night of the Living Dead* against its other competitor for the most influential horror movie: "Although few critics were able to see it at the time, there was far more to *Night of the Living Dead* than its visceral impact. *Psycho* might have recalibrated the focus of modern horror, but it was Romero who widened its scope. . . . This was a film that dragged American horror kicking and screaming into the modern age."

9   The suggestion of Hutchings, *Horror Film*, 170; see also Williams, *Cinema of George A. Romero*, 24–25: "Deciding to profit from his sister's vulnerability to childhood fears, he begins to scare her by taking on a voice which parodies once-threatening Karloff-Lugosi imagery from classical horror films now rendered camp. . . . Although certain forms of horror now become harmless and parodic, new ones arise to take their place."

10   The closing credits (at least on the DVD version) spell her name "Barbra," but most secondary works follow the more usual spelling "Barbara." I will follow the individual author's usage when quoting from them, without using "sic."

11   The exact nature of his injury does not quite make sense in this version. If he hit his head hard enough to kill himself, that would seem to cause enough brain damage to keep him from coming back as a zombie. And if he is only unconscious, then why doesn't the zombie attacking him start to eat him? The zombies in this film are quite intent on eating their victims, so it seems unlikely that one would immediately pursue another human before eating the first victim.

12   Cf. Waller, *Living and the Undead*, 283–84: "What Romero emphasizes is both the sheer physical effort required to kill just one of the living dead and the utter lack of supernatural assistance for man."

13 Williams, *Cinema of George A. Romero*, 27, interestingly connects this to moments in the later films where the living show some connection or sympathy to the undead: "This is the first appearance of a compelling gaze between humans and zombies, which will occur throughout the trilogy. Despite the barriers separating both species, the looks often exchanged between hunters and hunted hint at some deep, unconscious connection between the living and the dead."

14 Cf. Waller, *Living and the Undead*, 284: "Quite the opposite of Barbara, Ben seems to become energized by the situation and the increasingly more difficult tasks he faces. . . . Romero focuses on Ben's constant movement as he completes his physical work."

15 Pirie, *Vampire Cinema*, 143; see also Waller, *Living and the Undead*, 283, on the sexism.

16 On the zombies as both human and monstrous, see Waller, *Living and the Undead*, 276: "The radio announcer who calls them 'assassins' or 'misshapen monsters' obviously has not seen the living dead and has settled for available labels. Yet when Barbara recounts her terrifying experience in the cemetery, she refers to her assailant as a 'man'—and she, too, is right. The first of the living dead that we see in the film is a man before he is a thing; he is one of *us* before we realize that he is one of *them*" (emphasis in original).

17 See Waller, *Living and the Undead*, 287: "Tom, the 'kid,' becomes the spokesperson for the virtues of collective action. With reasonable arguments, he tries to settle the conflict between Ben and Harry, because 'we'd be a lot better off if all three of us were working together.'"

18 Cf. Waller, *Living and the Undead*, 278: "The living dead—without a leader—increase, press forward, force their way into the farmhouse like some sort of mob."

19 Cf. Higashi, "Horrors of the Vietnam War," 182–84, who relates their watching television newscasts of the zombie terror to Americans of the time getting graphic, violent images of the Vietnam War beamed into their living rooms via television.

20 Waller, *Living and the Undead*, 274.

21 The count given by Dillard, "Not Like Just a Wind," 15.

22 Pirie, *Vampire Cinema*, 145.

23 On the film's relation to contemporary events, esp. the Vietnam War and the civil rights movement, see Maddrey, *Nightmares in Red, White, and Blue*, 122: "The year [1968], heralded a revolution in cinema—independent filmmakers were suddenly unwilling to reassure audiences of a 'better tomorrow,' as Hollywood studio films had for decades. Instead, they reflected the chaos of life in America, where wartime casualties at home and abroad were being routinely delivered, via television, into living rooms across the country for mass consumption"; Williams, *Cinema of George A. Romero*, 21: "But, on national release, the film caught the mood of an America in turmoil." See also Higashi, "Horrors of the Vietnam War," esp. 180-86; Hoberman and Rosenbaum, *Midnight Movies*, 112; Russell, *Book of the Dead*, 71.

24 Cf. C. Derry, "More Dark Dreams: Some Notes on the Recent Horror Film," *American Horrors: Essays on the Modern American Horror Film*, ed. G. A. Waller (Urbana: University of Illinois Press, 1987), 162-75, esp. 163: "Among the most common of all dreams, particularly among children, is the dream in which one is chased by a large dog or monster and, as if drugged or in slow-motion, one can't seem to lift one's feet to run—an archetypal scene replicated in recent films such as *Night of the Living Dead* (1968) and *The Omen* (1976)"; Newman, *Nightmare Movies*, 2-3: "*Night of the Living Dead* adopts the logic of the nightmare, the sensation that, no matter how you run, you'll never get away from the monster behind you."

25 E.g., Newman, *Nightmare Movies*, 6: "Even the budgetary necessity of black-and-white filming is exploited. Decades of newsreels, newspapers, TV documentaries and still photographs have conspired to give the impression that, though real life is in color, black and white is more realistic"; Russell, *Book of the Dead*, 67: "Intriguingly, this restraint helped increase rather than diminish the film's impact, foregrounding the one thing that's always the inevitable focus of any zombie movie, the human body itself." See also the connection with "naturalism" observed by Williams, *Cinema of George A. Romero*, 23.

26 Thus Dillard, "Not Like Just a Wind," 17; and Pirie, *Vampire Cinema*, 143. Higashi, "Horrors of the Vietnam War," 182; Hoberman and

Rosenbaum, *Midnight Movies*, 121; and Williams, *Cinema of George A. Romero*, 24, get the temporal setting correct (a surprise in Williams, whose analysis is marred by so many factual gaffes). The scene was actually filmed in November, as reported by Gagne, *Zombies That Ate Pittsburgh*, 33, thereby contributing to the critics' confusion, for there are very few leaves left on the trees.

27 Daylight savings had just become law in the United States in 1966, under something ominously called The Uniform Time Act. See http://webex-hibits.org/daylightsaving/e.html (accessed September 23, 2005).

28 See Dillard, "Not Like Just a Wind," 18, 25: "The farmhouse has its symbolic uses, too, but they are minimal. There are in one of its rooms several mounted animal heads, innocent enough in themselves, but that do take on certain symbolic overtones in the context of the equally dead but moving human figures around the house and the posse with its hunting rifles. But Romero's only functional use of these heads is for a cheap shock. . . . After the shock cuts when Barbara enters the house and starts at the animal heads, the film moves into its longest speech"; Fraser, "Watching Horror Movies," 46: "The fragmentariness is likely to be increased, too, by those old but still effective standbys, the subject camera movement . . . cross-cuttings from hunted to hunter, and ominous juxtapositions and contrasts"; Hoberman and Rosenbaum, *Midnight Movies*, 122: "Noticeably influenced by the suspense (and point-of-view shots) of Alfred Hitchcock's movies—a quick montage of stuffed animal heads when Barbara first enters the farmhouse living room is derived from a scene between Tony Perkins and Janet Leigh in *Psycho*; the successively larger close-ups of the decaying corpse, joined by subjectively timed jump cuts, are taken directly from *The Birds*"; Williams, *Cinema of George A. Romero*, 26: "As she moves into another room, a montage of quick shots reveals animal heads on the wall with disorientating effect. Barbara has not only left a kitchen where humans once prepared meat for consumption but also enters another room where trophies ironically foreshadow the fate of the entire human species. These shots thus symbolize a reverse world where humans change from being consumers to a hunted species facing consumption."

29 See Waller, *Living and the Undead*, 285: "Earlier, Ben startles both us and Barbara when he first appears in the film, suddenly looming forward diagonally in a disorienting close-up before he saves her life. The introduction of Harry and Tom is even more ironic." These camera angles are made more ironic by the fact that Romero is imitating the movie *Frankenstein* that he parodied in the first scene, as observed by Newman, *Nightmare Movies*, 2: "Romero may reject the rickety surrealism of the *Frankenstein* graveyard, but his films are full of the tilted camera angles and eccentric by-play favored by James Whale, director not only of *Frankenstein*, but also of *The Old Dark House, The Invisible Man* and *Bride of Frankenstein*."

30 Cf. Williams, *Cinema of George A. Romero*, 27–28: "The men's entry initially suggests another form of threatening violence. But they are humans not zombies. The very manner of their introduction, however, suggests little difference between either species. The film will soon depict the presence of violence among humans as the main threat to safety as Harry enters Ben's world."

31 I owe this observation to V. Sobchack (*Screening Space, The American Science Fiction Film*, 2nd ed. [New York: Ungar, 1987], 189–90): "Apart from the content of the newscasts, the way in which the set itself is photographed is drastically at odds with the cinematography of the rest of the film. It is shot straight on, centered symmetrically in the screen, while everything else in the film is viewed from either grotesque or uncomfortable angles. . . . The magic of the media is, indeed, black. For the public is totally credulous and trusting while the media is electronic, apathetic, and finally immune to private experience."

32 See Hutchings, *Horror Film*, 188–89: "Repeatedly in 1970s horror, private, domestic and familial dramas are connected with contemporary institutions, be these state, military, legal, scientific or media-related, but without the dramas being wholly subsumed into those institutions (which is often what happened in 1950s monster movies). This is already apparent in *Night of the Living Dead*, a film that contrasts the private tribulations of the characters trapped inside the house with public events such as television broadcasts and the climactic activities of the posse"; Sobchack,

Screening Space, "In a deadly quiet and parodic reversal of radio and TV appearances in traditional SF films, the radio and TV in this film demonstrate a total lack of connection with the characters in peril."

33 The label of Clover, *Men, Women, and Chainsaws,* 236.

34 Cf. Waller, *Living and the Undead,* 290: "In *Night of the Living Dead,* no God, father, or president, no military, scientific, political, or religious form of authority guarantees or in any way promotes the survival of the living."

35 Cf. the more general comments at the beginning of D. E. Winter, "Less than Zombie," in *Splatterpunks: Extreme Horror,* ed. P. Sammon (New York: St. Martin's Press, 1990), 84–98, esp. 85, noting "one of splatterpunk's basic contentions: that the old horrors are tired, or irrelevant. The old monsters aren't really that important anymore. The *real* monsters are us" (emphasis in original).

36 Contra Skal, *Monster Show,* 357: "George Romero's *Night of the Living Dead* was well established by this time [the mid-seventies] as a fixture of the midnight movie circuit, a primal allegory of haves and have-nots (the 'living' and the 'dead') struggling over the control and occupancy of an emblematic house."

37 See Hutchings, *Horror Film,* 112: ". . . the hero's racial identity is never referred to by any of the characters in the film"; Wood, "Apocalypse Now," 93: "The film has often been praised for never making an issue of its black hero's colour (it is nowhere alluded to, even implicitly)." Dillard, "Not Like Just a Wind," 19, gives an optimistic interpretation of this: "Perhaps the only unusual thing about them is that no one of them ever comments about one of their numbers being black, especially in the light of his assuming a natural leadership. But even that lack of race prejudice in a tight situation may be more ordinarily American than we might suspect." On the other hand, Higashi, "Horrors of the Vietnam War," 180, sees Ben as part of a pattern of racist stereotypes in American films.

38 E.g., Pirie, *Vampire Cinema,* 143, calls Cooper a "bigot."

39 Cf. S. K. Dewan, "Do Horror Films Filter the Horrors of History?" *The New York Times,* B9, October 14, 2000: "George Romero's *Night of the Living Dead* (completed just days before the Rev. Dr. Martin Luther King

Jr. was assassinated) had policemen scouring the countryside with dogs at their side, mirroring photographs of Southern sheriffs spoiling for civil rights activists. The movie's black protagonist, Ben, is mistaken for a zombie and shot through the head, with the comment, 'That's another one for the fire.'"

40 The analysis of Wood, "Apocalypse Now," 93: "It is the function of the posse to restore the social order that has been destroyed; the zombies represent the suppressed tensions and conflicts—the legacy of the past, of the patriarchal structuring of relationships, 'dead' yet automatically continuing—which that order creates and on which it precariously rests."

41 Cf. Gagne, Zombies That Ate Pittsburgh, 90: "Night's Barbara is a product of the sixties, existing in a state of limbo on the outskirts of women's liberation; while she is not the traditional horror-movie screamer of the fifties, she can do little more than slip into a state of zombielike catatonia when confronted with the living dead."

42 Cf. Waller, Living and the Undead, 286: "By all counts, Ben is less cowardly, less self-centered, less obnoxious, and much more capable, inventive, and heroic than Harry."

43 The phrase of Hutchings, Horror Film, 112, who goes on to tie this in with contemporary films more generally: see Hutchings, Horror Film, 175.

44 Cf. Gagne, Zombies That Ate Pittsburgh, 26: "Petty human squabbles within the tiny farmhouse begin to outweigh the zombie threat outside as Ben and Harry argue incessantly"; and Waller, Living and the Undead, 281: "Romero also suggests that the living have a certain propensity for murderous violence, territorialism, and irrationality—qualities that immediately surface during a crisis."

45 Cf. Williams, Cinema of George A. Romero, 28: "[Ben] also egotistically reveals his own masculinist desires for property and control. . . . it [Night of the Living Dead] clearly recognizes that the competitive arena of patriarchal aggression is no solution for the besieged humans."

46 Cf. Waller, Living and the Undead, 285–86: "What Night of the Living Dead finally suggests, however, is that these human beings are indeed a threat to Ben's survival. . . . As soon as other people besides Barbara appear, Ben's simple struggle to survive becomes complicated by questions and conflicts about territory, authority, and responsibility—questions that

quite obviously do not worry the living dead"; Williams, *Cinema of George A. Romero*, 22: "The human survivors never unite to defeat the zombies. They are constantly at each other's throats and attempt to devour each other in an ironically metaphorical version of the outside assault by their living dead opponents. Indeed, the dead appear more united than the living in terms of their concentrated focus on a specific aim."

47 Cf. Carroll, *Philosophy of Horror*, 141: "Ben, the black hero, is for staying upstairs and trying to hold off the zombie attack, while the acrimonious Harry Cooper argues for staying in the cellar. This argument is not simply a matter of tactics; it is a battle of wills pitched over who is to be 'boss'"; Dillard, "Not Like Just a Wind," 22: "The living people are dangerous to each other, both because they are potentially living dead should they die and because they are human with all of the ordinary human failings. Ben kills Harry because his cowardice has risked Ben's life, and the clash of egos between Ben and Harry endangers the lives of all the others throughout the film"; Russell, *Book of the Dead*, 68: "The problem of the dead returning to life actually seems quite containable if only Ben and Cooper— and on a much larger scale the infighting authorities in Washington— could stop arguing for long enough to formulate a plan of action. For Romero, this is the way the world ends: not with a bang, but with a series of whimpering arguments that invite a chaotic collapse of the social order into arguments, fistfights and dispassionate news reports."

48 The film of which was coincidentally distributed by the same company as distributed *Night of the Living Dead*, as reported in Gagne, *Zombies That Ate Pittsburgh*, 39.

49 On the film's rejection of marriage and family, see Waller, *Living and the Undead*, 292: ". . . in the cellar we see the death not just of husband and wife, but of the family"; Wood, "Apocalypse Now," 93: "Their destruction at the hands of their zombie daughter represents the film's judgment on them and the norm they embody."

50 On romantic love in the film, see Dillard, "Not Like Just a Wind," 23: "Tom and Judy die because they have the courage to try to help the whole group escape and because they love each other"; Gagne, *Zombies That Ate Pittsburgh*, 27: "Young love doesn't get much more revolting than this";

Waller, *Living and the Undead*, 288: "Needless to say, romantic love is neither the means nor the prerequisite for survival in *Night of the Living
Dead*. Again, as so often in the film, an overwhelming, blackly comic irony
pervades the sequence: Judy's desire to remain by the side of her boyfriend
helps cause both their deaths."

51 As noted by Dillard, "Not Like Just a Wind," 28; Pirie, *Vampire Cinema*,
143-45; Twitchell, *Dreadful Pleasures*, 268; and generalized to other horror films by Wood, *American Nightmare*, "Introduction," 17-18.

52 Cf. Shaviro, "Contagious Allegories," 91: "Even as dread pulses to a cli-
max, as plans of action and escape fail, and as characters we expect to survive are eliminated, we are denied the opportunity of imposing
redemptive or compensatory meanings. There is no mythology of
doomed, heroic resistance, no exalted sense of pure, apocalyptic negativity. The zombies' lack of charisma seems to drain all the surrounding circumstances of their nobility"; Waller, *Living and the Undead*, 295-96:
"What we realize is that, however flawed and unsuccessful he has proven
himself to be, Ben remains the closest any of the human beings in *Night
of the Living Dead* come to being a resourceful, brave, principled man of
action, to being the sort of hero that is found in stories as diverse as
Stoker's *Dracula*, *The Thing*, and *Salem's Lot*."

53 Carroll, *Philosophy of Horror*, 198. See also Maddrey, *Nightmares in Red,
White, and Blue*, 123-24: "*Night of the Living Dead* is an indictment of
modern life in America. It conveys the anxieties of life in a time of theological and political uncertainty, suggesting that we as a nation are overwhelmed by faceless, irrational and blindly destructive forces, and are
incapable of creating a united front to drive them back"; Russell, *Book of
the Dead*, 69: "Aligning itself in direct opposition to the dominant
American patriarchal order of family, community, police and military,
Night of the Living Dead suggests that the whole of society is rotten to the
core. It's this maggot-ridden, flesh-eating putridity that's crawled back from
the grave to jab a decomposing finger of blame at us all."

54 On how widespread is the critique, see Gagne, *Zombies That Ate
Pittsburgh*, 38: "The film presents a hopeless world where nothing matters-
young love, heroism, traditional family values are meaningless . . . and the

struggle to survive is undermined by our own flaws and unwillingness to cooperate with each other"; Newman, *Nightmare Movies*, 4: "Love, the family, military capability and individual heroism are all useless"; Sobchack, *Screening Space*, 187: "*Night of the Living Dead* (George Romero, 1968) is a black comedy, a moral fable in which all virtue is singled out and rewarded with death"; Waller, *Living and the Dead*, 296: "Romero has shown us the failure of tradition and religious faith; the incompetence of the federal government, civil defense authorities, and the news media; the inadequacy of communal action and romantic love; and the vulnerability of the private home."

55 Cf. Dillard, "Not Like Just a Wind," 23: "Within that simple plot line, the characters exhibit traditional virtues and vices, but the good and the bad, the innocent and the guilty, all suffer the same fate: they all lose. . . . The plot is, then, one of simple negation, an orchestrated descent to death in which all efforts toward life fail."

56 On the denial of religion, see Waller, *Living and the Undead*, 282: "Traditional rituals offer her no protection, her veneration of the dead is pointless, and it makes no difference whether she demonstrates Christian faith. We realize by the end of *Night of the Living Dead* that Barbara's initial survival only guarantees that she will face a much more horrible and ironic fate at the hands of the undead."

57 On such an outcome from "disposing" of the dead, see Waller, *Living and the Undead*, 302: "All that will be altered are the hunters themselves, who may come to take extermination as a type of sport or may themselves become emotionless zombies as they carry out their work"; Williams, *Cinema of George A. Romero*, 29: "Although this strategy is necessary on one level, it also ominously reveals the perspective of an inhumane scientific establishment totally oblivious to the traumatic effects this will have on surviving family members. . . . Dr. Logan's world in *Day of the Dead* is not too far away." See also Caputi, "Films of the Nuclear Age," 103, who ties this in with the projected effects on survivors of a nuclear attack.

58 On Ben's complete failure, see Dillard, "Not Like Just a Wind," 27: "Ben loses his moral struggle as well as his practical one for survival; he surrenders to the darkness in himself and to that around him."

59 Cf. Dillard, "Not Like Just a Wind," 28: "Reason itself is negated, the traditional quality that separates man from the rest of nature."

60 Exceptions would be, e.g., the so-called "Prosperity Gospel" movement in Christianity, and the Nichiren Shoshu sect of Buddhism.

61 E.g., in *City of God*, book 1, chs. 8–12.

62 Cf. Caputi, "Films of the Nuclear Age," 103: "The disturbance represented by the ghouls is a mental one. They bespeak a monstrosity of consciousness"; Engall, "Fears for Horror and Hollywood," 160: "The film is really concerned with looking at the monster within all of us."

63 Though he notes his Catholic upbringing in Hoberman and Rosenbaum, *Midnight Movies*, 113.

64 See Maddrey, *Nightmares in Red, White, and Blue*, 125–26: "In almost all of his films, Romero exposes a spiritual void in America. . . . Romero believes that this deep-rooted malaise has been present in the American temperament since the 1960s: 'We've lost it in religion,' he says, 'We've lost it in sex. We've lost it even in our feelings about a city like New York. It's really gone and tarnished. We're trying to operate on a very realistic plane. I find that to be a very devastating thing as life goes on—you can't analyze it all. We're not meant to operate that way. You have to leave some room for emotion, and you have to leave some room for love and romance, or you're not really complete, and you find that you just want more.'" Romero clearly believes that religion has failed (after thousands of years), followed by the stunningly quick failure (after a decade) of all its supposed replacements.

65 Cf. Wood, "Apocalypse Now," 95: "The end of *Night of the Living Dead* implies that the zombies have been contained and are in process of being annihilated; by the end of *Dawn of the Dead* they have apparently over-run everything and there is nothing left to do but flee. Yet *Dawn* (paradoxically, though taking the cue from its title) comes across as by far the more optimistic of the two films."

66 Dillard, "Not Like Just a Wind," 15, quoting Richard McGuinness writing for *The Village Voice*.

67 Cf. Dillard, "Not Like Just a Wind," 27, 28: "*Night of the Living Dead*, however, expresses only human smallness and ineffectuality. . . . *Night of*

the Living Dead presents the bad with great force, but what good we reach in it is small and frail indeed."

Chapter 2

1   The release date of *Dawn of the Dead* is variously reported as 1978 or 1979. In the United States the release was delayed because of a controversy over the rating of the movie, which was threatened with the X rating usually reserved for sexual pornography. *Dawn of the Dead* was eventually released as unrated. See the discussions in Gagne, *Zombies That Ate Pittsburgh*, 97-100; Russell, *Book of the Dead*, 95. On the comparison of these films with sexual pornography, see Shaviro, "Contagious Allegories," 101: "Horror shares with pornography the frankly avowed goal of physically *arousing* the audience. If these 'base' genres violate social taboos, this is not so much on account of *what* they represent or depict on the screen as of *how* they go about doing it. Horror and porn are radically desublimating" (emphasis in original).

2   Ebert's review is on http://rogerebert.suntimes.com/ (accessed September 10, 2005).

3   See Wood, "Apocalypse Now," 91: "From this viewpoint, *Dawn of the Dead* emerges as the most interesting of the four films."

4   The most common amount given for the budget is $1.5 million, as in Gagne, *Zombies That Ate Pittsburgh*, 83; Loudermilk, "Eating *Dawn* in the Dark," 96; Russell, *Book of the Dead*, 95.

5   On the film's commercial success, see Gagne, *Zombies That Ate Pittsburgh*, 83, 100-101; Loudermilk, "Eating *Dawn* in the Dark," 96-97; Russell, *Book of the Dead*, 95. On the irony of such success, see T. Modleski, "The Terror of Pleasure: The Contemporary Horror Film and Postmodern Theory," in *Studies in Entertainment: Critical Approaches to Mass Culture*, ed. T. Modleski (Bloomington: Indiana University Press, 1986), 155-66, esp. 161: "There is a similar paradox in the fact that *Dawn of the Dead*, the film about zombies taking over a shopping center, has become a midnight favorite at shopping malls all over the United States."

6   On the image of the home in the first and second movie, cf. Waller, *Living and the Undead*, 284-85, esp. 308: "Romero will explore and test all three

of these conceptions of the mall through the remainder of *Dawn of the Dead*, in a manner comparable to his examination in *Night of the Living Dead* of the private home as refuge, fortress, and trap."

7   Waller, *Living and the Undead*, 321, also notes that Peter "initially appears in the film wearing a gas mask and holding an automatic rifle—an anonymous, faceless trooper ready to kill the living as well as the undead."

8   Cf. Waller, *Living and the Undead*, 301–2: "During the raid the two troopers witness how easily the living become innocent casualties, suicidal victims, and insane murderers. In fact, Peter and Roger meet only after they each have dissociated themselves from the other men and escaped alone to the basement."

9   Russell, *Book of the Dead*, 96 and 145, believes that the priest's ethnicity and Peter's "no more room in hell" speech are references to the Caribbean roots of the zombie myth.

10   Waller, *Living and the Undead*, 302, gives the same evaluation: "Horror movies are rife with acts of butchery, murder, and wild work, but I know of no scene comparable to this methodical destruction of these monstrous, pathetic, somehow still human things caged in the basement of the apartment house. This work is without question an act of extermination rather than of ritualized struggle or heroic self-defense."

11   Waller, *Living and the Undead*, 288, notes an allusion to America's fuel woes in the first movie, but does not note the more obvious reference here in *Dawn of the Dead*.

12   In real life, the Monroeville Mall, outside of Pittsburgh.

13   On Romero's self-conscious use of clichés, cf. Waller, *Living and the Undead*, 304: "This sequence parodies the many recent horror movies that use a moving hand-held camera to approximate the monster's point of view as it stalks its often helpless potential victim through a dark, mazelike setting. Stephen has, as it were, stumbled into the sort of chilling but predictable type of horror story that Romero's films always challenge and subvert."

14   Newman, *Nightmare Movies*, 200, mentions caviar and crackers as part of their mall diet, seeming to confirm this identification.

15   Cf. Waller, *Living and the Undead*, 310–11: "These [the many guns they procure] are not merely weapons for survival. They are the central icons in

the so-called male action genres of popular culture; they are the elements of style, the props for a grand performance. . . . As in war movies about the covert operations of a small group . . . or stories of a 'big caper,' in *Dawn of the Dead*, the plan is logical, imaginative, and difficult to carry out. . . . Romero has called this sequence 'high adventure.'"

16 Cf. S. Harper, "Zombies, Malls and the Consumerism Debate: George Romero's Dawn of the Dead," *Americana: The Journal of American Popular Culture* 1, no. 2 (2002): available at http://www.americanpopular-culture.com/journal/articles/fall_2002/harper.htm: "With the corpses of the exterminated zombies cleared away, the survivors indulge in a fantasy of purchase power. . . . Indeed, the film's scenes of carnival license are among its principle attractions, and they appear to have a particular resonance for the film's audience"; Williams, *Cinema of George A. Romero*, 92: "The live males are little better than small boys entranced at a new train set."

17 On the failure or even danger posed by the outside world, cf. Waller, *Living and the Undead*, 290: "As Romero will insist much more completely in *Dawn of the Dead*, there is no hope of being rescued by outside agencies."

18 Inexplicably, Hoberman and Rosenbaum, *Midnight Movies*, 127, incorrectly name the shooter Stephen.

19 Cf. Waller, *Living and the Undead*, 313: ". . . shopping has become a tedious, deadening routine."

20 On the bikers' senseless vandalism, cf. Loudermilk, "Eating *Dawn* in the Dark," 94: "After more than basics (like weapons and food), the raiders' gluttony includes cash, things once significant of cash value (jewelry, silver) and other pointless items (mannequin or bowling ball) taken for the sake of taking"; Waller, *Living and the Undead*, 317: "Finally, the motorcycle gang seems to be looting for the sake of looting. . . . the raiders are saturnalian revelers celebrating the end of civilization or at least the lifting of all extrapersonal sanctions on behavior."

21 On the possible hopefulness of the ending, cf. Newman, *Nightmare Movies*, 201: "No one wins the battles, but the ending is curiously upbeat for a post-*Night of the Living Dead* horror movie. . . . With a touch of hope, they fly off into the sunrise"; Waller, *Living and the Undead*, 322: "Fran and Peter have no set itinerary and no destination in mind. If they

move away from the camera as homeless, isolated exiles, their flight is at the same time a liberating entrance into a world of possibility as well as of danger and horror."

22 For a scholarly analysis of consumerism in the film, see Harper, "Zombies, Malls, and the Consumerism Debate," and Loudermilk, "Eating *Dawn* in the Dark," contra Beard, "No Particular Place to Go," 30, who denies this interpretation: "But *Dawn of the Dead* is not a satire on the Fordist consumer society, however much it thinks it is. It is a film unaware of its real political significance." For a sociological application of the image of "living dead," but without reference to the film, see G. Ritzer, "Islands of the Living Dead: The Social Geography of McDonaldization," *American Behavioral Scientist* 47, no. 2 (2003): 119–36. For a recent examination of malls as "sacred space," see J. Pahl, *Shopping Malls and Other Sacred Spaces: Putting God in Place* (Grand Rapids: Brazos Press, 2003).

23 Cf. Gagne, *Zombies That Ate Pittsburgh*, 87: "*Dawn*'s zombies are the ultimate 'consumers,' carried to the absurd extreme of consuming *people*! Zombie nurses, nuns, insurance salesmen, softball players, and so on all gravitate toward the mall . . . staring longingly through store windows at the film's human protagonists. Even when they're blocked out of the mall, the zombies continue to hang around the main entrances like shoppers waiting for a Washington's Birthday sale to begin!" (emphasis in original); Modleski, "Terror of Pleasure," 159: "In George Romero's *Dawn of the Dead*, the plot involves zombies taking over a shopping center, a scenario depicting the worst fears of the culture critics who have long envisioned the will-less, soul-less masses as zombie-like beings possessed by the alienating imperative to consume"; Williams, *Cinema of George A. Romero*, 91, 92–93: "Zombie attraction to the mall is redundant and unnecessary. But as their human lives were programmed by society, resulting in behavioral patterns becoming 'instinctive' or part of 'human nature,' their dead counterparts continue the same form of behavior. The living and the dead are united by desire and memory. . . . While the zombies remain the ultimate consumers who follow their instincts to the logical conclusion by killing and eating humans, Fran, Peter, Steve and Roger kill the living dead so that they can gain access to a lifestyle of conspicuous consumption."

24 On Peter's line, cf. Harper, "Zombies, Malls, and the Consumerism Debate": "This phrase—which oscillates suggestively between oxymoron and tautology—functions as a kind of shorthand for the troubled relations between human beings and zombies."

25 Dante, *Inferno*, 5.37–39. Cf. Shaviro, "Contagious Allegories," 86: "They are driven by a sort of vestigial memory, but one that has become impersonal and indefinite, a vague solicitation to aimless movement. . . . That is to say, they are nonholistic, deorganicized bodies: lumps of flesh that still experience the cravings of the flesh, but without the organic articulation and teleological focus that we are prone to attribute to ourselves and to all living things."

26 The consumer motto is invoked similarly in Russell, *Book of the Dead*, 91, and in Skal, *Monster Show*, 376: "Ellis' world of blood-soaked designer labels recognizably upgrades the voracious mall zombies in *Dawn of the Dead*: they shop till they drop, eat your brains, then shop some more." Cf. also Beard, "No Particular Place to Go," 30: "The zombies want to consume as much as their human counterparts; it's just that they've forgotten how."

27 The phrase of Barbara Kruger, as quoted in Shaviro, "Contagious Allegories," 93; also quoted in Loudermilk, "Eating *Dawn* in the Dark," 93.

28 Loudermilk, "Eating *Dawn* in the Dark," 93.

29 Cf. Loudermilk, "Eating *Dawn* in the Dark," 85: "Capitalism is over, that's the real apocalypse here. Its consumer citizenry—figuratively zombified by commercial culture—is literally zombified by those who once were us, our *simulacral doubles* as cannibal consumers" (emphasis in original); Russell, *Book of the Dead*, 94: "Pointedly lampooning the faux utopian logic behind the consumerist boom of the 1970s, the middle section of *Dawn of the Dead* places its four protagonists inside the zombie-free, empty enclosure of the mall, gives them all they could ask for (cash, food, sports facilities, gadgets and unlimited leisure time) and then quietly watches as they descend into abject misery and self-loathing. Apparently, the zombies aren't the only ones who've lost their souls"; Shaviro, "Contagious Allegories," 92: "The four protagonists hole up in the mall and try to recreate a sense of 'home' there. Much of the film is taken up by what is in effect their delirious shopping spree."

30 On the comparison of the bikers with our protagonists, see Shaviro, "Contagious Allegories," 92: "This consumers' utopia comes to an end only when the mall is invaded by a vicious motorcycle gang: a bunch of toughs motivated by a kind of class resentment, a desire to 'share the wealth' by grabbing as much of it as possible for themselves. They enter by force and then pillage and destroy, enacting yet another mode of commodity consumption run wild"; Waller, *Living and the Undead*, 317, who notes that "their looting of the mall is a parodic repetition of Fran, Stephen, Peter, and Roger's shopping spree"; Wood, "Apocalypse Now," 96: "The motorcycle gang's mindless delight in violence and slaughter is anticipated in the development of Roger; all three groups are contaminated and motivated by consumer-greed (which the zombies simply carry to its logical conclusion by consuming *people*)" (emphasis in original).

31 Cf. Gagne, *Zombies That Ate Pittsburgh*, 89: "Ironically, once *Dawn's* protagonists have the mall and can take whatever goodies they want, they become obviously *bored*, which is one of the film's most significant insights" (emphasis in original); Newman, *Nightmare Movies*, 200: "With the zombies out of the way, the survivors find themselves at something of a loose end. They toy idly with an abundance of luxuries they don't really want, and start getting on each other's nerves. . . . The heroes' survival has become a parody of the vanished society rather than an outlaw alternative. The characters dress up in expensive clothes, play poker with real money that means less than matchsticks and spread caviar on their cream crackers, but soon get bored stiff"; Williams, *Cinema of George A. Romero*, 93: "After indulging themselves in the material gains like victors following a colonial conquest, the humans become bored and decadent. They behave in a listless manner paralleling the zombies who once inhabited the mall. Furthermore, their rise in material status also reproduces the typical pattern of the rise and decline of most human civilizations and religions in moving from barbarism to bored decadence."

32 On the scene, see Wood, "Apocalypse Now," 96: "The pivotal scene is the parody of a romantic dinner, the white couple, in evening dress, cooked for and waited on by the black, with flowers and candlelight, the scene build-

ing to the man's offer and the woman's refusal of the rings that signify traditional union."

33 Cf. Williams, *Cinema of George A. Romero*, 93: "The former lovers grad-
ually lose the vitality of their emotional relationship and become little better than a stereotypical married couple passively enduring a relationship
which is already dead and buried. Romero significantly illustrates this by a
slow zoom-out showing Steve awake in bed while Fran stares listlessly into
space. They resemble a bored and frustrated couple in an Antonioni film."

34 Cf. Harper, "Zombies, Malls, and the Consumerism Debate": "As she
applies her lipstick, she adopts the vacant gaze of the stereotypical female
consumer who sees in the department store dummy an image of her objec-
tified, commodified self. Fran becomes a human zombie, no more alive
than the conspicuous mannequin heads on which the camera mockingly
alights in a series of objective shots. As she makes herself up, she absent-
mindedly toys with a pistol, indicating her implication in the film's system
of commodity fetishism. In short, despite her own earlier warnings to the
men, Fran becomes a cultural dummy. Although it is fleeting, Fran's nar-
cissism attests to the zombifying power of commodity fetishism on even the
liveliest characters."

35 Cf. Waller, *Living and the Undead*, 314: "Striking 'provocative' poses with
a six-gun, Fran resembles a painted mannequin or a poor imitation of a
gangster's moll or a child costumed as an adult. Over the mall's loudspeakers, a voice calls all 'shoppers' to pay attention, and Fran looks up as
if she realizes the extent to which she has become the willing, predictable
'shopper'—the prisoner who can no longer see the bars of her prison."

36 Waller, *Living and the Undead*, 320, observes this of the very end of the
movie: "Ironically, the mall's clock chimes over and over, marking the
hour for a crowd of shoppers who will never again worry about the passage of time."

37 Cf. S. Harper, "Zombies, Malls, and the Consumerism Debate: George
Romero's *Dawn of the Dead*," *Americana: The Journal of American
Popular Culture* 1, n. 2 (2002): "Fran helps the men defend the mall; she
also takes responsibility for herself and others" (http://www.americanpopu-
larculture.com/journal/articles/fall_2002/harper.htm).

38 Cf. Waller, *Living and the Undead*, 314–15: "For unlike the automatistic zombies who still fill the parking lot and press against the entrances of the mall, the well-fed, safe, comfortable human beings inside this fortress have the freedom to choose."

39 Cf. Gagne, *Zombies That Ate Pittsburgh*, 87: ". . . only Fran seems to recognize that the mall represents a lifestyle that must be forsaken if they are to survive"; Harper, "Zombies, Malls, and the Consumerism Debate": "Of the film's characters, however, only Fran voices the film's moral insight. . . . Fran is expressing, albeit rather preachily, Romero's own perspective: far from endorsing consumerism, she highlights the tendency of human beings to become cultural dupes"; Williams, *Cinema of George A. Romero*, 91: "Despite consumerism's goal of targeting female shoppers by lavish displays of material goods, *Dawn of the Dead* ironically reveals that the mall has more fascination for the three males than the solitary female who accompanies them on the journey."

40 Cf. Shaviro, "Contagious Allegories," 89: "In contrast, white American males come off badly in all three films."

41 Waller, *Living and the Undead*, 310.

42 The fur coats are also other corpses with which they surround themselves: cf. Waller, *Living and the Undead*, 311: "The mall—refuge or promised land or prison—belongs to the living. However, in making it safe and habitable, they have, figuratively at least, closed themselves in and surrounded themselves with corpses." Only Harper, "Zombies, Malls, and the Consumerism Debate," notes the significance and superfluity of the coats.

43 Cf. Waller, *Living and the Undead*, 308: "Fran sees the mall neither as a convenient, well-stocked hideout nor as an earthly paradise."

44 Cf. Gagne, *Zombies That Ate Pittsburgh*, 90: "One of the more interesting societal aspects of the trilogy is Romero's evolution of women's roles over the course of the three films. . . . Fran is somewhere in between, pregnant and untrained, but a survivor"; Shaviro, "Contagious Allegories," 88: "The woman protagonist in *Dawn* rejects the subordinate role in which the three men, wrapped up in their male bonding fantasies, initially place her; she becomes more and more active and involved as the film progresses"; Williams, *Cinema of George A. Romero*, 87–88: "Romero's heroine Fran

. . . exists in an earlier stage of development from her successor in *Day of the Dead* but in an advanced stage of existence from her predecessor, Barbara in *Night of the Living Dead. . . .* Fran will experience a more liberating sense of personal development and eventual freedom no matter how insecure its future may be"; Wood, "Apocalypse Now," 96: "But in the course of the film she progressively assumes a genuine autonomy, asserting herself against the men, insisting on possession of a gun, demanding to learn to pilot the machine."

45 On the scene's racism, cf. S. Harper, "Zombies, Malls, and the Consumerism Debate": ". . . the scene invites the audience to consider zombiedom as a condition associated with both racial oppression and social abjection and, therefore, sanctions socio-political interpretations of the film as a whole"; see also Hoberman and Rosenbaum, *Midnight Movies*, 127.

46 Representative Richard Baker (R - La.), as reported in the *Washington Post*, http://www.washingtonpost.com/wpdyn/content/article/2005/09/09/A R2005090901930.html (accessed September 15, 2005), which also reports that the congressman has objected that this was not what he meant.

47 See Williams, *Cinema of George A. Romero*, 97, and Wood, "Apocalypse Now," 96, for the possible homosexual overtones of the friendship.

48 On their relationship, cf. Waller, *Living and the Undead*, 304: "Peter and Roger are a confident, effective team who speak the same language, share ideas, and perfectly complement each other."

49 On the failure of traditional relationships and the formation of a new, see Wood, "Apocalypse Now," 96: "In place of *Night*'s dissection of the family, *Dawn* explores (and explodes) the two dominant couple-relationships of our culture and its cinema: the heterosexual couple (moving inevitably towards marriage and its traditional male/female roles) and the male 'buddy' relationship with its evasive denial of sexuality"; and Waller, *Living and the Undead*, 321: "The couple that survives in *Dawn of the Dead*—a black man and a pregnant white woman—is not the traditional heterosexual couple (Fran and Stephen come closest to filling the role of the new Adam and Eve) or the pair of male buddies (like the team of Roger and Peter), but potentially a new type of partnership."

50 On their possible future relationship, see Russell, *Book of the Dead*, 96: "But if they do live long enough to reach another safe haven, Romero seems to be hinting at the possibility of a progressive new beginning for the human race as black man and (pregnant) white woman head off in hope of a fresh start. Perhaps they might even found some radical interracial utopia. As the only two characters who have managed to keep their heads throughout the preceding action, it seems fair to say that Fran and Peter represent mankind's last, best hope"; Wood, "Apocalypse Now," 96: "Instead of the restoration of conventional relationship-patterns, we have the woman piloting the helicopter as the man relinquishes his rifle to the zombies"; and Waller, *Living and the Undead*, 321–22: "Fran—carrying within her the prospect of new life—has been the most perceptive of the group, and Peter has been the most skillful and the most inclined to regard her as an equal. . . . Perhaps since Fran is piloting the helicopter and Peter has left behind his rifle, this couple is also escaping from the limiting roles fostered by a racist and sexist society that has now been destroyed." Gagne, *Zombies That Ate Pittsburgh*, 91; Russell, *Book of the Dead*, 96; and Williams, *Cinema of George A. Romero*, 96, all recount the original ending, in which both Peter and Fran commit suicide. Gagne describes how this ending was abandoned partly because Fran was to decapitate herself with the helicopter blades, and the effect apparently didn't look as "good" (if that's the right word) as Romero wanted. So, on the one hand, he was being a morbid perfectionist, but at the same time, he also describes himself as something of an old softy for the characters he had given "life" to: "I just woke one day and decided to let them go simply because I liked them too much" (Gagne, *Zombies That Ate Pittsburgh*, 91).

51 The pettiness is also noted by Loudermilk, "Eating *Dawn* in the Dark," 90: "The four . . . deny this stranger a cigarette, only to light up as soon as he's gone. Precious commodity, what may be one's last pack of cigarettes."

52 The irony of the city's name is noted by Waller, *Living and the Undead*, 302, and Williams, *Cinema of George A. Romero*, 88.

53 Cf. Waller, *Living and the Undead*, 310: "Each man can also become the victim of his own fantasies of action and adventure."

54 Suggested by Waller, *Living and the Undead*, 321: "In the end Peter must 'opt to survive' and literally surrender his rifle to climb aboard the helicopter. . . . As far as we can tell, the living cannot completely escape the burden of killing in order to survive, but in the conclusion of *Dawn of the Dead* Romero suggests that the rifle must be discarded like a vestige of a previous existence. Considered in the context of the ongoing story of the confrontation between the living and the undead, this action summarizes Romero's rejection in *Night of the Living Dead* and *Dawn of the Dead* of the idea of sacred weapons and ritualized violence that can redeem and regenerate."

55 Suggested by Waller, *Living and the Undead*, 321: "When Peter leaves his rifle behind he seems to be heeding the advice given to him and Roger by an old Puerto Rican priest in the public housing project. The frail, crippled, understatedly courageous priest emerged like a specter in the basement when the two troopers were discussing whether or not to 'run.' Instead of admonishing the men to have faith and to follow the ways of tradition, the priest cryptically warned Peter and Roger that 'we must stop the killing or we lose the war'"; and Williams, *Cinema of George A. Romero*, 90, 98: "The priest articulates the need for a rational strategy to deal with a situation become increasingly out of control. He also urges the cessation of violence. . . . It is tempting to see this figure as embodying another incarnation of the director as enunciator, especially in relation to Romero's Catholic upbringing. . . . Peter no longer needs any weapon to affirm his new sense of identity."

56 Cf. Newman, *Nightmare Movies*, 200: "The main dangers in the film come from violent humans: the racist SWAT psycho, the redneck posse from *Night* and a mindless gang of motorcycle crazies who destroy the ghoul-free haven the four central characters establish in a huge shopping mall"; Waller, *Living and the Undead*, 315: "Both groups [posses and bikers] ultimately pose a threat to the heroes that is at least equal to the threat posed by the undead."

57 On their likely degeneration into lawlessness and destructiveness, cf. Waller, *Living and the Undead*, 300: "The hunters and soldiers will be dangerous and unpredictable indeed when they fully realize that the social

contract has been nullified and that they are not just playing at self- and civil defense"; Williams, *Cinema of George A. Romero*, 90: "With grotesque male figures such as those living on a diet of beer and violence, humanity will certainly 'lose the war.'"

58 Cf. Grant, "Taking Back *The Night of the Living Dead*," 71: "In *Dawn*, Roger becomes so taken with the sporting pleasure of killing zombies that he acts recklessly and, as a result, is fatally bitten"; Shaviro, "Contagious Allegories," 89: "The two white men among the group in *Dawn* both die as a result of their adolescent need to indulge in macho games or to play the hero"; Waller, *Living and the Undead*, 310, 316: "In this world, killing is inevitable—thus Fran must learn to shoot—but Roger endangers himself and the entire group as soon as he begins to kill for the sake of pleasure or revenge, for the sake of killing itself. . . . For Roger, the destruction of the zombies becomes more and more like a game, a new sort of sport (like it also is for the redneck hunters). When Roger's life is actually threatened by the living dead, he retaliates by seeking out victims, as if he foolishly believes that somehow he can settle the score."

59 Cf. Waller, *Living and the Undead*, 305: "Only a few of the creatures actually look monstrous, with gaping wounds, disfigured faces, or missing limbs."

60 Emphasized by Waller, *Living and the Undead*, 307, 312–13, contra Beard, "No Particular Place to Go," 30, who, for some reason, denies this perspective: "Raw, blown apart, exposed, they have been completely desubjectified (they do no not even qualify for a point-of-view shot)."

61 Cf. Williams, *Cinema of George A. Romero*, 92: "She [Fran] intuitively realizes the dangerously infectious nature of violent behavior."

62 Wood, "Apocalypse Now," 96–97.

63 Cf. Loudermilk, "Eating *Dawn* in the Dark," 92: ". . . the more basic lesson Fran and Peter will learn from Roger and Steve is that the desire for more than what you need induces survival-compromising myopia. Peter and Fran survive because they resist—better than the others—the consumption of comforts that can never solve their problems"; Shaviro, "Contagious Allegories," 88: "All these characters are thoughtful, resourceful, and tenacious; they are not always right, but they continually debate possible courses of action, and learn from their mistakes. They seem to be

groping toward a shared, democratic kind of decision making"; Williams, *Cinema of George A. Romero*, 87, 97: "Human beings may survive, die or join a growing army of zombies depending upon the degree of self-realization contained within their capitulation to what appears to be a life-threatening deterministic situation. . . . Peter and Fran represent two characters who intuitively recognize these dangerous mechanisms of human behavior and attempt to move in different directions"; Wood, "Apocalypse Now," 96: "The two who die are those who cannot escape the constraints of their conditioning, the survivors are those who show themselves capable of autonomy and self-awareness."

64 Cf. Gagne, *Zombies That Ate Pittsburgh*, 88: "With the mall, Romero offers another variation on his magic-versus-reality theme—it stands as a symbol for the cheap, materialistic values that so often take precedence over traditional romantic, moral, and spiritual ideals in the twentieth century."

Chapter 3

1 See Romero's comments in T. Williams, "An Interview with George and Christine Romero," *Quarterly Review of Film and Video* 18, no. 4 (2001): 397–411, esp. 397. Many of the concepts explored in the original *Day of the Dead* script but abandoned in the final version—as described in Gagne, *Zombies That Ate Pittsburgh*, 148—would then be postponed until *Land of the Dead.*

2 Cf. Gagne, *Zombies That Ate Pittsburgh*, 151, who describes the bunker as "an acutely claustrophobic setting akin to the farmhouse in *Night of the Living Dead*"; Newman, *Nightmare Movies*, 210: "*Day of the Dead* needs these slapstick horrors because it is otherwise an unrelievedly intense, grim movie. Although the bunker is larger than the locales of the earlier films, and purposely built for such a calamity, it is an even more claustrophobic and uncomfortable setting"; Shaviro, "Contagious Allegories," 94: "Everything in this hellish, underground realm of the living is embattled, restricted, claustrophobically closed off"; Williams, *Cinema of George A. Romero*, 133, describes it as an "underground military installation resembling the claustrophobic confines of *Night of the Living Dead*'s farmhouse."

3   Cf. Russell, *Book of the Dead*, 144: "The development of the special effects industry allows Savini [the special effects artist in charge of effects in both *Dawn of the Dead* and *Day of the Dead*] to really push the gore to the limit, giving the film a bleak nastiness that's suitably chilling. . . . The tone is darker, edgier and far more depressing than before."

4   Cf. the description of Engall, "Fears for Horror and Hollywood," 161, on how *Night of the Living Dead* somehow avoids feeling claustrophobic: "Most of the film is shot in the confines of the house, yet the story never feels constrained by the location."

5   Russell, *Book of the Dead*, 143–47, interprets his accent as a reference back to the Caribbean voodoo roots of the zombie myth.

6   See Williams, "An Interview with George and Christine Romero," 404.

7   In an otherwise favorable review, J. Bowen, "*Day of the Dead*," http://orbitalreviews.com/movies/DayofDead.html, also criticizes the ending, though he does not note the ambiguity. Williams, *Cinema of George A. Romero*, 132, makes much the same criticism of the opening dream sequence: "The opening image appears redundant to the rest of the film, laying itself open to the 'It's only a dream' type of dismissal." He also notes the ambiguity of the dream-ending (Williams, *Cinema of George A. Romero*, 139–40). See also the *New York Daily News* review quoted in Gagne, *Zombies That Ate Pittsburgh*, 168, that refers to the "unbelievably cheap cop-out of an ending." On the other hand, the ending is praised in Gagne, *Zombies That Ate Pittsburgh*, 155, quoting a review by Dave Kehr in *Chicago* magazine: "It's the very thinness and arbitrariness of the conclusion that marks it as somehow miraculous, an inexplicable touch of grace."

8   Cf. Shaviro, "Contagious Allegories," 94: "A shot near the beginning shows dollar bills being blown about randomly in the wind: a sign that even commodity fetishism has collapsed as an animating structure of desire."

9   Cf. Williams, *Cinema of George A. Romero*, 131: "Furthermore, like Fran in *Dawn of the Dead*, Sarah is the film's main point of character identification."

10   Gagne, *Zombies That Ate Pittsburgh*, 153, calls it the "most grisly scene in the film."

11 E.g., Bowen, "Day of the Dead"; A. X. Miller, "Day of the Dead," *Rolling Stone* 931, September 18, 2003, 84.

12 Cf. Newman, *Nightmare Movies*, 210: "Romero reveals not only his proven skills as a director of action and personal unease, but a command of poetically profane language that makes many of the dialogue scenes more forcefully shocking than the special effects horrors. Particularly uncomfortable is the series of explicit and roundabout threats made by Rhodes and his men against Sarah, the only woman in the group, who is sexually unavailable."

13 Cf. Grant, "Taking Back *The Night of the Living Dead*," 71–72: "The internecine conflict among the living in *Day* is obviously motivated by the threat to phallic control represented by the presence of the professional woman—she is . . . a 'traumatic presence,' but significantly, Romero refuses to allow her to be 'negated'"; Shaviro, "Contagious Allegories," 89: "These white males' fear of the zombies seems indistinguishable from the dread and hatred they display toward women"; Williams, *Cinema of George A. Romero*, 131: "Penetrating the futile and superficial face of social masculinity, she [Sarah] vainly urges the importance of cooperation during two sequences in the film."

14 Cf. Shaviro, "Contagious Allegories," 88: "In both *Dawn* and *Day*, the women end up establishing tactical alliances with black men who are not blindly self-centered in the manner of their white counterparts."

15 I presume that Romero would have stated that Sarah was pregnant if such information was essential to the meaning of the film, but, in light of the previous film, there are hints of it: she keeps taking pills for some unexplained reason, she is shown gagging and almost vomiting, and she is shown marking the days off of a calendar, the way Fran is shown doing so in the previous movie.

16 Romero as quoted by Beard, "No Particular Place to Go," 31, and Grant, "Taking Back *The Night of the Living Dead*," 74. See also Gagne, *Zombies That Ate Pittsburgh*, 152: "Bub becomes increasingly more sympathetic and *human* than the sadistic Rhodes as his dormant soul is reawakened" (emphasis in original); Newman, *Nightmare Movies*, 209: "Although physically more monstrous than ever . . . they [the zombies] are otherwise more human. Whereas the monsters of the earlier films were

silent and implacable, the zombies of *Day* wail in hunger and despair, are mainly bullied and abused by the living, and begin to exhibit individual personality traits"; and Russell, *Book of the Dead*, 147: "Bub's blessed with faint stirrings of memory and, as a result, humanity." On the other hand, Williams, *Cinema of George A. Romero*, 136, rather inexplicably discounts Bub's increasing humanity as mere appearance or conditioning.

17 Cf. Gagne, *Zombies That Ate Pittsburgh*, 154: "The zombie cries out in a heart-wrenching display of emotional torment . . . and his eyes are filled with a vengeful fury as he lifts a pistol out of its holster."

18 On the complementarity of the two sets of bad characters, see Williams, *Cinema of George A. Romero*, 135: "He [Logan] represents the insanity of a scientific establishment which also mirrors Rhodes' embodiment of the violently mad military mind."

19 Cf. Williams, *Cinema of George A. Romero*, 135: "He [Logan] works on specimen after specimen like a vivisectionist gone mad and shares the same pleasure in tearing apart helpless victims like his zombie counterparts."

20 On the obvious comparison with real life scientists who lost all sense of morality, see Williams, *Cinema of George A. Romero*, 135: "Logan's attitudes thus parallel those of other scientific establishments who ignored their responsibilities to society and eagerly worked with totalitarian regimes."

21 On the kinds of behaviorist experiments Logan has been performing, see Williams, *Cinema of George A. Romero*, 136–37.

22 On her character, see Shaviro, "Contagious Allegories," 88: "The woman scientist in *Day* is established right from the start as the strongest, most dedicated, and most perspicacious of the besieged humans."

23 Cf. Gagne, *Zombies That Ate Pittsburgh*, 151: "The primary threat to their survival is not the flesh-eating ghouls wandering above but the intense conflict raging below; they are literally at each other's throats"; Russell, *Book of the Dead*, 144–45: "As in *Night* and *Dawn*, it is the stupidity of the living that is the greatest threat, with the zombies simply capitalizing on the petty squabbles. *Day* proves once and for all that the real horror in this world isn't the returning dead, but the inhumanity of the living and the inherent rottenness of contemporary society."

24 Cf. Loudermilk, "Eating *Dawn* in the Dark," 88, who detects this in the earlier *Dawn of the Dead*: "Personal identity and consumer identity seem to
be two sides of the same coin in a capitalist society, both usurped by *Dawn*'s
dead; and American history, and all history, is rendered meaningless."

25 Dante, *Inferno*, 11.22–27.

26 The persuasive suggestion of Russell, *Book of the Dead*, 145: "In *Day of
the Dead*, however, Romero returns to the zombie's cultural heritage establishing John as a link to the Caribbean and also as the chief explicator of
the apocalypse—something that his biblical Christian name hints at. . . .
Day transforms this Caribbean black male hero into a saviour who *guarantees* meaning, rather than brings about its collapse" (emphasis in original).
On the closeness of this outlook to Romero's own, see Gagne, *Zombies
That Ate Pittsburgh*, 152: "Romero's longing for a 'higher plane of existence' is expressed in John's own mystical, quasi-religious explanation of
the plague."

27 The description of Harper, "Zombies, Malls, and the Consumerism
Debate." See also the grandiloquent description of Williams, *Cinema of
George A. Romero*, 138: "Bill and John both know the difference between
their own form of magic and the world of outside reality. But, rather than
symbolically drowning themselves in irrational fantasies which leave them
vulnerable to the onslaughts of a world of powerful reality, they nourish
their ideals as utopian values while being fully aware of the dangerous
world outside."

28 Cf. Russell, *Book of the Dead*, 147: "The film ends with an upbeat scene
that shows Sarah, John and McDermott safely ensconced on a (presumably) zombie-free island in the Caribbean. In Romero's hands, the zombie
movie has come full circle, inverting its origins so that the Caribbean
becomes a place of safety and civilization while the American mainland is
the site of primitive ghoulish cannibalism. Civilization and savagery have
exchanged places and the implicit suggestion is that what we once considered civilized was never actually civilized at all."

29 Cf. Gagne, *Zombies That Ate Pittsburgh*, 155, again quoting Kehr: "For
George Romero, man is the animal who, on those rare occasions when he
wants to, can pull himself up."

30 Cf. Williams, *Cinema of George A. Romero*, 133: "They also embody minority groups often denigrated by a racist and patriarchal society. . . . However, as in all his films, Romero respectfully invests these outsider characters with indisputable qualities of human dignity."

Chapter 4

1 Russell, *Book of the Dead*, 184, interprets the ads negatively, as a sign that the producers were trying to deflect the accusation that they had not done justice to Romero's masterpiece, though even he goes on to admit that "it was also reverential of its source material, glossily effective and more breathlessly exciting than any American horror movie of the previous decade."

2 Cf. the similar description of the original *Night of the Living Dead* in Waller, *Living and the Undead*, 301: "In these two opening sequences Romero, like many other storytellers who offer what W. Warren Wagar calls 'terminal visions,' emphasizes how quickly the institutions of society and the preconceptions of the citizen can be short-circuited."

3 Dante, *Inferno*, 4.33–35.

4 See my discussion in *The Heart Set Free: Sin and Redemption in the Gospels, Augustine, Dante, and Flannery O'Connor* (New York: Continuum, 2005), 67–102.

5 The film has therefore been called "reactionary" by M. Degiglio-Bellemare, "Review of *Land of the Dead*," *Journal of Religion and Film* 9, no. 2 (2005), http://www.unomaha.edu/jrf/Vol9No2/Reviews/LandDead.htm (accessed November 10, 2005): 4, who believes the director is equating the zombies with terrorists "closing in on the US from the outside." It is an intriguing suggestion, but hardly seems borne out in the film, where the zombies, exactly as in Romero's vision, are horrifying because they are our neighbors, family, and friends, and the vast majority shown in the film are middle-class Americans of various ages and races.

6 It is also very telling in a post-9/11 world that many of them are rescue personnel, as noted by Russell, *Book of the Dead*, 192: "The fact that the redux version of *Dawn of the Dead* concentrates on a group of heroes led by emergency service workers—a nurse, a policeman, and (at a push) a couple of security guards—seems rather significant in the post-9/11 world."

7   Frequently observed, as in Wood, "Apocalypse Now," 93; Waller, *Living and the Undead*, 291–92.

8   Though Wood, "Apocalypse Now," 95, detects it there as a parody: "They [the zombies] are no longer associated with specific characters or character-tensions, and the family as a social unit no longer exists (it is only reconstituted in parody, when the injured Roger becomes the-baby-in-a-pram, wheeled around the supermarket by his 'parents' as he shoots down zombies with childish glee." This interpretation is followed by Williams, *Cinema of George A. Romero*, 94: "Even before Roger's death, the quartet already began to resemble a bourgeois family out on a shopping spree with the injured Roger appearing like a baby in a mall shopping cart."

9   I had overlooked the name of the fort, until Victor Gibbs pointed it out in an e-mail correspondence (November 5, 2005).

10 In this sense, the film very much harkens back to the original *Night of the Living Dead*. See Russell, *Book of the Dead*, 69: "No accident, then, that the film opens with a young couple's journey to visit the grave of their dead father—this is a world completely lacking in patriarchal authority"; Waller, *Living and the Undead*, 290: "In *Night of the Living Dead*, no God, father, or president, no military, scientific, political, or religious form of authority guarantees or in any way promotes the survival of the living."

11 In an otherwise negative evaluation of the film, Russell, *Book of the Dead*, 185, notes the aptness of this choice of music.

12 In this sense, the film returns to a more classical, pre-Romero vision of horror movies, as described by Fraser, "Watching Horror Movies," 47: "And once the possibility of splatter effects had been opened up, an interesting tension was established wherein one partly *wanted* horrible things to happen, for their shock effect, and yet at the same time did not want them to happen to everyone. So that one stayed alert for possible clues as to who in some sense 'deserved' to become victims" (emphasis in original).

13 In this, the remake is very different from Romero's original vision in *Night of the Living Dead*, which, as noted by Waller, *Living and the Undead*, 296, shows "the inadequacy of communal action and romantic love."

14 Dante, *Inferno*, 4.41–42.

Chapter 5

1   As reported on http://www.usatoday.com/life/movies/news/2005-06-20-
    land-of-dead_x.htm. Russell, *Book of the Dead*, 187, gives the budget as
    only $15 million and calls the amount "near insulting."

2   Cf. Dargis, "Not Just Roaming": "In 'George A. Romero's *Land of the
    Dead*,' an excellent freakout of a movie, the living no longer have the
    advantage or our full sympathies"; Russell, *Book of the Dead*, 190: "It's the
    first film in the series to explicitly ask us to sympathize with the zombies
    themselves and it extends Romero's living dead mythology in a way which
    none of his imitators have ever managed to do."

3   Cf. Shaviro, "Contagious Allegories," 87–88, in reference to the earlier
    films: "They can be regarded both as monstrous symbols of a violent,
    manipulative, exploitative society and as potentially remedies for its ills—all
    this by virtue of their apocalyptically destructive, yet oddly innocuous,
    counterviolence. They frighten us with their categorical rapacity, yet allure
    us by offering the base, insidious pleasures of ambiguity, complicity, and
    magical revenge."

4   Cf. the description of Dargis, "Not Just Roaming": "The tower, which
    appears to have been modeled on a Vegas hotel, complete with the usual
    feedlots, luxury stores and glassy-eyed shoppers, rises above the devastated
    metropolis like a threat and a promise. Outside its locked doors, amid
    atmospheric squalor, the huddling masses distract themselves with bread
    and circuses, while one man agitates for revolution." Romero's depictions
    of both the wealthy enclave of Fiddler's Green and the impoverished and
    debauched nightclub seem influenced by the dystopian sci-fi films of the
    80s and 90s, such as *Blade Runner* (1982), *RoboCop* (1987), and *Total
    Recall* (1990), which depict shocking disparities between safe havens for
    the wealthy, surrounded by underground slums of misery and violence.
    These also contain blackly ironic television advertisements for the "good
    life," like those for Fiddler's Green.

5   Degiglio-Bellemare, 8.

6   Dargis, "Not Just Roaming."

7   Cf. S. Klawans, "Alien Nation," *Nation* 281, no. 4 (August 1, 2005): 41–44,
    esp. 44, where he calls Kaufman an "all-purpose realtor, corporate czar and

crime boss." Russell, *Book of the Dead*, 190, makes the reference much more explicit and historically contextualized: "Presenting Kaufman as a composite of George W. Bush and Defense Secretary Donald Rumsfeld, Romero makes his criticism of the regime more than transparent."

8   Dargis, "Not Just Roaming."

9   Cf. Russell, *Book of the Dead*, 186: "What was threatened before in Romero's series has finally come to pass: the living are now more like monsters than the living dead."

10   John Milton, *Paradise Lost*, ed. C. Ricks (New York: Signet, 1968), 1.263.

11   Cf. Russell, *Book of the Dead*, 189: "With the apartments of Fiddler's Green a more luxurious take on the shopping mall enclave from *Dawn of the Dead*, it's obvious that Romero has lost none of his anti-consumerist fervour even when taking a major Hollywood studio's dollar."

12   The connection suggested by Russell, *Book of the Dead*, 189.

13   I was first alerted to this by the "Trivia" section for *Land of the Dead* on the Internet Movie Database site: http://www.imdb.com/title/tt0418819/ (accessed November 14, 2005). The lyrics are from "Brobdingnagian Bards," http://www.thebards.net/music/lyrics/Fiddlers_Green.shtml (accessed November 14, 2005).

14   Cf. Degiglio-Bellemare, "*Land of the Dead*," 7: "Romero's new film offers a very important statement on the reality of 'lockdown America,' with its gated communities, its stark class divisions, and its racial demarcations."

15   Degiglio-Bellemare, "*Land of the Dead*," 5, calls them "*lumpenproletariat.*"

16   Dargis, "Not Just Roaming."

17   Cf. Dargis, "Not Just Roaming": "For Cholo and some of the others, there's much fun to be had popping wheelies on motorcycles while blowing holes through the zombies, even if the ghouls, still dressed in the clothes in which they died—a cheerleader's outfit, a butcher's apron—look uncomfortably human."

18   Cf. Klawans, "Alien Nation," 44: "In *Land of the Dead*, America's small-town past comes back as parody, horror and ideal all in one: haunting the modern city, preying on it, showing it an aspiration higher than anything a Kaufman would offer his clients."

19   The suggestion of Degiglio-Bellemare, "*Land of the Dead*," 6.

20 "Brobdingnagian Bards."
21 Dante, *Inferno*, 34.136–39.

Conclusion

1 Clover, *Men, Women, and Chainsaws*, 235–36, speculates that vampire and zombie movies will be the last great hope of edgy, controversial, low-budget horror movies, though she worries that even these have become too mainstream.

2 Cf. the description of Dargis, "Not Just Roaming": "What has changed since corpses roamed the cemetery in '*Night of the Living Dead*' crudely pockmarked with sores and dripping movie blood is the special-effects makeup, which in the new film is alternately frightfully real and obscenely beautiful. Here, Mr. Romero . . . creates gruesome demons right out of Bosch and Goya."

3 Cf. the optimistic appraisal of Russell, *Book of the Dead*, 192: "It [the zombie movie] seems unlikely to be ousted anytime soon. As the West wages its war on Terror and makes imperial incursions into the Middle East, the zombie's role as a veiled commentary on relations between colonial occupier and native subjects and its more contemporary role as a symbol of the mass destruction of the First World may yet have a place in many, many nightmares."

BIBLIOGRAPHY

Aizenberg, E. "'I Walked with a Zombie': The Pleasures and Perils of Postcolonial Hybridity." *World Literature Today* 73, no. 3 (1999): 461–66.

Arnzen, M. A. "Who's Laughing Now? The Postmodern Splatter Film." *Journal of Popular Film and Television* 21, no. 4 (1994): 176–84.

Augustine. *The City of God*. Trans. H. Bettenson. Penguin Books, 1972.

Balun, C. "I Spit in Your Face: Films That Bite." In *Splatterpunks: Extreme Horror*, 167–83. Edited by P. Sammon. New York: St. Martin's Press, 1990.

Beard, S. "No Particular Place to Go." *Sight and Sound* 3, no. 4 (1993): 30–31.

Benjamin, W. *Illuminations*. Edited by H. Arendt. Translated by H. Zohn. New York: Schocken Books, 1969.

Bowen, J. *Review of Day of the Dead*, directed by George A. Romero. Orbital Reviews. http://orbitalreviews.com/movies/DayOfDead.html (accessed October 15, 2005).

Bringsjord, S. "The Zombie Attack on the Computational Conception of Mind." *Philosophy and Phenomenological Research* 59 (1999): 41–69.

Britton, A. "The Devil, Probably: The Symbolism of Evil." In *American Nightmare: Essays on the Horror Film*, 34–42. Edited by R. Wood and R. Lippe. Toronto: Festival of Festivals, 1979.

Brooks, M. *The Zombie Survival Guide: Complete Protection from the Living Dead*. New York: Three Rivers Press, 2003.

Caputi, J. "Films of the Nuclear Age." *Journal of Popular Film and Television* 16, no. 3 (1988): 100–107.

Carroll, N. *The Philosophy of Horror, or, Paradoxes of the Heart.* New York: Routledge, 1990.

Chalmers, D. J. *The Conscious Mind: In Search of a Fundamental Theory.* New York: Oxford University Press, 1996.

Clover, C. J. *Men, Women, and Chain Saws: Gender in the Modern Horror Film.* Princeton: Princeton University Press, 1993.

Cottrell, A. "Sniffing the Camembert: On the Conceivability of Zombies." *Journal of Consciousness Studies* 6 (1999): 4-12.

Dante. *The Divine Comedy: Inferno.* Translated by M. Musa. New York: Penguin Books, 1971.

Dargis, M. "Not Just Roaming, Zombies Rise Up: Review of *Land of the Dead.*" *The New York Times,* June 24, 2005. http://www.nytimes.com/page/movies /index.html (accessed November 13, 2005).

Davis, W. *Passage of Darkness: The Ethnobiology of the Haitian Zombie.* Chapel Hill: University of North Carolina Press, 1988.

———. *The Serpent and the Rainbow.* Simon & Schuster, 1985.

Degiglio-Bellemare, M. "Review of *Land of the Dead.*" *Journal of Religion and Film* 9, no. 2 (2005). http://www.unomaha.edu/jrf/Vol9No2/ Reviews/Land Dead.htm (accessed November 10, 2005).

Deleuze, G., and F. Guattari. *Anti-Oedipus: Capitalism and Schizophrenia.* Translated by R. Hurley, M. Seem, and H. R. Lane. Minneapolis: University of Minnesota, 1983.

Dendle, P. *The Zombie Movie Encyclopedia.* Jefferson, NC: McFarland, 2000.

Dennett, D. C. "The Unimagined Preposterousness of Zombies." *Journal of Consciousness Studies* 2 (1995): 322-26.

———. "The Zombic Hunch: Extinction of an Intuition?" In *Philosophy at the New Millennium,* 27-44. Edited by A. O'Hear. Cambridge: Cambridge University Press, 2001.

Derry, C. "More Dark Dreams: Some Notes on the Recent Horror Film." *American Horrors: Essays on the Modern American Horror Film,* 162-75. Edited by G. A. Waller. Urbana: University of Illinois Press, 1987.

Dewan, S. K. "Do Horror Films Filter the Horrors of History?" *The New York Times,* October 14, 2000, B9.

Dillard, R. H. W. *Horror Films.* Monarch, 1976.

———. "*Night of the Living Dead:* It's Not Like Just a Wind That's Passing Through." In *American Horrors: Essays on the Modern American Horror Film,* 14-29. Edited by G. A. Waller. Urbana: University of Illinois Press,

1987. (Originally appeared as R. H. W. Dillard, *Horror Films*. New York: Monarch, 1976, 55-81.)

Engall, P. "George A. Romero's Fears for Horror and Hollywood: The Underbelly of the Monster." *Metro Magazine* 133 (2002): 158-63.

Fraser, J. "Watching Horror Movies." *Michigan Quarterly Review* 24, no. 1 (1990): 39-54.

Freeland, C. A. *The Naked and the Undead: Evil and the Appeal of Horror*. Boulder: Westview Press, 2002.

Gagne, P. R. *The Zombies That Ate Pittsburgh: The Films of George A. Romero*. Dodd, Mead, 1987.

Grant, B. K. "Taking Back the *Night of the Living Dead*: George Romero, Feminism and the Horror Film." *Wide Angle: A Film Quarterly of Theory, Criticism, and Practice* 14, no. 1 (1992): 64-76. Reprinted in *The Dread of Difference: Gender and the Horror Film*, 200-212. Edited by B. K. Grant. Austin: University of Texas Press, 1996.

Greene, R., and K. S. Mohammad, eds. *The Undead and Philosophy*. Peru, IL: Open Court, forthcoming.

Guzeldere, G. "Varieties of Zombiehood." *Journal of Consciousness Studies* 2 (1995): 326-33.

Hantke, S., ed. *Horror Film: Creating and Marketing Fear*. Jackson: University Press of Mississippi, 2004.

Harper, S. "Zombies, Malls and the Consumerism Debate: George Romero's *Dawn of the Dead*." *Americana: The Journal of American Popular Culture* 1, no. 2 (2002). http://www.americanpopularculture.com/journal/articles/fall_2002/harper.htm.

Higashi, S. "*Night of the Living Dead*: A Horror Film about the Horrors of the Vietnam War." In *From Hanoi to Hollywood: The Vietnam War in American Film*, 175-88. Edited by L. Dittmar and G. Michaud. New Brunswick, NJ: Rutgers University Press, 1990.

Hoberman, J., and J. Rosenbaum. *Midnight Movies*. New York: Harper & Row, 1983.

Hutchings, P. *The Horror Film*. New York: Pearson Longman, 2004.

Jancovich, M., ed. *Horror: The Film Reader*. New York: Routledge, 2001.

Kirk, R. "Reply to Don Locke on Zombies and Materialism." *Mind* 86 (1977): 262-64.

——. "Sentience and Behaviour." *Mind* 81 (1974): 43-60.

——. "Why There Couldn't Be Zombies." *Aristotelian Society Supplement* 73 (1999): 1-16.

——. *Zombies and Consciousness*. New York: Oxford University Press, forthcoming.

——. "Zombies vs. Materialists." *Aristotelian Society Supplement* 48 (1974): 135–52.

Klawans, S. "Alien Nation." *Nation* 281, no. 4 (August 1, 2005): 41–44.

Locke, D. "Zombies, Schizophrenics, and Purely Physical Objects." *Mind* 83 (1976): 97–99.

Loudermilk, A. "Eating *Dawn* in the Dark: Zombie Desire and Commodified Identity in George A. Romero's *Dawn of the Dead.*" *Journal of Consumer Culture* 3, no. 1 (2003): 83–108.

Maddrey, J. *Nightmares in Red, White, and Blue: The Evolution of the American Horror Film*. Jefferson, NC: McFarland, 2004.

Marcus, E. "Why Zombies Are Inconceivable." *Australasian Journal of Philosophy* 82 (2004): 477–90.

Marton, P. "Zombies vs. Materialists: The Battle over Conceivability." *Southwest Philosophy Review* 14 (1998): 131–38.

Miller, A. X. "Day of the Dead." *Rolling Stone*, September 18, 2003, 84.

Milton, J. *Paradise Lost*. Edited by C. Ricks. New York: Signet, 1968.

Modleski, T. "The Terror of Pleasure: The Contemporary Horror Film and Postmodern Theory." In *Studies in Entertainment: Critical Approaches to Mass Culture*, 155–66. Edited by Tania Modleski. Bloomington: Indiana University Press, 1986.

Moody, T. "Conversations with Zombies." *Journal of Consciousness Studies* 1 (1994): 196–200.

Newman, K. *Nightmare Movies: A Critical Guide to Contemporary Horror Films, 1986–88*. New York: Harmony, 1988.

Paffenroth, K. *The Heart Set Free: Sin and Redemption in the Gospels, Augustine, Dante, and Flannery O'Connor*. New York: Continuum, 2005.

Pahl, J. *Shopping Malls and Other Sacred Spaces: Putting God in Place*. Grand Rapids: Brazos Press, 2003.

Perry, J. *Knowledge, Possibility, and Consciousness*. Cambridge, MA: MIT Press, 2001.

Pirie, D. *The Vampire Cinema*. New York: Crescent Books, 1977.

Polger, T. "Zombies explained." In *Dennett's Philosophy: A Comprehensive Assessment*, 259–86. Edited by A. Brooks, D. Ross, and D. Thompson. Cambridge, MA: MIT Press, 2000.

Prince, S., ed. *The Horror Film*. New Brunswick, NJ: Rutgers University Press, 2004.

Ritzer, G. "Islands of the Living Dead: The Social Geography of McDonaldization." *American Behavioral Scientist* 47, no. 2 (2003): 119–36.

Russell, J. *Book of the Dead: The Complete History of Zombie Cinema.* Surrey, UK: FAB Press, 2005.

Shaviro, S. "Contagious Allegories: George Romero." In *The Cinematic Body*, 83–105. Minneapolis: University of Minnesota Press, 1998.

Silver, A., and J. Ursini, eds. *Horror Film Reader.* New York: Limelight Editions, 2001.

Skal, D. J. *The Monster Show: A Cultural History of Horror.* Rev. ed. New York: Faber & Faber, 2001.

Skokowski, P. "I, Zombie." *Consciousness and Cognition* 11 (2002): 1–9.

Slater, J. *Eaten Alive! Italian Cannibal and Zombie Movies.* London: Plexus, 2002.

Sobchack, V. *Screening Space: The American Science Fiction Film.* 2nd ed. New York: Ungar, 1987.

Sommers, T. "Of Zombies, Color Scientists, and Floating Iron Bars." *Psyche* 8 (2002). http://psyche.cs.monash.edu.au/v8/psyche 8 22 sommers.html (accessed July 25, 2005).

Squires, R. "Zombies vs. Materialists II." *Aristotelian Society Supplement* 48 (1974): 153–63.

Stalnaker, R. "What is it like to be a Zombie?" In *Conceivability and Possibility.* Edited by T. Gendler and J. Hawthorne. New York: Oxford University Press, 2002.

Thomas, N. J. T. "Zombie Killer." In *Toward a Science of Consciousness II.* Edited by S. Hameroff, A. Kaszniak, and A. Scott. Cambridge, MA: MIT Press, 1998.

Twitchell, J. B. *Dreadful Pleasures: An Anatomy of Modern Horror.* New York: Oxford University Press, 1985.

Vatnsdal, C. *They Came from Within: A History of Canadian Horror Cinema.* Winnipeg, MB: Arbeiter Ring, 2004.

Virilio, P. *Speed and Politics: An Essay on Dromology.* Translated by M. Polizzotti. New York: Columbia University Press, 1986.

Wagar, W. W. *Terminal Visions: The Literature of Last Things.* Bloomington: Indiana University Press, 1982.

Waller, G. A., ed. *American Horrors: Essays on the Modern American Horror Film.* Urbana: University of Illinois Press, 1987.

——. *The Living and the Undead: From Stoker's "Dracula" to Romero's "Dawn of the Dead."* Urbana: University of Illinois Press, 1986.

Wells, P. *The Horror Genre.* London: Wallflower Press, 2001.

Williams, T. *The Cinema of George A. Romero: Knight of the Living Dead.* London: Wallflower Press, 2003.

———. "An Interview with George and Christine Romero." *Quarterly Review of Film and Video* 18, no. 4 (2001): 397–411.

Winter, D. E. "Less than Zombie." In *Splatterpunks: Extreme Horror*, 84–98. Edited by P. Sammon. New York: St. Martin's Press, 1990.

Wood, R. "Apocalypse Now: Notes on the Living Dead." In *American Nightmare: Essays on the Horror Film*, 91–98. Edited by R. Wood and R. Lippe. Toronto: Festival of Festivals, 1979. (Reprinted in R. Wood, *Hollywood from Vietnam to Reagan.* New York: Columbia University Press, 1986, 114–21.)

Wood, R., and R. Lippe, eds. *American Nightmare: Essays on the Horror Film.* Toronto: Festival of Festivals, 1979.

INDEX